RISEN

FINDING HOPE IN THE EMPTY TOMB

CLIFFORD GOLDSTEIN

Pacific Press®
Publishing Association

Nampa, Idaho | www.pacificpress.com

Cover design by Steve Lanto
Cover illustration from Sermonview.com
Inside design by Aaron Troia

Purchase additional copies of this book by calling toll-free 1-800-765-6955 or by visiting https://adventistbookcenter.com.

Library of Congress Cataloging-in-Publication Data

Names: Goldstein, Clifford, author.
Title: Risen : finding hope in the tomb / Clifford Goldstein.
Description: Nampa, Idaho : Pacific Press Publishing Association, 2020. |
    Includes bibliographical references. | Summary: "A study on the philosophical and scientific reasoning behind theories for and against Jesus' resurrection"— Provided by publisher.
Identifiers: LCCN 2020037804 | ISBN 9780816366361 (paperback) |
    ISBN 9780816366378 (e-book edition)
Subjects: LCSH: Jesus Christ—Resurrection.
Classification: LCC BT482 .G65 2020 | DDC 232/.5—dc23
LC record available at https://lccn.loc.gov/2020037804

November 2020

Contents

In 1971, American Tom Robbins wrote a goofy and dumb book that many of us loved despite its goofiness and dumbness. Called *Another Roadside Attraction*, it paraded across its pages implausible characters doing implausible things, such as Plucky Purcell, who infiltrates an order of monk assassins and gets assigned to the Vatican. There, plundering all the gold that he can stuff into his greedy pockets in the catacombs after an earthquake hits Rome, Plucky comes across the corpse of Jesus Christ in a sealed chamber ruptured open by the quake.

"It looked, to be sure, nothing like the milky portraits we had been shown in Sunday school, looked hardly at all like the handsome gentleman with the Aryan profile and the five-hundred-watt glow who effulged at us from calendars in Protestant parlors all over Dixie."[1] (At least that description is better than all the paintings that color Jesus as a white Anglo-Saxon Protestant poster boy, while the only Jewish-looking character is a hooked-nosed Judas sneering over his bag of money.)

Plucky steals the body and smuggles it to America. However, when the grand-high-muckety-mucks fear what may happen if people realize that Jesus hadn't really been resurrected, they attempt to track down Plucky and the body before word gets out, and Western civilization collapses.

It's hard to imagine Tom Robbins taking his characters or his plot seriously, even if he wanted to ask serious questions about the beliefs and assumptions of our society, which were being pummeled, trampled, and stomped on at that time because of, among other things, the American pummeling, trampling, and stomping on the North Vietnamese. However, even if Western civilization could survive the debunking of Christ's resurrection, Christianity certainly couldn't.

Or, at least, that was the fear.

Over the years, though, the resurrection of Jesus Christ has come under sustained attack but not from the usual suspects, such as the much-ballyhooed new atheists—Richard Dawkins, Daniel Dennett, or Sam Harris. Rather, biblical scholars, many professed Christians, have been writing books and papers and sponsoring seminars that put the resurrection of Jesus Christ in the same class as Orpheus descending to the underworld.

For example, one of the most well-known New Testament scholars of the Resurrection is John Dominic Crossan, author of more than twenty-eight books on Jesus, Paul, and the New Testament. He is also a popular lecturer who, between numerous academic appointments, has appeared on TV and radio broadcasts all over the world. In 2020, he was a professor emeritus of Religious Studies at DePaul University in Chicago.

And what does the eminent scholar say about Christ's resurrection? The empty tomb could be explained, he argues, not because Jesus Christ arose from Joseph's tomb as Conqueror of the grave—the act upon which so many hurting souls pin their hopes—but because Jesus never made it to Joseph's tomb to begin with.

Instead, the renowned Dr. Crossan pronounces, Christ's corpse was most likely thrown in a shallow grave and later eaten by "scavenging animals."[2]

Not as dramatic as Plucky Purcell's Vatican adventures but just as implausible.

---

1. Tom Robbins, *Another Roadside Attraction* (New York: Bantam Books, 1971), 259.
2. John Dominic Crossan, *Jesus: A Revolutionary Biography* (New York: HarperOne, 1994), 180.

Love can do all but raise the Dead.
                                    —Emily Dickinson

Your dead shall live;
Together with my dead body they shall arise.
Awake and sing, you who dwell in dust;
For your dew is like the dew of herbs,
And the earth shall cast out the dead.
                                    —Isaiah 26:19

To Demand a Miracle

In 216 BC, in the notorious battle of Cannae, Carthaginian general Hannibal Barca, who led his army across Europe, through the Alps, and into Italy, routed the Romans, killing fifty-five thousand to seventy-five thousand and losing about six thousand of his own men. More soldiers died at Cannae than on any other day of battle in Western history.

Yet today our eyes can float over the placid fields of Cannae quietly sprouting life where tens of thousands had died. Who were those fathers, sons, brothers whose dreams, hopes, and passions vanished on a scream or a moan thousands of years ago, and not the residue of a dream, a hope, a passion lingering in their chemical remains?

That's just one battle. Who can keep track of all the wars (not battles, *wars*) since 216 BC? And natural disasters? How many of us know, for instance, that a famine in North Vietnam killed a million people in 1945? What kind of world is this in which one million people starve to death, and others don't know about it? And of those million men, women, children, and babies who slowly withered back into the ground that so betrayed them, do we know a single name?

And even if some do now, soon who will?

"Look, Lola," wrote Louis-Ferdinand Céline, "do you remember a single name, for instance, of any of the soldiers killed in the Hundred Years War? . . . Did you ever try to find out who any of them were? . . . No! . . . You see? You never tried. . . . As far as you're concerned, they're as anonymous, as indifferent, as the last atom of that paperweight."[2]

Meanwhile, think about how close, how immediate and essential our sense of self is. We know existence only through our own consciousness. "Everything begins with consciousness," wrote Albert Camus, "and nothing is worth anything except through it."[3]

Consciousness is the knowledge of life; it is how our life appears to us, how it is experienced and known, which is why we cling so fervently to it, as did the billions of dead before us whose consciousness was just as real, just as immediate, and just as precious to each one of them as ours is to us. Yet each one of those people's consciousnesses has evaporated into what can be best described by the periodic table of elements, nothing more. And each one of ours will as well—*a thought that terrorizes us.*

Many ancient Roman tombstones read: *I wasn't, I was, I am not, I don't care.* But we do care now. We care greatly now. *We are*, and the realization that one day *we won't be* is as acid on the soul. Who, having had moments where they thought that they were about to die, wasn't petrified, horrified, panicky? Everything else vanishes except hard cold death—*your* hard, cold death.

And the specter of death is, really, the specter of meaninglessness, the fear that "all that we suffered through having existed shall be forgotten as though it had never existed."[4] Death leaves us nothing; that is, it leaves us as nothing and with nothing.

"What can they be worth?" wrote Nikolai Gogol about the dead. "Just consider: why, they are dust, you know. Do you understand, they are nothing but dust? Take the most worthless, humblest article, a simple rag, for instance. But even the rag has a value: rags are bought for making into paper, anyway, but what I am speaking of is of no use for anything."[5]

However much we intellectualize death, philosophize about it, memorize cute and pithy maxims regarding it, we hate and fear it as almost nothing else. *Death is part of life*, we say. That's one of those pithy maxims, and it happens to be one of those pithy maxims that are wrong too. Death isn't part of life; it's the undoing of life, the negation of life, the opposite of life. It's the one thing that can make life as meaningless as roadkill.

A dead raccoon beside the road is too bad; a dead human beside the road is worse, but in a thousand years (or even 150), what's the difference, especially when no one knows or cares?

Cal was a seventeen-year-old senior in high school near Miami Beach in the 1970s. He hustled, parking cars at hotels and restaurants that lined the island like broken keys on a piano. Mile after mile of concrete, steel, and glass pulsated with packets of rational flesh crying out for something, if not knowing what, and surely not finding it in Miami Beach, no matter the good package deals that got them there to begin with.

One afternoon, before starting the four o'clock shift, Cal pulled up to the Newport Beach Hotel (now the Newport Beachside Hotel and Resort) on 163rd Street. Police lights, flashing blue and red on green-and-white cruisers, cordoned off the street up the block from the hotel. An ambulance, red light silently pulsing, eased in past the police cars.

"What happened?" Cal asked.

About half a block from the hotel was a small field where a helicopter tour originated. The chopper came in a bit too tilted, and its blade separated some schnook on the sidewalk from his head.

The next day Cal returned to work early. He walked up the street. The chopper was gone; only a small shed, the helicopter-tour office, remained. Gruesomely enough, Cal looked for blood, which from a beheading should have been profuse, but found none. Not on the sidewalk. Not on the grass. Not on the street.

Cal watched as mothers pushed strollers past the field. Kids skateboarded on the sidewalk. A convertible left a trail of music, laughter, and exhaust fumes in its wake. People meandered on by, as on any Florida afternoon, even though a day before a universe of desire, passion, thoughts, dreams, hopes, plans, loves, and fears simmering in that man's head had, at the speed of a chopper-blade spin, spilled out with blood that was now washed away.

Cal had often walked past the chopper field to get dinner at the Rascal House, just up the street. A few tweaked twists of fate and it could have been him headless, and people would walk by just as they did that day as if Cal had never existed at all.

Time and space seemed out of kilter. Cal touched his neck, then went to work parking cars. Later that night, he stood behind the hotel, the black sky over the ocean looking like a dimmed chandelier. His thoughts were already bruised, not so much by the death or by how macabre but by how quickly it was gone. Vanished. Unreal. Hundreds of people today would pass by that exact spot, oblivious to the reality that yesterday, right here, a man had been beheaded.

Cal looked at the stars; their distances mocked him with meaninglessness, *his* meaninglessness. What could he mean amid a cosmos so big and enduring when he was so small and fleeting, and when a man could die and the next day most everyone not know or care? Time (the little he had) and space (the little he occupied) made him feel less than zero.

Dread, starting (it felt like, anyway) in his chest, lodged in his head. The realization, painful like a sliver under his skull, that his life didn't matter struck him with a clarity that Cal had never before experienced. Maybe he had never thought about it much before. But then and there—the stars shining as they had done before he had been born and would shine after he had died (his birth, life, and death not changing a cloud overhead, much less the stars)—though he didn't want to admit it and though deep down the realization filled him with terror, callous and unkind logic showed him how little his life meant.

Cal shook his head to dislodge the dread, cast it away and all would be good again. But the dread followed like a shadow. Could his life really mean nothing? No, it had to mean something. Or maybe he thought that it had to mean something only because he wanted it to.

Done musing under the stars, Cal returned to work, not so sure why.

I t's a cross, kind of, between a sad love story (boy meets girl, boy and girl fall in love, girl dies) and science fiction (girl freezes her brain in the hope of living forever).

Kim S., a young woman in her early twenties, had asked her boyfriend to bring the Advil. *Another dreaded headache.* But Advil didn't solve the problem, which turned out to be a brain tumor that promised only death.

But if Mother Nature wanted to play witch, then Kim S. would use the marvels of technology to outwit her. When Kim S. died, her brain would be put in the deep freeze, so that after fifty, one hundred, one thousand years, whenever the technology obliged, scientists would thaw it, upload the neural connections—the connections that create* thoughts, emotions, identity, those things that make us who we are—into a supercomputer. That way her personality, her essence, and her consciousness, yes, Kim S. herself, would not only come back to life but (as long as they could keep swapping out computer hardware) she could live forever.

With silicon chips and hard drives, who needs Mother Nature after all?

Freeze your brain? Upload the neural connections? Live (live?) inside a computer? And if they make a backup, which one is really Kim S. and which one is the copy? This is an AD twenty-first-century version of the fifteenth century BC Egyptian pyramids, and who'd bet the farm that it's going to work any better for Kim S. than it did for Pharaoh Tutankhamen?

This isn't a time to judge the unfortunate young lady. You'd have to be there yourself, with your own mortality shoving its whiskered face into yours as it did hers (as opposed to some distant thing that you know will come but never quite accept) to appreciate the desperation revealed in this sad science nonfiction love story.

Until then, we push off the ugly specter of death, even if it still taints every living moment. Like eggplant and oysters, we die, but unlike them, we know it, an altogether tough rub for beings hardwired well enough to cringe before the gap between the bit of time that we limp upon the ground and the eternity that grinds us into that ground.

"For it is not to be doubted," wrote Blaise Pascal, "that the duration of this life is but a moment; that the state of death is eternal, whatever may be its nature."[7] Pascal, who died in 1662 at the age of 39, had in the year 2020 a life-to-death ratio of 39:358 (that is, he was dead 358 years compared to being alive only 39)—and counting. George Washington comes in at 67:231; Julius Caesar, at 66:2063.

The point?

We exist here mostly dead.

Time magazine ran a cover article in 2013 titled "Can Google Solve Death?" The kicker read, "The search giant is launching a venture to extend the human

---

* Supposedly.

life span. That would be crazy—if it weren't Google."[8]

Extending the human life span is one thing (giving up Bloody Marys for wheatgrass juice would do the trick too), but these few extra years are as far from solving death as adding three inches to a yard is from infinity. Another few years, or decades, would be fine (if you could avoid Parkinson's, Alzheimer's, osteoporosis, arthritis, and other debilitating diseases along the way), but longevity isn't immortality.

Wrote Donna Tartt in *The Secret History*:

> "And if beauty is terror," said Julian, "then what is desire? We think we have many desires, but in fact we have only one. What is it?"
>
> "To live," said Camilla.
>
> "To live for*ever*," said Bunny, chin cupped in palm.[9]

To live *forever*?

Maybe most people don't dwell on living forever, but that's the only alternative to dying forever. And dying forever is what makes our existence here, ultimately, no different from raccoon roadkill, with the exception that, as opposed to the raccoon, we *know* that we will die. And that death, and our foreknowledge of it, is the one absolute that makes all the fleeting contingencies of our lives absurd in a way that even the raccoon's wasn't.

C al, Kim S., Cannae—what does it matter? In the long run, we're all dead anyway. For thousands of years, thinkers have engaged in all sorts of linguistic and logical gymnastics in the futile quest for philosophical certainty about something, anything—the nature of reality, the meaning of life, whatever—even though one certainty alone has stared them down from the start, and that is death.

Benjamin Franklin said that you can't avoid death and taxes. Wrong. There have been plenty of tax cheats, but death cheats? Good luck with that. Sure, some things are worse than death, but whatever they are, they must be pretty bad when death is deemed better.

Annie Dillard wrote about the time her father "tried to explain why men on Wall Street had jumped from skyscrapers when the stock market crashed: 'They lost everything!'—but of course, I thought they lost everything only when they jumped."[10]

Suicide, genocide, accident, and old age, death annuls all things and everything, even the only thing most people leave behind—the memory of them, though in most cases, even that gets vaporized in the void of ether as well.

Is there, then, no hope, no answer but only the inevitability of death?

Well, according to the Bible . . .

The Bible?

That Book, of necessity, brings in God, who Himself comes with a host of concepts and presuppositions that some can't abide: "I want atheism to be true," wrote Thomas Nagel, "and am made uneasy by the fact that some of the most intelligent and well-informed people I know are religious believers. It isn't just that I don't believe in God and, naturally, hope that I'm right in my belief. It's that I hope there is no God! I don't want there to be a God; I don't want the universe to be like that."[11]

Like what? Like one that leaves us "nothingness after death—the huge solace of thinking that for our betrayals, greed, cowardice, murders we are not going to be judged"?[12]

We might not be Joseph Goebbels or even Idi Amin, but who doesn't live with dirty secrets, ugly deeds that we hope will vanish into the grave with our corpses or dissolve into the air with our ashes, as opposed to being openly judged by an all-knowing, all-seeing Deity? However much people might really want God deep down, deeper still is the fear of what His existence might entail: a transcendent Being whom we might have to answer to, a frightening prospect for a race bone rotten enough to know, even without conscious knowledge of God's law, that we're two-legged rats or, as one tribe of cannibals described us, "food that talks."[13]

As the apostle Paul wrote two thousand years ago: "For since the creation of the world God's invisible qualities—his eternal power and divine nature—have been clearly seen, being understood from what has been made, so that people are without excuse" (Romans 1:20, NIV).

Without excuse?

No wonder people fear a universe "like that." They ought to. The God who created the cosmos, from electrons to galaxies and all in between, possesses power that we can't fathom. So fathom this instead: standing before this God with every nasty fantasy, every warped act, and every unkind utterance on display. Fathom standing before the One for whom all lame and cheap excuses and rationalizations glimmer under a light so bright it exposes even what your own subconscious has concealed from you in self-defense.

What are your odds?

That's why Jesus of Nazareth and His resurrection from the dead offer us—entities as rank as depicted here—our only hope in a universe that, despite Thomas Nagel's fear, is, in fact, just "like that."

W e who must die," wrote W. H. Auden, "demand a miracle."[14]
What else? Freezing your brain in the hope that some computer geek
will later upload your neural connections to a hard drive? Or, as some have been
trying, transfusions of young blood into old bodies? If "the life of the flesh is in the
blood" (Leviticus 17:11), then shouldn't an endless supply of young blood keep
old flesh endlessly alive? The logic works; good luck with the technology, though.

Auden's right. We who must die demand a miracle. Otherwise what? Roadkill,
that's what. Fortunately, we have been given a miracle, many actually, in the
Gospels.

Miracles? *Come on.*

No, you come on. Who hasn't had a whiff of the miraculous, an inkling of
something beyond chemicals and formulas, a hint that reality's much more than
what your high-school biology textbooks taught?

Even when faced with great suffering, humans endeavor to hold out hope that
something good will happen. For instance, under Soviet Communism, Anna
Akhmatova wrote:

> By day, from the surrounding woods,
> cherries blow summer into town;
> at night the deep transparent skies
> glitter with new galaxies.
>
> And the miraculous comes so close . . .
> something not known to anyone at all,
> but wild in our breast for centuries.[15]

If you're open to the possibility of the miraculous, the hopeful notion that
more's here than appears here ("something not known to anyone at all"), then
lucky you. Logic is on your side.

In *Conjuring the Universe*, atheist Peter Atkins claims that the universe arose
from nothing. And to be sure that we know what he means by "nothing,"* he
explains: "From now on, by nothing I shall mean absolutely nothing. I shall
mean less than empty space. . . . This Nothing has no space and no time. This
Nothing is absolutely nothing. A void devoid of space and time. Utter emptiness.
Emptiness beyond emptiness. All that it has, is a name."[16]

And from here, he annunciates his goal: "I want to show that nothing is the
foundation of everything."[17]

---

* He explicates so much on this definition of "nothing" because other books about the universe
arising from nothing actually have their "nothings" as things such as false vacuum patches, quantum
fluctuations, or gravity, which, simply, beg the question: Where did these so-called nothings come
from? Atkins, with his definition, seeks to avoid that trap.

Because Atkins denies the existence of God, the everything-from-nothing theory remains his only logical recourse.

Why?

"Imagine," writes physicist Sabine Hossenfelder, "theoretical physicists proved there is only one, ultimate law of nature that could have created us. Finally, everything would make sense: stars and planets, light and dark, life and death. We would know the reason for each and every happenstance, know that it could not have been any different, could not have been better, could not have been worse. We'd be on par with nature, able to look at the universe and say, 'I understand.' "[18]

Not so fast, because whatever this "ultimate law of nature"—no matter how primal or brutally factual—is, the question remains, *Why this formula instead of another?* But whatever explains that specific formula must be explained by something before it, and on and on forever into infinity.

Only two options (it seems) save us from this infinite regress.

First, an eternally existent God who needs no explanation because He always existed.

Or nothing, which needs no explanation because, after all, it's nothing.

Because Atkins rules out Deity, his only option is that nothing, a "void devoid of space and time. Utter emptiness. Emptiness beyond emptiness," created the universe. But to label that idea even as irrational is to give it more credence than it deserves. "The doctrine," wrote David Bentley Hart, "that there is nothing apart from the physical order, and certainly nothing supernatural—is an incorrigibly incoherent concept, and one that is ultimately indistinguishable from pure magical thinking."[19]

Thus, God as the Creator is the most, even only, logical option.

And because this God created space, time, matter, energy, and all the natural laws that govern them, He must be greater than those laws. He is not bound by them but beyond and above them. That's why the miraculous is logical. It is simply God—who created and sustains the natural laws—occasionally acting outside of, or even beyond, the natural laws that He created and sustains. It's like a painter who, painting mostly in one style, on rare occasion paints in another or even goes into another art form completely.

If Picasso were outside of, beyond, and transcendent to a piece of canvas that he painted on, how much more so would the Creator of the universe be outside of, beyond, and transcendent to the universe He had created? And thus, when He willed, He acted above and beyond the laws that He Himself created and sustains. That's, perhaps, all that a miracle is.

"A better analogy," writes theologian Edward Feser, "might be to think of the world as music and God as the musician who is playing the music. Divine conservation of the ordinary, natural course of things is comparable to the musician's playing the music according to the written score as he has it before his mind. God's causing a miracle is comparable to the musician temporarily departing from the score, as in the sort of improvisation characteristic of jazz."[20]

Logic doesn't mean that miracles have to happen but only that they could. And for beings like us "who must die," we can be glad that they have—especially the miracle of Jesus' resurrection, for only from it do we have the hope of our own.[21]

---

1. See Patrick N. Hunt, *Hannibal* (New York: Simon and Schuster, 2017), 144, 145.

2. Louis-Ferdinand Céline, *Journey to the End of the Night* (New York: New Directions, 1983), 54.

3. Albert Camus, *The Myth of Sisyphus* (Toronto: Vintage Books, 1955), 18.

4. Donald Justice, "There Is a Gold Light in Certain Old Paintings," in *Collected Poems* (New York: Alfred A. Knopf, 2004), 278.

5. Nikolai Gogol, *Dead Souls,* trans. Constance Garnett (New York: Modern Library, 1936), 75.

6. "Man is the only being that knows death; all others become old, but with a consciousness wholly limited to the moment which must seem to them eternal." Oswald Spengler, *Decline of the West* (New York: Alfred A. Knopf, 1986), 89.

7. Blaise Pascal, *Pensées,* trans. W. F. Trotter (Mineola, NY: Dover Pub., 2003), 59.

8. Harry McCracken and Lev Grossman, "Can Google Solve Death?" *Time,* September 30, 2013, cover.

9. Donna Tartt, *The Secret History* (New York: Penguin Books, 1993), 42; emphasis in the original.

10. Annie Dillard, *The Annie Dillard Reader* (New York: HarperCollins, 1994), 243.

11. Thomas Nagel, *The Last Word* (New York: Oxford University Press, 1997), 130.

12. Czeslaw Milosz, *Road-Side Dog,* trans. Czeslaw Milosz and Robert Hass (New York: Farrar, Straus and Giroux, 1998), 22.

13. Thomas Ligotti, *The Conspiracy Against the Human Race* (New York: Penguin Books, 2018), 154.

14. W. H. Auden, *For the Time Being*, in *Collected Poems* (New York: Vintage Books, 1991), 353. The whole stanza is worth reading:

> We who must die demand a miracle.
> How could the Eternal do a temporal act,
> The Infinite become a finite fact?
> Nothing can save us that is possible:
> We who must die demand a miracle.

15. Anna Akhmatova, " 'Everything Is Plundered . . . ,' " in *Poems of Akhmatova*, ed. and trans. Stanley Kunitz with Max Hayward (New York: Houghton Mifflin, 1973), 73.

16. Peter Atkins, *Conjuring the Universe: The Origins of the Laws of Nature* (Oxford, UK: Oxford University Press, 2018), 28.

17. Atkins, 17.

18. Sabine Hossenfelder, *Lost in Math: How Beauty Leads Physics Astray* (New York: Basic Books, 2018), 99.

19. David Bentley Hart, *The Experience of God: Being, Consciousness, Bliss* (London: Yale University Press, 2013), 17.

20. Edward Feser, *Five Proofs of the Existence of God* (San Francisco: Ignatius Press, 2017), 243.

21. Portions of this chapter are adapted from Clifford Goldstein, "The Produce of the Dead," Cliff's Edge, *Adventist Review*, October 19, 2017, https://www.adventistreview.org/church-news/story5553-cliffs-edge-the-produce-of-the-dead; "The Irrationality of Doubt," Cliff's Edge, *Adventist Review,* July 20, 2018, https://www.adventistreview.org/church-news/story6316-the-irrationality-of-doubt/.

Light-Years and Inches

The painter Willem de Kooning, who lived in New York City, often spent time in rural North Carolina. One evening he and his wife exited a party and walked outside. The sky was cloudless, and the stars sizzled.

"It was a sight never seen in the city, where the reflected glare blanked out the stars and only a slice of the sky was visible from a loft window. 'Let's get back to the party,' de Kooning said suddenly. 'The universe gives me the creeps.' "[1]

The creeps?

Sure, a place measured in light-years when we're used to measuring in feet and inches would seem creepy. And then, squatting for millennia at the center of the universe (or so we thought), only to be ingloriously exiled to the fringes of one galaxy out of trillions—our egos have taken a hit.

"The life of a man," lamented David Hume, "is of no greater importance to the universe than that of an oyster."[2]

That depends upon the universe actually. In a meaningless, purposeless, and godless one, you could make that argument, perhaps[3] (though even then, *an oyster?*). But not in the universe depicted in Scripture like this: "Then Joseph, being aroused from sleep, did as the angel of the Lord commanded him and took to him his wife, and did not know her till she had brought forth her firstborn Son. And he called His name Jesus" (Matthew 1:24, 25).

Humanity is so important that the God who created the universe* became part of it. (Compared to what it took to make the universe in the first place, becoming part of it would be easy.) The One whose creation is measured in light-years shrank into Someone measured in feet and inches. Willem de Kooning, limited by the laws of nature, couldn't transform himself into one of his creations. But God, not limited by those laws, could—and did, and that's who Jesus of Nazareth was. The Creator became a person, a human being who, as one of us, has thus linked Himself to us with ties that will never be broken.

Christ, God Himself, in a sense shrinking down and becoming one of us—this is the foundation of the gospel. But only the foundation. There's much more.

---

* John 1:1–3, talking about Jesus as Creator, says: "In the beginning was the Word, and the Word was with God, and the Word was God. He was in the beginning with God. All things were made through Him, and without Him nothing was made that was made." Anything that once didn't exist but then came into existence was created by Jesus.

Sometimes, something floods us with a momentary sense of happiness or hopefulness—a curtain floating on a warm breeze, a whiff of freshly washed hair, an act of unselfish kindness—causing a flush of goodness so big and near that our skin laughs (that's what tingles are), and we know that all is going to be good. Like Anna Akhmatova, who, though suffering, could still inscribe into other souls words about something not known nor fully understood "but wild in our breast for centuries."

The incarnation of Jesus shows us that these moments of hope, when the "miraculous comes so close" and transcends the harsh and pricking facts in our faces now—these are not mere spasms of sentimental chemicals that come and go like sneezes or heartburn. Rather, they are emotional snapshots from the greater reality beyond the narrow and temporary one that's being staged, as if we were characters in a play who didn't know that we were in a dramatic production and that a greater reality existed outside the stage.

Sure, a cosmos measured in light-years can overwhelm creatures measured in feet and inches. However, this contrast reveals the extent of the Creator's love. God reached across the forbidding vastness of space, past galaxies and superclusters of galaxies, and—instead of continuing on past us and past the galaxies and superclusters of galaxies on the other side of us—He stopped among us and assumed the same biology and chemistry as us. According to the laws of physics, information itself would take billions of years to cross the known cosmos (try wrapping your mind around that idea), and yet this same distance wasn't too vast for God's love to traverse every inch of it and, in so doing, embrace humanity.

After all, two trillion (2,000,000,000,000) galaxies burnish the cosmos. Approximately one hundred million (100,000,000) stars comprise each galaxy. Two trillion galaxies of one hundred million stars each come to two hundred quintillion (200,000,000,000,000,000,000) stars. Meanwhile, astronomers are discovering planets that orbit other stars, much like Earth, Venus, Jupiter, and the other planets of our solar system do ours. If every one of the two hundred quintillion stars had planets orbiting them, we'd be in neuron-snapping numbers.[4]

And the distances also mock our minds. At speeds of 186,000 miles per second (about seven times around the earth), light takes hundreds, thousands, millions even billions of years to reach many of these galaxies, some so wide that light, zipping along at 186,000 miles per second, would still need thousands of years to get from one side of a galaxy to the other.

Our nearest galactic neighbor, the Andromeda galaxy, is 2.5 million light-years away. So, at 186,000 miles per second, for 2.5 million years . . . well, you do the math.

This is just the known universe, what's capturable with our telescopes and theories. If the universe is infinite, then our telescopes and theories will, eventually, fizzle out somewhere in the cosmos but, technically, no closer to the edge than when they started. (If the universe is not infinite, what's immediately outside its edge—what's it made of, what's its color and its texture, how far does it extend, and what comes after?)

Nothing created can be greater than what created it. A painting by Pablo Picasso was never deeper, richer, and greater than Picasso. Whatever went into the painting existed first in Picasso, who remained outside of the painting and, in a real sense, transcended it. Thus, the God who created the cosmos, two trillion galaxies, each shimmering with billions of stars (themselves very complicated structures), is greater, outside of, and transcendent of this cosmos. Which leaves us in an epistemological pickle: If we can barely comprehend the cosmos, how can we understand its Creator?

Revelation, of course, teaches us things that our senses, piggybacked on reason, can't, such as, "In the beginning was the Word, and the Word was with God, and the Word was God. He was in the beginning with God. All things were made through Him, and without Him nothing was made that was made" (John 1:1–3).

The God who created all that was created, the two hundred quintillion stars and everything else—did what? He shrank down and became a human baby, lived in perfect obedience to the Father, and then, "according to His own purpose and grace which was given to us in Christ Jesus before time began" (2 Timothy 1:9), offered Himself as a divine-human sacrifice for the sins of a single species on one planet among the two hundred quintillion (200,000,000,000,000,000,000,000) stars.

The next time you look up at the night sky blistering in starlight, as did de Kooning, think of the incarnation of Jesus and try to imagine a love so great that, though originating light-years beyond those stars, it reached past them and embraced us in our mere feet and inches.

Herman Cohen, a Jewish philosopher, believed that despite centuries of persecution in Europe, the Jews should forget about establishing a homeland of their own. Instead, they should take the great legacy bequeathed to them from the Hebrew Scriptures—the legacy of ethical monotheism—and using those lofty ideals, work to better their respective communities, wherever they were. For Cohen (who died in 1918), one country in particular, in the heart of Europe, offered the perfect environment for his utopian vision. This was a country where the Jews, having already had a long history there, not only would be fully accepted but also would be free to help create a just and prosperous society that, surely, could stand as a model for what the Jews could become in Europe.

What country?

Guess.

According to custom, a political leader, having turned on the Christmas tree lights, would utter some or another platitude: "These are the most hopeful times in all the years since Christ was born in Bethlehem. . . . Today, as never before, man has in his possession the capacities to end war and preserve peace, to eradicate poverty and share abundance, to overcome the diseases that have afflicted the human race and permit all mankind to enjoy their promise in life on this earth."[5]

Thus spake President Lyndon Baines Johnson in 1964 as he was about to escalate the Vietnam War.

In his Vietnam memoir, Philip Caputo wrote about the idealism of his youth; responding to John F. Kennedy's call to "ask not what your country can do for you, but what you can do for your country," Caputo thought that he could do something for his country by fighting in Vietnam. Before long, officers were offering grunts beer for every Vietcong they killed. "That is the level to which we had sunk from the lofty idealism of a year before," he wrote. "We were going to kill people for a few cans of beer and the time off to drink them."[6]

Unfortunately, even when people mean well, things often go south—that's fallen human nature. (*Everyone has a plan*, said heavyweight boxing champion Mike Tyson, *until he gets punched in the face*.) And what's it called when people don't mean well?

It's called world history.

For millennia, humans have debated moral theory. Are morals absolute? Relative? Universal? Cultural? Is something moral because God says it's moral, or does God say it's moral because it is?

Moral? If only people would be so, whatever the theory behind it.

But then there's Jesus, who once asked His enemies: "Can any of you prove me guilty of sin?" (John 8:46, NIV). None could. And that's because Jesus of Nazareth was the only human (out of billions) who never sinned and never violated the moral foundation of God's creation—the Ten Commandments. Those inclined to deem this old law code hopelessly antiquated ought to ask someone whose home has been burglarized (Exodus 20:15) or whose child has been murdered (verse 13) how antiquated the Ten Commandments are. What better way for God to show humanity how to live than for God Himself to become a human and live as He wanted humans to?

Jesus became not only an infant but also an adult who lived in flawless obedience to His Father. Jesus was humanity's perfect model. "He who says he abides in Him ought himself also to walk just as He walked" (1 John 2:6). Yet even if we follow Him, no matter how perfectly, that no more solves the dilemma of sin than if, having committed murder, we stop committing murder, even perfectly. The questions of guilt, justice, and punishment remain.

That's why Jesus just didn't come to Earth, present a perfect model (*Here is what I have done. Go and do likewise.*), and then happily shuttle heavenward. However amazing in and of itself, that condescension still wouldn't have been enough to solve the problem of death any more than a written law pardons the violation of that law. On the contrary, the written law is what makes the violation of the law the violation to begin with. "What shall we say then? Is the law sin? Certainly not! On the contrary, I would not have known sin except through the law. For I would not have known covetousness unless the law had said, 'You shall not covet' " (Romans 7:7).

That's why, even after all He had already done, none of it would count without the cross.

Jesus of Nazareth was not alone when crucified outside Jerusalem. Two criminals were with Him too. "They crucified two rebels with him, one on his
right and one on his left" (Mark 15:27, NIV). At first, both derided Jesus, as
did the Romans and the religious leaders. "In the same way the rebels who were
crucified with him also heaped insults on him" (Matthew 27:44, NIV; see also
Mark 15:32).

One then had a change of heart.

One of the criminals who hung there hurled insults at him: "Aren't you the
Messiah? Save yourself and us!"

But the other criminal rebuked him. "Don't you fear God," he said, "since
you are under the same sentence? We are punished justly, for we are getting
what our deeds deserve. But this man has done nothing wrong."

Then he said, "Jesus, remember me when you come into your kingdom"
(Luke 23:39–42, NIV).

However harsh life could be under Rome, the Romans were sticklers for the law.
They weren't going to crucify someone for stealing bread in order to feed hungry
children. They didn't even want to crucify Jesus and did so only at the instigation
of corrupt priests. Neither of these criminals was like Victor Hugo's Jean Valjean.[7]
One of them even admitted that they deserved to be tortured and executed.

Despite the horrendous pain of the crucifixion, the cold fear of his impending
demise, and the cacophony of insults, mockery, and calumny, this wretched man,
seeing Jesus as *HaMaschiach*,* uttered: "Jesus, remember me when you come into
your kingdom."

And what did Jesus answer?

Well, friend, I'd like to help you, but you shouldn't have been a robber? Or, maybe,
*Sorry, brother, but you shouldn't have been cursing Me when we were first brought
here?* Did Jesus repeat what He had preached earlier, that "unless your righteousness exceeds the righteousness of the scribes and the Pharisees, you will by no
means enter the kingdom of heaven" (Matthew 5:20)? Did Jesus rebuke the
robber with the commandment about not stealing (Exodus 20:13)? Did Jesus
quote for the Jew the psalm about having clean hands and a pure heart (Psalm
24:4)? Did Jesus throw in this man's face any of his sins and crimes?

No. Jesus looked at this broken, dying sinner who had nothing to offer God, a
man who even by Roman standards was worthy of death, and without any caveat
or fine print, Jesus flat-out promised him, "You will be with Me in Paradise"
(Luke 23:43). In other words, *Despite your sins, despite your crimes, despite your
defective character, and despite your unworthiness—I'm telling you right now, at this
moment—you have salvation in Me.*

---

* *HaMaschiach* is the transliteration of the Hebrew word for the Messiah.

Talk about a real-time, living-color, and 3-D representation of salvation by faith alone. "Therefore we conclude that a man is justified by faith apart from the deeds of the law" (Romans 3:28). This man's only relationship to the law was to have transgressed it, *and yet Jesus promised Him eternal life anyway?*

How could that be?

Because, with His impending death, Jesus bore in Himself the penalty for this man's sins and crimes, while at the same time, Jesus' own perfect life, His own perfect record of law-keeping, was credited to this man by faith—the faith revealed in his words to Jesus. Thus, the thief on the cross was now accounted before God as though he had never sinned to begin with.

Where else in Scripture is salvation so clearly portrayed? Jesus was getting what the robber deserved so that the robber could have what Jesus deserved. Christ became "a curse for us" (Galatians 3:13) so that the righteousness of God could be given to us: "For He made Him who knew no sin to be sin for us, that we might become the righteousness of God in Him" (2 Corinthians 5:21).

No wonder that the thief didn't need any works to be saved. What works could add to what Jesus did for him?

Yes, Jesus, the One who had existed above, beyond, and outside the creation, became part of the creation, starting as a fetus in a Jewish womb. Yes, Jesus then lived a sinless life in a sinful world, the perfect Example for us, and He offers us that sinless life instead of our sinful ones. Yes, Jesus died on the cross, paying in Himself the punishment for all of our evil so that we never have to pay it ourselves.

Yet all of this was still not enough. *Not enough?* As astonishing as His death was, at least as far as our long-term prospects are concerned, it would have been a nice but meaningless and ultimately futile gesture. Why? Because our fate would remain no different from that of the roadkill raccoon, whom we met in the first chapter, without His resurrection.

In 1973, Ursula K. Le Guin wrote "The Ones Who Walk Away From Omelas,"[8] a story about a city brimming with happiness and delight. The utopian tale begins by depicting a summer festival with children riding horses in a race as part of the celebration in Omelas.

"The air of morning was so clear that the snow still crowning the Eighteen Peaks burned with white-gold fire across the miles of sunlit air, under the dark blue of the sky. There was just enough wind to make the banners that marked the racecourse snap and flutter now and then."[9]

The narrator even gives readers room to customize the bliss of Omelas for ourselves. Despite the well-being and joy already revealed, we're allowed to mold our own vision of what this utopia should be.

"Omelas sounds in my words like a city in a fairy tale, long ago and far away, once upon a time. Perhaps it would be best if you imagined it as your own fancy bids, assuming it will rise to the occasion, for certainly I cannot suit you all."[10]

Amid the pleasure of Omelas, the narrator concedes that in the cellar of one of "the beautiful public buildings," a small child is locked away in wretchedness where it has been kept for years in isolation from any human touch except for an occasional kick by the warder. The dark room of captivity is empty but for "a couple of mops, with stiff, clotted, foul-smelling heads,"[11] which the child fears. The imp's age is hard to tell because its growth has been stunted. The child hadn't always lived there; it can even vaguely remember sunlight and its mother's voice.

"The child used to scream for help at night, and cry a good deal, but now it only makes a kind of whining, 'eh-haa, eh-haa,' and it speaks less and less often. It is so thin there are no calves to its legs; its belly protrudes; it lives on a half-bowl of corn meal and grease a day. It is naked. Its buttocks and thighs are a mass of festered sores, as it sits in its own excrement continually."[12]

The people of Omelas know that the child is there, that it has to be there, and that "their happiness, the beauty of their city, the tenderness of their friendships, the health of their children, the wisdom of their scholars, the skill of their makers, even the abundance of their harvest and the kindly weathers of their skies, depend wholly on this child's abominable misery."[13]

Hence, Le Guin's utopian tale of Omelas, a place so much better than what we experience here except, that is, for the unfortunate child upon whose wretchedness all Omelasian joy, prosperity, and peace depend.

This story is an example of *utilitarian calculus*—the notion that we can justify any deed by the amount of pleasure or good, in contrast to the amount of pain or evil, it causes. "The greatest good for the greatest number," that idea, which, though it sounds reasonable, proves how deceptive reason can be. After all, wouldn't this calculus justify enslaving one million people for the peace, happiness, prosperity, and joy of twenty-five million? Or a hundred thousand slaves for the peace, prosperity, and joy of fifty million? Ten thousand for fifty million?

Plug in the numbers. Which work for you?

This thinking is common because it sounds so reasonable, so sensible, so, well, utilitarian. It's nothing new either. "Then one of them, named Caiaphas, who was high priest that year, spoke up, 'You know nothing at all! You do not realize that it is better for you that one man die for the people than that the whole nation perish' " (John 11:49, 50, NIV).

Though not a bad calculation itself, one man for an entire nation, the numbers get better because, as John says, Christ's death wasn't for the whole Hebrew nation alone but for "the scattered children of God" (verse 52, NIV)—that is, for all people who will be redeemed. In fact, technically, it was for the whole world.

In reality, instead of our hope depending upon a wretched child locked in a basement, according to the gospel, our hope is dependent upon a wretched Christ on the cross. When humanity violated the moral freedom God had given it, only the death of One equal with God, Christ Himself,* could pay the penalty for that violation. Though the narrator never explained why the child had to suffer for the sake of Omelas, Scripture is clear about why Christ had to suffer: "God made him who had no sin to be sin for us, so that in him we might become the righteousness of God" (2 Corinthians 5:21, NIV). " 'He himself bore our sins' in his body on the cross, so that we might die to sins and live for righteousness; 'by his wounds you have been healed' " (1 Peter 2:24, NIV).

The gospel is Christ in the basement of Omelas for us. Only unlike the child, Christ went voluntarily; unlike those who, upon finding out about the child, leave the city ("the ones who walk away from Omelas"), the Lord—having computed the utilitarian calculus—knew that the suffering of Christ on our behalf was more than worth it.

But again, without the Resurrection, that suffering would have been for nothing and, certainly, not for us.

* Though this isn't the place to deal with the divinity of Christ, numerous texts, such as John 1:1–3; 8:58; and Philippians 2:5–11, testify that He is God.

In the 1990s, signs and bumper stickers appeared in Brooklyn and Israel that read *Moshiach Now. Moshiach* is Yiddish for *Messiah.* These Orthodox Jews thought the Messiah was about to appear.

This was not, of course, the second coming of Jesus but rather the first coming of Rabbi Menachem Mendel Schneerson, known as the Lubavitcher Rebbe* or just the Rebbe, the spiritual leader of the Chabad-Lubavitcher dynasty of ultra-Orthodox Jews. For decades, from his iconic headquarters in Brooklyn, the Rebbe guided his movement, which, under his spiritual and practical leadership, expanded from Bangalore to Richmond and to parts in between (there's a Chabad house in Kinshasa, Congo). As one of the most influential Jewish religious leaders of the twentieth century,[†] Schneerson was so revered that some Chabadniks[‡] claimed that he was the long-awaited Messiah.

Yes, for many, the Messiah had come. And he (*Yechi HaMelek!*[§]) was living at 770 Eastern Parkway, Brooklyn, New York. Though he never claimed to be *Moshiach*, in the early 1990s, Messianic fervor among some Lubavitch reached a critical mass: Rebbe Schneerson was not only the Messiah but would soon reveal himself as such to the world. Wrote biblical scholar Michael Brown: "And so a movement began within Lubavitch— including a petition drive—announcing the belief that the seventh Lubavitcher Rebbe, Menachem Mendel Schneerson, was, in fact, the long-awaited Messiah."[14]

Then, on 3 Tammuz 5754 (June 2, 1994), Rabbi Menachem Mendel Schneerson upped and died, but not the Messianic fervor around him. On the contrary, it increased. Why? Because many claimed that, according to the Hebrew Scriptures, the Messiah had to first die and then, after being resurrected, He would reign as King *Moshiach*.

A Messiah who dies and is then resurrected?

In 2002, Lubavitch high-school girls sang:

Redemption has arrived
That's what the Rebbe prophesied
Moshiach has come
It's already begun. . . .

The world will gather passionately
To the Rebbe in 770[¶]
In the *Beis Hamikdash***
We know it can't be long

---

* *Rebbe* is Yiddish for the Hebrew *rabbi*, which means "teacher" or "master."

† In 1994, he was awarded a Congressional Gold Medal for "outstanding and lasting contributions toward improvements in world education, morality, and acts of charity." See An Act to Award a Congressional Gold Medal to Rabbi Menachem Mendel Schneerson, H.R. 4497, 103rd Cong. (1994), https://www.govinfo.gov/content/pkg/BILLS-103hr4497rds/html/BILLS-103hr4497rds.htm.

‡ Informal nickname for members of the Chabad movement.

§ A Yiddish phrase that some followers applied to him, which meant, "Long live the King!"

¶ That is, 770 Eastern Parkway, his Brooklyn headquarters.

** The third temple.

Why has so much time gone by?
The question brings tears to our eyes
Rebbe dear Rebbe
We know you are alive.[15]

Eight years after his passing, some Lubavitch were singing about Schneerson: "We know you are alive"!

In 2007, the Israeli newspaper *Haaretz* ran an article titled "The Lubavitcher Rebbe as a God."[16] The gist of the article, written by a skeptical reporter, was that some of the Rebbe's most devoted followers believed the Rebbe was God. The author quoted one Messianic Lubavitcher as saying about the Rebbe: "God chose to imbue this world with life through a body. So that's how we know the Rebbe can't have died, and that his actual physical body must be alive. The Rebbe is the conjunction of God and human. The Rebbe is God, but he is also physical."[17]

A divine Messiah who assumed a human body, dies in that body, but then comes back to life? Sounds like Jews for Jesus, not Hasidim, which explains why many other Jews, including other Orthodox, even other Chabadniks, were appalled. The theology of a dead and then resurrected Messiah sounds frighteningly like what the Christians have been saying for almost two thousand years about Jesus.

A statement released in 1996 by the Rabbinical Council of America reads: "In light of disturbing developments which have recently arisen in the Jewish community, the Rabbinical Council of America in convention assembled declares that there is not and has never been a place in Judaism for the belief that Mashiach Ben David [Messiah son of David] will begin his Messianic Mission only to experience death, burial, and resurrection before completing it."[18] The notion of Schneerson as the Messiah was bad enough (especially when, having been afflicted with a stroke in 1992, he was unable to speak and was confined to a wheelchair) but then, after his death, to claim that Schneerson was going to be resurrected and reign as *Moshiach*?

Though controversy still exists regarding the late Rebbe from 770 Eastern Parkway, Brooklyn, not that far away, at 121-83 Springfield Boulevard—that is, the Montefiore Cemetery, Queens—Rebbe Schneerson remains where they first placed him.

The same, however, can't be said about Jesus of Nazareth.

*T*ime magazine ran an article in 1979 about a new book by a theologian who affirmed the veracity of Jesus' bodily resurrection.[19] Considering the theological atmosphere of that time, infused with higher criticism and the naturalistic presuppositions that dominated it—a theologian affirming something as unscientific as a man, three days dead, being resurrected was remarkable enough.

But that's only half the story, the least interesting half. The theologian who affirmed Jesus' resurrection wasn't a New Testament scholar at Princeton or from the Moody Bible Institute, but an Orthodox Jew, a Holocaust survivor who lived in Israel.

His name was Pinchas Lapide, and he was not a Messianic Jew nor a Jew for Jesus or the like. He was, instead, a scholar who, though never publicly accepting Jesus as the Jewish Messiah, claimed, based on the historical evidence, that he believed in the bodily resurrection of Jesus of Nazareth as depicted in the New Testament.

In regard to the question about how the earliest followers of Jesus, Christ's first disciples, could overcome their horrible disappointment when Jesus was killed, and in such an ignominious manner as well, Lapide writes: "The answer of the apostles was brief and unambiguous: The resurrection of Jesus from the dead."[20]

And Lapide accepts that answer: Jesus of Nazareth rose from the dead, and "the resurrection belongs to the category of the truly real and effective occurrences, for without a fact of history there is no act of true faith."[21]

Lapide goes on, saying, "This means that the Risen One came in order to bless Israel. The unavoidable conclusion that forces itself on us from these facts is that the Easter event, in whatever way one wants to understand it, was primarily and chiefly a Jewish faith experience."[22]

The key phrase in those two sentences is "in whatever way one wants to understand it." And Lapide understands it in a way that allows him, he says, to believe in the resurrection of Jesus—"the unavoidable conclusion that forces itself on us"—but without believing that Jesus is the Jewish Messiah.

Lapide takes the position, not a particularly logical one, that, though not the Messiah, Jesus was preparing the way of the Messiah. "Jesus," he writes, "therefore, without doubt, belongs to the *praeparatio messianica* of the full salvation which is still in the future. He was 'a paver of the way for the King Messiah,' as Maimonides calls him, but this does not mean that his resurrection makes him the Messiah of Israel for the Jewish people."[23]

Again, however questionable, even absurd, the logic of this position (one rabbi, upset with Lapide's position, said, "If I believed in Jesus' resurrection I would be baptized tomorrow"[24]), the question remains: What was the evidence that caused this Jewish scholar to believe in the resurrection of Jesus?

Even when still children, we face the coldness of our own temporality. Not a morbid fear of death necessarily, but simply the logical realization of death's inevitability, which is so apparent that you don't need to be a twentieth-century French atheist to experience what twentieth-century French atheists termed "existentialist dread"—the fact that our lives, so temporal and hard to begin with, could be purposeless as well.

Annie Dillard depicted this dread from her own young girl's perspective:

Loss came around with the seasons, blew into the house when you opened the windows, piled up in the bottom desk and dresser drawers, accumulated in the back of closets, heaped in the basement starting by the furnace, and came creeping up the basement stairs. Loss grew as you did, without your consent; your losses mounted beside you like earthworm castings. No willpower could prevent someone's dying. And no willpower could restore someone dead, breathe life into that frame and set it going again in the room with you to meet your eyes. That was the fact of it. The strongest men and women who had ever lived had presumably tried to resist their own deaths, and now they were dead.[25]

About her last point, to restore "someone dead" and to "breathe life into that frame"—here is precisely what the promise of Christ's resurrection is all about. It happened to Jesus, and the promise is that it will happen to those redeemed by Him as well. However, in the immediate context of Annie Dillard's concern, it's hard to argue with the pain caused by a loss that engulfs us.

Loss—it is part and parcel of existence, built into the fabric of physical reality, actually. It's so real that it can be described with mathematical formulas. It's a law of physics: the second law of thermodynamics, also known as entropy, which in the simplest terms means that, left to themselves, things go from bad to worse. And whatever the numbers in the formula come to, for humans, the fear is that they threaten to make our lives mean zero.

"All is nothingness in the world," wrote Giacomo Leopardi, "including my despair, which any man who is wise but also calmer, and I myself certainly at a quieter time, will see as vain, irrational, and imaginary. Wretched me! Even this pain of mine is vain, nothing. After a certain time it will pass and turn to nothing, and leave me in a universal emptiness, a terrible apathy that will not even let me lament."[26]

The apostle Paul reflected on this theme himself, the idea being that if this life is all that there is, if nothing's beyond, then why not just have fun now because it all comes to naught. "Let us eat and drink, for tomorrow we die!" (1 Corinthians 15:32). But his larger point was to argue that, in the bodily resurrection of Jesus, people have the promise of their own resurrection; that is, the promise of eternal life in an entirely new existence.

This resurrection was so central, Paul wrote, that "if there is no resurrection of the dead, then Christ is not risen. And if Christ is not risen, then our preaching is empty and your faith is also empty. . . . For if the dead do not rise, then Christ is not risen. And if Christ is not risen, your faith is futile; you are still in your sins!" (verses 13–17).

Notice, Paul didn't say that if Christ were not incarnated, or not sinless, or even if Christ were not crucified, then their faith would be empty and vain. Christ could have been all of those things, yet if He had not been resurrected, then everything that they hoped for and believed in meant nothing. In short, the foundation of Christianity rested on trusting that a Man who had been beaten, whipped, crucified, killed, stabbed, wrapped in grave clothes, and put in a tomb on Friday, which was closed in by a boulder and sealed, had, on the following Sunday, been brought back to life, freed from the tomb, and then appeared in His resurrected fleshly body to numerous people—some of whom struggled to believe that it was Him.

And if some people who actually saw Him in person, in the flesh, struggled to believe, what about the millions, billions, who never saw Him in that manner?

Why should they believe?

Yes, it's written in the Bible, and Christians accept the Bible. But, still, they are asked to believe and trust that their entire hope rests upon a single supernatural event that unfolded in a three-day period that (for us now) was almost two thousand years ago.

That takes faith, yes.

But what if Christ's bodily resurrection and the hope that it offers is not only the most logical explanation for what happened but the *only* logical one? What if it's so logical and heavily laden with evidence that the great leap of faith comes, not in believing in His resurrection but, actually, in denying it?[27]

1. Mark Stevens and Annalyn Swan, *De Kooning: An American Master* (New York: Alfred A. Knopf, 2004), 264.

2. David Hume, *On Suicide* (New York: Penguin Books, 2005), 4.

3. "Man is alone in a cold and alien universe," Morris Kline, *Mathematics: The Loss of Certainty* (Oxford, UK: Oxford University Press, 1980), 353.

4. See Elizabeth Howell, "How Many Stars Are in the Universe?" Space.com, May 18, 2017, https://www.space.com/26078-how-many-stars-are-there.html.

5. Kevin M. Schultz, *Buckley and Mailer: The Difficult Friendship That Shaped the Sixties* (New York: W. W. Norton, 2015), 139.

6. Philip Caputo, *A Rumor of War: The Classic Vietnam Memoir* (New York: Picador, 1996), 311.

7. See Victor Hugo's *Les Misérables*, first published in 1862.

8. Ursula K. Le Guin, "The Ones Who Walk Away From Omelas," in *The Wind's Twelve Quarters* (London: Gollancz, 2015), 254–262.

9. Le Guin, 256.

10. Le Guin, 257.

11. Le Guin, 259.

12. Le Guin, 260.

13. Le Guin, 260.

14. Michael L. Brown, *Resurrection* (Lake Mary, FL: Charisma House, 2020), 12.

15. David Berger, *The Rebbe, the Messiah, and the Scandal of Orthodox Indifference* (London: Littman Library of Jewish Civilization, 2008), xxxiii, xxxiv.

16. Saul Sadka, "The Lubavitcher Rebbe as a God," *Haaretz*, November 2, 2007, https://www.haaretz.com/1.4804959.

17. Sadka, "Lubavitcher Rebbe."

18. Brown, *Resurrection*, 3.

19. "Religion: Resurrection?," *Time*, May 7, 1979, 87.

20. Pinchas Lapide, *The Resurrection of Jesus: A Jewish Perspective*, trans. Wilhelm C. Linss (Eugene, OR: Wipf and Stock, 2002), 70.

21. Lapide, 92.

22. Lapide, 45, 46.

23. Lapide, 152.

24. "Religion: Resurrection?," 87.

25. Annie Dillard, *The Annie Dillard Reader* (New York: HarperCollins, 1994), 209, 210.

26. Giacomo Leopardi, *Zibaldone*, ed. Michael Caesar and Franco D'Intino, trans. Kathleen Baldwin et al. (New York: Farrar, Straus and Giroux, 2015), 75.

27. Portions of this chapter are adapted from Clifford Goldstein, "Light Years and Inches," Cliff's Edge, *Adventist Review*, August 3, 2018, https://www.adventistreview.org/church-news/story6372-light-years-and-inches; "The Calculus of the Cross," Cliff's Edge, *Adventist Review*, September 11, 2017, https://www.adventistreview.org/church-news/story5443-cliffs-edge-the-calculus-of-the-cross-goldstein; and "The Thief on the Cross and the 'Everlasting Gospel,' " Preparation for the End Time, in *Adult Sabbath School Bible Study Guide*, May 21, 2018, https://absg.adventist.org/pdf.php?file=2018:2Q:SE:PDFs:EAQ218_08.pdf.

Jesus, Dead

For Jesus to have been resurrected from the dead, He had to have died. Which happened at the cross.* Though debate exists about most everything with Jesus, few deny that Jesus of Nazareth was crucified by the Romans.

The Romans, after all, crucified lots of people, including Jews. Though cruel, this punishment was hardly unusual. Crucifixion had been a time-honored practice before Jesus and continued after Him. Though the Romans didn't originate this form of "justice" (the Persians, Macedonians, Carthaginians, and others had already been doing it), they gave it their own cultural twist. It was deemed the worst way to die, something reserved mostly for the dregs of society—that is, slaves, pirates, political insurgents, and traitors.

One of the earliest reports of mass crucifixions occurred after the Third Servile War (73–71 BC), the famous slave revolt against Rome led by Spartacus, which ended in defeat for the slaves but only after some stunning victories against their Roman masters. The six thousand survivors were crucified en masse along the Appian Way—a major road between Rome and the port city of Brindisi.

The most infamous example of Roman mass crucifixions appears from the pen of the historian Josephus, who described what the Romans did during the siege of Jerusalem in AD 70, in which Titus ordered five hundred Jews crucified a day.

So they were first whipped, and then tormented with all sorts of tortures before they died, and were then crucified before the wall of the city. This miserable procedure made Titus greatly to pity them, while they caught every day five hundred Jews; nay, some days they caught more; yet did it not appear to be safe for him to let those that were taken by force go their way; and to set a guard over so many, he saw would be to make such as guarded them useless to him. The main reason why he did not forbid that cruelty was this, that he hoped the Jews might perhaps yield at that sight, out of fear lest they might themselves afterwards be liable to the same cruel treatment. So the soldiers out of the wrath and hatred they bore the Jews, nailed those they caught, one after one way, and another after another to the crosses, by way of jest; when their multitude was so great, that room was wanting for the crosses, and crosses wanting for the bodies.[1]

A Jew crucified by Romans in Judea in the first century AD is, then, no big deal (except, of course, if you happened to be the Jew crucified). And the account of Jesus on the cross—from the scourging (Mark 15:15), the beating (Matthew 27:30), the Crucifixion (Luke 23:33), and the sign over His head (John 19:19)—accurately depict Roman executions.

Thus, the death in the first century AD of a Jewish Galilean peasant on a Roman

* The question about whether Jesus really died on the cross will be dealt with in more detail later in the book.

cross in the province of Judea under the reign of Pontius Pilate should have, in and of itself, been nothing extraordinary.

Except for one detail—who that Galilean peasant was: Jesus of Nazareth, the One who created the created world. "In the beginning was the Word, and the Word was with God, and the Word was God. He was in the beginning with God. All things were made through Him, and without Him nothing was made that was made" (John 1:1–3).

The One through whom "all things were made"—He was crucified by a small segment of that creation?

God, *on a cross*?

Yes, which explains why, however ordinary crucifixion in Roman Judea was, the crucifixion of Jesus wasn't ordinary.

Whatever hoopla surrounds the birth announcements of the world's most illustrious babies, nothing beat Jesus' birth announcement:

And suddenly there was with the angel a multitude of the heavenly host praising God and saying:

> "Glory to God in the highest,
> And on earth peace, goodwill toward men!" (Luke 2:13).

Angels?

Why not? Can we be so narrow-minded, so enslaved to the intellectual dominion of scientific materialists who must reject this story out of hand? The universe is so big, and we are so small. "Consider," wrote Raymond Tallis, "the relative volumes of our heads (4 litres) and of the universe (4×10^{23} cubic light years)."[2] And what are we in our smallness in contrast to the bigness of the universe other than a mass of cells that consume other cells until consumed by other cells ourselves?

Scripture paints a reality so much bigger and grander and richer than where our eyes, ears, and physics formulas and test tubes can take us. And so how foolish to make what a few pounds of water, blood, chemicals, and neurons snug inside a helmet of bone—all programmed by our short and very subjective contact with a sliver of reality—how foolish to make only what this organ can grasp or understand the limits of all reality.[3]

Scripture points us to something greater than the physical world as we now understand it, at least scientifically, which is why the existence of angels, of intelligent beings from another part of the creation, shouldn't be hard to believe in. (Can we actually think that we are, in all the cosmos, the only intelligent life?) Old and New Testament Scripture is suffused with the reality of angelic powers—that is, nonearthly life who, undoubtedly, come from another part of the creation. (Genesis 32:1; 2 Samuel 24:17; 1 Kings 19:5; Job 4:18; Psalms 91:11; 104:4; Daniel 6:22; Zechariah 4:1; Matthew 1:20; Mark 1:13; Luke 1:30; John 20:12; Acts 10:3; 1 Corinthians 4:9; 2 Thessalonians 1:7; Hebrews 1:5; 13:2; 2 Peter 2:4—these are only a smattering of biblical references to angelic powers.)

In addition, the New Testament records the following teachings on angels by Paul, Jesus, Peter and John. Paul wrote, "But even if we, or an angel from heaven, preach any other gospel to you than what we have preached to you, let him be accursed" (Galatians 1:8). Jesus told His followers, "But of that day and hour no one knows, not even the angels in heaven" (Mark 13:32). Finally, we read about "principalities and powers in the heavenly places" (Ephesians 3:10), about "angels and authorities and powers" (1 Peter 3:22) in heaven, about supernatural beings who in heaven sing:

"Holy, holy, holy,
Lord God Almighty,
Who was and is and is to come!" (Revelation 4:8).

And if heavenly beings were there at Christ's birth—beings who knew Him when He had "the glory which . . . [He] had with You [God] before the world was" (John 17:5)—they were surely there at His death too. What must have gone through their minds as they viewed their Lord, the One who had created them (Colossians 1:16), the One whom they had worshiped in heaven (Nehemiah 9:6; Hebrews 1:6), suffering the cruelty and taunts of the very people He had been dying for? These are intelligences who knew Christ when He reigned in heaven; now, they see Him dying under the curse of sin here on Earth.

It was as if inanimate nature itself was impacted. "Now from the sixth hour until the ninth hour there was darkness over all the land" (Matthew 27:45). And other supernatural events unfolded as well: "Then, behold, the veil of the temple was torn in two from top to bottom; and the earth quaked, and the rocks were split, and the graves were opened; and many bodies of the saints who had fallen asleep were raised; and coming out of the graves after His resurrection, they went into the holy city and appeared to many" (verses 51–53).

Darkness, suddenly, in the middle of the day? An earthquake? Rocks split? Graves open? The veil of the temple torn? All of this during the crucifixion of Jesus?

No wonder, then, the Roman centurion (of all people), the head of the guards, and others there could cry out, "Truly this was the Son of God!" (verse 54).

However common crucifixion was, nothing was common about the crucifixion of Jesus. The supernatural, made manifest at His birth and then throughout His life, was manifest at His death as well—a precursor to the miracle upon which all of our hope rests, and that is the resurrection of Jesus.

A bitter, twisting irony permeates Jesus' death. No matter how often Jesus had told His closest cohorts that He would be handed over and killed, only to rise on the third day, they frankly didn't believe it. "The Son of Man is being betrayed into the hands of men, and they will kill Him. And after He is killed, He will rise the third day" (Mark 9:31; see also Mark 10:34; Luke 18:32; 24:46; Matthew 20:19)—just one of the numerous times He told them.

Though Peter, James, John, Mary, and others of the inner circle didn't believe, how ironic that His biggest enemies, the scribes and Pharisees, did. Or rather, they believed that something out of the ordinary, even supernatural, could happen on the third day.

And why not? For years, the deeds and words of Jesus had played out in real-time 3-D flesh and blood all through the nation. These leaders surely had seen for themselves or heard reports of the paralytic healed (Matthew 9:1–8), the boy blind from birth given sight (John 9), the crowds fed (Matthew 14:13–21), and Lazarus rotting in death raised (John 11:1–53). How many people, once broken and bent with sickness and disease, were now brought before them whole and upright in health, singing praises to the Man, Jesus of Nazareth, who had done this for them? The land shimmered with the fruit of Christ's ministry, which was so powerful that many believed that He must have been from God—a prophet, the returned Elijah, or even the Messiah.

And what about the time they sent men to arrest Jesus, only to be told that they wouldn't do it because "no man ever spoke like this Man!" (John 7:46)? And not only did Jesus have powerful words but His deeds also backed up those words, and these men knew it too.

Thus, no matter how hard hearted, no matter how cold and furious they had been toward and about Him, the supernatural reality surrounding Jesus couldn't be denied. After the resurrection of Lazarus, "the chief priests and the Pharisees gathered a council and said, 'What shall we do? For this Man works many signs. If we let Him alone like this, everyone will believe in Him, and the Romans will come and take away both our place and nation'" (John 11:47, 48). They didn't deny the miracle or dismiss it as a trick but admitted it was one of "many signs" that He did.

Then, too, how must the crowds—not the small crowd that said, "Crucify Him, crucify Him!" but the other crowds, the crowds of those who, through the years, had been healed or had their children, their siblings, or their parents healed or ministered to by Jesus—how did they feel about their beloved Healer and Teacher being crucified by these religious leaders? How many of them, as did the thief on the cross, started putting things together about who Jesus really was?

The story of Jesus, both of His miracles and, later, of His death, was out, having spread to the wider community. Pilate, hearing that Jesus was a Galilean, had Him sent over to Herod, who was in Jerusalem at that time. "Now when

Herod saw Jesus, he was exceeding glad; for he had desired for a long time to see Him, because he had heard many things of Him, and he hoped to see some miracle done by Him" (Luke 23:8). The accounts of Jesus and His miracles had permeated even the walls of Herod's palace.

Then, after the death of Jesus, the two disciples on the road to Emmaus, when talking (unbeknownst to them) to Jesus, asked Him:

> "Are You the only stranger in Jerusalem, and have You not known the things which happened there in these days?"
>
> And He said to them, "What things?"
>
> So they said to Him, "The things concerning Jesus of Nazareth, who was a Prophet mighty in deed and word before God and all the people, and how the chief priests and our rulers delivered Him to be condemned to death, and crucified Him. But we were hoping that it was He who was going to redeem Israel. Indeed, besides all this, today is the third day since these things happened" (Luke 24:18–21).

Their question—"Are You the only stranger in Jerusalem, and have You not known the things which happened there in these days?"—revealed how well known the events surrounding His death must have been. Jesus, they proclaimed, was a prophet mighty "in deed and word." These words testify to the power of Christ's ministry. They said that He did these things "before God and all the people." The people knew that He was a miracle worker, and His life and witness were so popular that they, among others, were hoping that this Jesus would "redeem Israel."

Notice the contrast that these disciples then presented. Jesus, a prophet mighty in deed and word, was delivered to death by "the chief priests and . . . rulers." They directed the blame for His death right on the leaders, where it belonged. Pilate had wanted to free Jesus, and Pilate's wife even had a dream about "that just Man" (Matthew 27:19), but only because of the goading of the chief priests and rulers was "that just Man," as opposed to Barabbas, crucified.

With their consciences (perhaps) seared with the memory of His "many signs," with the echo of Judas's cry ringing in their ears, "I have sinned by betraying innocent blood" (verse 4), as well as Christ's cry, "It is finished!" (John 19:30), and "Father, 'into Your hands I commit My spirit' " (Luke 23:46), and the centurion's, "Certainly this was a righteous Man!" (verse 47)—these leaders, probably more fearful of Jesus dead than alive, did what, ironically enough, made the evidence for Him only more powerful than when He was walking, teaching, and doing miracles before their faces.

H umans are capable of rational thought, unlike animals, but we're not dominated by it. Imagine how differently the final draft of our lives would play out if our decisions were rational instead of based on fear, greed, passion, and other emotions that spark in our chemical heads.

Take, for instance, what the religious leaders did out of their fear of Jesus, dead: "On the next day, which followed the Day of Preparation, the chief priests and Pharisees gathered together to Pilate, saying, 'Sir, we remember, while He was still alive, how that deceiver said, "After three days I will rise." Therefore command that the tomb be made secure until the third day, lest His disciples come by night and steal Him away, and say to the people, "He has risen from the dead." So the last deception will be worse than the first' " (Matthew 27:62–64).

Besides all the miracles of His ministry, what about the earthquake when He was on the cross? Or the darkness over the land? Or the veil in the temple torn at the moment of Christ's death? (See Mark 15:38.) No wonder these men were scared of Jesus even when He was dead. They had good reason to be.

But to put a guard around the tomb? In case—what? The disciples steal the body? And then what? Claim that Jesus had been resurrected from the dead? When the people asked, Where is the risen Jesus? they could say, Just take our word for it. (That would have been convincing, wouldn't it?)

Thieves have been robbing graves since time immemorial, not usually to take the corpse (though in 1978 Charlie Chaplin's body was dug up and held for ransom) but to steal artifacts, especially when, as with the Egyptian pharaohs, people were interred with a lot of booty. Thus, had the disciples stolen His body, Christ's empty tomb would no more prove that He had been resurrected than an empty pair of shoes means that their owner has been raptured to heaven.

What, then, were these leaders thinking? They weren't thinking, at least from reason, logic, and common sense but, instead, from fear.

First, they went to Pilate, but when? The day after the "Day of Preparation"— that is, the Sabbath. Obviously, their fear of Jesus allowed them little Sabbath rest, which is why they crossed a Gentile's threshold, inviting defilement, in order to try to squelch that fear.

Second, what did they warn Pilate? That Jesus said: "After three days I will rise." Three days after what? Jesus had more than once said that He would "be rejected by the elders and chief priests and scribes, and be killed, and be raised the third day" (Luke 9:22). Thus, the first part of that prediction had just been fulfilled right before their eyes. These men wanted to assure themselves, if nothing else, that the last part wouldn't be as well.

And Pilate, knowing that Jesus was innocent and no doubt remembering his wife's warning (Romans were big into dreams), must have been scared, too, because he agreed, saying: "You have a guard; go your way, make it as secure as you know how" (Matthew 27:65).

As secure as possible? Why? So that some grave robbers couldn't steal a corpse and claim that it rose from the dead? Sounds as if these leaders, burdened with guilty consciences, were afraid that something other than a few disgruntled disciples would stage a deception "worse than the first." And what would that "worse" deception be? Proclaim that Jesus had arisen from the dead, though they would never be able to produce Him, even while having to find some way to dispose of His rotting corpse so that no one could find it?

And so Pilate and the chief priests had a seal put around the stone that closed the tomb where Christ had been buried and then set a guard before it. That would have prevented grave robbers, for sure, if that was why they were afraid. But they were really afraid that some other miracle would occur (after all, look at all the other miracles that already had happened). The seal and guard were irrational actions by irrational men that, ironically enough, gave the world more rational reasons to believe in the resurrected Christ.

---

1. Flavius Josephus, *Josephus: The Complete Works*, trans. William Whiston (Nashville, TN: Thomas Nelson, 1998), 863, 864.

2. Raymond Tallis, "On *Logos*," *Philosophy Now* 117 (December 2016/January 2017), https://philosophynow.org/issues/117/On_Logos.

3. Or as W. O. Quine wrote, "How we, physical denizens of the physical world, can have projected our scientific theory of that whole world from our meagre contacts with it: from the mere impacts of rays and particles on our surfaces and a few odds and ends such as the strain of walking uphill." Raymond Tallis, *Logos: The Mystery of How We Make Sense of the World* (Newcastle Upon Tyne, UK: Agenda, 2018), loc. 146–149, Kindle.

The Christ Event

One account of Jesus' resurrection goes as follows: soldiers were guarding the tomb where Jesus had been buried that Friday when two personages descended from heaven. The stone that closed the sepulcher moved by itself, opening the way into the tomb. The two heavenly personages entered, but soon three came out. The two from above were holding up the third, only now their heads extended so far upward that they reached heaven while the head of the third man reached even higher.

Then a cross, apparently all by itself, exited the tomb right behind them. A voice from heaven uttered a question, to which the cross, able to speak, answered.

Here's the narrative itself:

(34) When the Sabbath morning dawned, a crowd came from Jerusalem and the surrounding area that they might see that the tomb had been sealed. (35) But during the night in which the Lord's day dawned, while the soldiers were stationed in pairs to keep watch, a great voice came from heaven. (36) And they saw the hea[v]ens open and two men descend from there, having a great radiance and approaching the tomb. (37) Then, the same stone which had been put in the entrance rolled away from it and gave way partially. And the tomb was opened and both young men went in. . . .

(38) Then, seeing this, these soldiers woke up the centurions and elders, for they themselves were all there to keep watch. (39) And while they were describing what they had seen, again they saw three men coming out from the tomb, two supporting the other and a cross following them. (40) The heads of the two reached up to the heavens and the head of the one they were leading by the hand went beyond the heavens. (41) And they heard a voice from heaven saying, "Did you preach to those who sleep?" (42) Obediently, there was heard from the cross, "Yes."[1]

What is this moronic story? Certainly, this account isn't what had persuaded people such as Pinchas Lapide to believe in the resurrection of Jesus, was it?

Of course not.

Instead, this drivel came from an ancient source (exactly how ancient is disputed). Though called the Gospel of Peter, it's neither a Gospel nor by Peter. And most important, it's not part of the New Testament canon; that is, it's not in the Bible and not one of the accounts upon which belief in Christ's resurrection rests.

Though mention is made of it by some early church personages—Origen (AD 140–253), Eusebius (AD 263–339), and Theodoret (AD 392–457)—who exactly wrote this account, when, and why is unknown. Only in the 1800s and later have fragments been found, which is why we have it today.

Scholarly debate continues regarding this piece of work (and that's what it is, "a piece of work"). What's interesting, however, is the stark contrast between this Resurrection story and the biblical versions by Matthew, Mark, Luke, John, and other New Testament writers.

Of course, any account of someone resurrected from the dead reaches into the realm of the supernatural, which, by itself, evokes incredulity, especially in a modern culture dominated by scientific materialism—itself not a completely rational and logical worldview.

However, to repeat: one needs only to believe in God to have logical reasons for believing in the supernatural. The God who created space, time, matter, and energy—that is, the physical world and the natural laws that move that world and the things in it—is greater than that world and those laws, which means that He can act outside those laws when He wills. When He does, as with the resurrection of Jesus, that's what a miracle is, plain and simple. (Though, if nothing's plain and simple about natural phenomena, how much more so for supernatural ones?) This truth doesn't mean that miracles *have* to happen, only that no inherent logical contradiction exists if they do.

Fortunately, though we have to believe in miracles in order to believe in the resurrection of Jesus, we are not asked to believe in heads reaching from Earth to heaven or walking and talking crosses, as in the Gospel of Peter.

What, then, are we asked to believe, and why does it make so much sense to believe and, even better, to rejoice in the hope that this belief offers?

In contrast to the grossly misnamed "Gospel of Peter" of unknown authorship, the earliest known written account of Christ's resurrection comes from the apostle Paul, who, to this day, is the most influential expositor on the meaning of Christ crucified. Western history, essentially world history, has been changed by Paul's writings, especially on Christ's death.

However central Christ's death was to Paul, and it was—"For I determined not to know anything among you except Jesus Christ and Him crucified" (1 Corinthians 2:2)—unless Christ were raised from the dead, the Christian hope was, Paul wrote, "empty" (1 Corinthians 15:14) and "futile" (verse 17). For Paul, the hope that this miserable existence, with all of its toils, suffering, disappointments, and at times, maddening absurdity, is not the whole picture (which, if it were, would make our existence empty and futile) is found in the resurrection of Jesus.

Otherwise, things can be pretty dismal.

As Raymond Tallis expressed it: "Lacking the hope of resurrection and the full illumination of an after-life, we unbelievers must live with the knowledge that our extraordinary capacity for comprehending the world is an incomplete mitigation of our helplessness, and of the darkness that surrounds our light, of the ignorance that bounds our knowledge and of the senselessness that delimits the sense we make of things."[2]

Struggling in darkness, senselessness, helplessness, ignorance, and without hope? (Tallis said it, not me.) According to Paul, though Christ was crucified, and though He sacrificed Himself to pay for human sin (Galatians 1:4; Ephesians 5:1, 2; Isaiah 53:11), unless He was resurrected, then, yes, Tallis's lament was correct.

Paul, though, believed in the resurrection of Jesus; in a letter to the Corinthian church, Paul penned what's, perhaps, Scripture's earliest exposition of Christ's death and resurrection:

> For I delivered to you first of all that which I also received: that Christ died for our sins according to the Scriptures, and that He was buried, and that He rose again the third day according to the Scriptures, and that He was seen by Cephas, then by the twelve. After that He was seen by over five hundred brethren at once, of whom the greater part remain to the present, but some have fallen asleep. After that He was seen by James, then by all the apostles. Then last of all He was seen by me also, as by one born out of due time (1 Corinthians 15:3–8).

For close to two millennia, every word, syllable, punctuation mark, thought, claim, and nuance of these five verses have been examined, parsed, analyzed, scrutinized, memorized, and every other *-ized*. For our present purposes, however, these words sweepingly summarize what is euphemistically called "the Christ event," upon which Christians rest their great hope that this spasm of cell life and protein metabolism, known as humanity—or as the late Stephen Hawking referred to us, a "chemical scum"[3]—that this existence isn't the end. But, rather, the eternal life that humans were originally to have been created with will eventually be given to us because of what Christ did.

And what did He do?

According to Paul, as expressed above, Christ died and was then buried. After three days, He rose from the dead, all according to what had been predicted in the Old Testament. Christ, then, was seen by various people, Paul included.

However quick and to the point Paul's summary, it holds some crucial keys to not only understanding what happened but also why it makes so much sense to believe that it did.

Paul's declaration, believed to be an early creedal statement, was first uttered within, perhaps, five years of the events it recounts. Here it is again:

> For I delivered to you first of all that which I also received: that Christ died for our sins according to the Scriptures, and that He was buried, and that He rose again the third day according to the Scriptures, and that He was seen by Cephas, then by the twelve. After that He was seen by over five hundred brethren at once, of whom the greater part remain to the present, but some have fallen asleep. After that He was seen by James, then by all the apostles. Then last of all He was seen by me also, as by one born out of due time (verses 3–8).

What Scripture gives here is a broad, sweeping version of events. *A version.* That term is important in understanding the biblical accounts of Christ's resurrection. *Accounts.* That word is important too. There are various accounts, various versions, of Christ's death, resurrection, and post-resurrection appearances.

In four English sentences, a single long Greek one, Paul wrote a kind of flyover view of what Matthew, Mark, Luke, and John taught in more detail. In four English verses, Paul writes about what the Gospel writers sometimes took chapters to do. Luke used about sixty verses for the events after the death of Jesus, His resurrection, and His post-resurrection appearances. If you include Luke's depiction of Christ's death, which Paul also mentions, then Luke's version used about seventy verses to express what Paul did in four.

This meant, of course, that Luke included events that Paul couldn't, even though Paul brought out events that Luke didn't. Paul wrote things that others ignored, such as Christ's appearance to him (Paul himself) and to James, while he left out a lot of what the others, such as John, include. These differences are important in making sense of what happened because, together, they paint a powerfully convincing picture of the death, Resurrection, and post-Resurrection appearances.

Various accounts and various versions? This is nothing new in the Gospels or even the New Testament letters, where the authors come at things, often the same things, with different perspectives, motives, angles, and emphases; some add details that others ignore or depict with a different slant.*

Far from discrediting the accounts, the differences are, for the most part, explainable and, in fact, lend credibility in that they show that these men didn't get together and conspiratorially concoct a false narrative.

Instead, what we get is a compelling picture of the events, which could be broadly expressed as follows: Jesus of Nazareth was nailed to the cross. After He died, His body was removed by two men who were not open followers of Jesus when He was alive and who placed Him in the tomb of one of the two, Joseph of Arimathea. After sunset, the beginning of the Sabbath, a guard was put in front of the sepulcher, the idea being to keep the followers of Jesus from stealing His corpse. On Sunday morning, Jesus rose from the dead. The guard fled the tomb and reported what happened to the religious leaders. Jesus then appeared to different people, women first, and then, eventually, to many others over the course of weeks before ascending to heaven.

This summary is parallel to Paul's but with one big difference. Paul's emphasis wasn't so much on Christ's death and resurrection as it was on His appearance to others afterward. According to Paul, Christ was seen by Cephas (Peter), the Twelve, then by five hundred others "at once," then by James, then the apostles, and finally, by Paul himself. This emphasis parallels all four Gospel accounts in that none depicted the Resurrection itself. Instead, their main focus was on when, where, how, and to whom Jesus had appeared after the Resurrection.

And here's where the power of the story is found: An empty tomb proves only that the tomb was empty (not proof itself of a resurrection). But in the Gospels and in Acts, the resurrected Jesus makes His appearance over and over, numerous times, to numerous people in different places. The historical evidence is so strong that even skeptics—those who don't believe that the Resurrection happened—are forced to admit that many people *believed* that they saw the resurrected Jesus, and a good chunk of anti-Resurrection apologetics attempts to explain what could have caused all of these different people to *believe* that they had seen a resurrected Jesus. And in response, a

---

* One interesting example is the story of the thieves on the cross. Matthew and Mark have them both reviling Jesus: "Even the robbers who were crucified with Him reviled Him with the same thing" (Matthew 27:44); "Even those who were crucified with Him reviled Him" (Mark 15:32). John mentions them both but says nothing else about them or what they did when crucified with Jesus. In contrast, Luke has one of the thieves accepting Jesus as the Savior. "But the other, answering, rebuked him, saying, 'Do you not even fear God, seeing you are under the same condemnation? And we indeed justly, for we receive the due reward of our deeds; but this Man has done nothing wrong.' Then he said to Jesus, 'Lord, remember me when You come into Your kingdom' " (Luke 23:40). Some argue that these accounts contradict each other, but that's an unwarranted conclusion. Matthew and Mark bring in an element that both Luke and John ignored, while Luke brought in an element that none of the others mentioned: the second thief accepting Jesus as the Messiah. At first glance, the different accounts, the different versions, appear contradictory but, on closer examination, they aren't. This is similar to what we find with the various versions of Christ's resurrection and post-resurrection appearances.

good chunk of this book looks at those arguments to see whether they work or whether, instead, the most logical explanation for the sightings is that, yes, Jesus did rise from the dead.

1. Peter Kirby, "Gospel of Peter," Early Christian Writings, accessed June 23, 2020, http://www .earlychristianwritings.com/text/gospelpeter-andrewbernhard.html.

2. Raymond Tallis, *Logos: The Mystery of How We Make Sense of the World* (Newcastle Upon Tyne, UK: Agenda, 2018), loc. 4251, Kindle. Or this, written in an earlier century by the poet Hölderlin: "Oh, you wretches who feel all this, who, even as I, cannot allow yourselves to speak of man's being here for a purpose, who, even as I, are so utterly in the clutch of the Nothing that governs us, so profoundly aware that we are born for nothing, that we love a nothing, believe in nothing, work ourselves to death for nothing only that little by little we may pass over into nothing—how can I help it if your knees collapse when you think of it seriously? Many a time have I, too, sunk into these bottomless thoughts, and cried out; Why do you lay the axe to my root, pitiless spirit?—and still I am here." Quoted in Sue Prideaux, *I Am Dynamite!* (New York: Random House, 2018), 33.

3. This quote is attributed to Stephen Hawking in a 1995 TV program called *Reality on the Rocks: Beyond Our Ken*. The quotes goes, "The human race is just a chemical scum on a moderate size planet, orbiting round a very average star in the outer suburb of one among a billion galaxies." Of course, it's self-refuting because no chemical scum could make that kind of statement. After all, it's only chemical scum.

Risen

However central to the Christian faith the Resurrection is; however much our only hope of anything beyond dissipation into subatomic obscurity rests upon that Resurrection, the Bible never depicts the actual event itself. Scripture gives graphic descriptions of His death, burial, and His post-resurrection appearances. It tells that Jesus was killed, wrapped "in a clean linen cloth" (Matthew 27:59), and placed in a tomb sealed by a rock and surrounded by Roman guards. But the resurrection itself, the event of Jesus coming back to life, being stripped of the cloth, exiting the tomb sealed by the rock, and escaping the Roman guard is never depicted.

Only Matthew comes close, but even he does not show the event itself: "And behold, there was a great earthquake; for an angel of the Lord descended from heaven, and came and rolled back the stone from the door, and sat on it. His countenance was like lightning, and his clothing as white as snow. And the guards shook for fear of him, and became like dead men" (Matthew 28:2–4).

An angel of the Lord. An earthquake. The stone rolled away. The guards shaking in fear, becoming like dead men. We're not told what becoming like dead men meant, but if nothing else, they fell to the ground. If they saw Jesus Himself rise, then perhaps some who had taken part in the abuse and murder of Jesus would have then seen Him rise from the dead. If that wouldn't put the fear of God in them, what would?

For whatever reason, the account leaves out the resurrection of Jesus. These verses say only that the angel came down, moved the stone, sat on it, and the soldiers, scared, became like dead men.

That's it? Nothing else happened? The rest must be inferred, which isn't hard because of what followed.

The story of the guard picks up a few verses later:

> Now while they were going, behold, some of the guard came into the city and reported to the chief priests all the things that had happened. When they had assembled with the elders and consulted together, they gave a large sum of money to the soldiers, saying, "Tell them, 'His disciples came at night and stole Him away while we slept.' And if this comes to the governor's ears, we will appease him and make you secure." So they took the money and did as they were instructed; and this saying is commonly reported among the Jews until this day (verses 11–15).

They told the leaders "all the things that had happened." What, exactly, happened? Implicit in this account is the idea that the guards saw the Resurrection. If not, what? An angel came down from heaven, moved the stone, sat on it, and the guards fainted from fear? The next thing they knew, the tomb was empty? Maybe, while the Romans were unconscious, the angel took away the body of

Jesus? Maybe the disciples did? Or someone else stole it? Whatever happened, the body of Jesus was obviously gone.

An angel from heaven coming down, the men fainting from fear, and the tomb being empty would have been disconcerting enough to the religious leaders. But that they "gave a large sum of money to the soldiers" to keep those men quiet implied that whatever the soldiers told them disturbed them plenty. Again, unless the soldiers themselves had seen the Resurrection, then all they knew was an angel came and the tomb was empty. It didn't, of necessity, mean that Jesus had been resurrected. However, the actions of the religious leaders suggest that something else happened that they didn't want to get out.

The irony is incredible. The chief priests had posted the guard in order to stop, they said, the disciples from stealing Jesus' corpse. *But now they pay the same Roman guard to declare that the disciples did steal the corpse?* In their thinking, that story was better than whatever the guards had told them. Which was what? Not just that the body was gone but, obviously, that Christ had been resurrected.

Some scoff at the idea of Gentiles—Romans and soldiers—being the first witnesses to Christ's resurrection. Why? What a powerful symbol of the gospel going to the Gentile world. In Matthew's Gospel, the first people at the death of Jesus to declare faith in Him were Roman soldiers: "So when the centurion and those with him, who were guarding Jesus, saw the earthquake and the things that had happened, they feared greatly, saying, 'Truly this was the Son of God!' " (Matthew 27:54). If Gentiles were witnesses to His death, why not also to His resurrection?

Scripture does not describe the exact details of the resurrection of Jesus, and if the first to see the Resurrection were Romans, perhaps even some who had crucified Him, so what? In the end, the most powerful evidence for the Resurrection wasn't the event itself but the appearances that followed.

I n his depiction of Christ's post-resurrection appearances (1 Corinthians 15:3–
9), Paul does not mention the women whom Christ had appeared to first and
who first proclaimed not only the empty tomb but also the risen Lord (unless
one counts what the Roman guard told the Jewish leaders, which, it seems, had
to be that Christ was resurrected). Paul ignores what Matthew, Mark, Luke, and
John make central: the women who saw Jesus first.

This difference serves as another example of how the Bible writers, recounting
the story of Jesus' resurrection, focused on events that others left out or emphasized differently. Luke, for instance, spends more than twenty verses (Luke 24:13–
35) on what Mark spent only two (Mark 16:12, 13) and Matthew and John
spent none—Jesus meeting two disciples on the road to Emmaus. Commenting
on this, John Lennox observes, "The narratives are often compressed; and one
might be tempted to think that they contain contradictory elements, if unaware
of the complexities of the situation, and the fact that there were different groups
of people going to and coming from the tomb of Christ, not only from different
directions and by different routes, but also at different times."[1]

This reality becomes important in harmonizing the appearances of Jesus after
His death.

Matthew, Mark, Luke, and John all have women, basically, at center stage and
in starring roles in the early post-Resurrection appearances. All four Gospels also
place women at the cross and at the death of Jesus (Matthew 27:55, 56; Mark
15:40, 41; Luke 23:49; John 19:25), and three list some women at the burial:
"And the women who had come with Him from Galilee followed after, and they
observed the tomb and how His body was laid" (Luke 23:55; see also Matthew
27:61; Mark 15:47). Paul, for reasons that will be looked at later, never mentions
them.

The women next appear early on the first day of the week, Sunday morning,
with spices to anoint the body. Jesus had already been interred, and John states
that "Nicodemus, who at first came to Jesus by night, also came, bringing a
mixture of myrrh and aloes, about a hundred pounds" (John 19:39).

Though no biblical record exists of Nicodemus accepting Jesus as the Messiah,
even after his secret night meeting with Jesus (John 3:1–21), Nicodemus is seen
again, now if not openly professing faith in Jesus, then at least seeking to get
Him some fair treatment. As excitement about Jesus was mounting, the leaders
had wanted to arrest Him:

Nicodemus (he who came to Jesus by night, being one of them) said to
them, "Does our law judge a man before it hears him and knows what he
is doing?"

They answered and said to him, "Are you also from Galilee? Search and
look, for no prophet has arisen out of Galilee" (John 7:50–52).

However much Nicodemus's sympathies were revealed here, they became more apparent after Christ's death: he was willing to attend to the body of Jesus, working, it appears, with Joseph of Arimathea to remove Jesus from the cross, wrapping Him in linen and applying spices—the idea being that the spices would help cover the stench of a rotting corpse. (Another irony: Christ's disciples were nowhere to be seen while these two prominent Jews attended to Christ's body.)

Why, then, did the women come on Sunday morning with more spices, especially when Nicodemus already had brought so many? One theory is that, because Christ's death was later in the day, His burial was rushed to get it done before Sabbath, and these women wanted to do more for Him as soon as they could. This would have been on Sunday morning when they would have light (Sabbath ended on Saturday at sundown when it would have been too dark to work).

Whatever the reason for coming to "anoint Him" (Mark 16:1), the women were first at the tomb with spices, which implies that they expected Jesus to be good and dead. Despite all that Jesus had said about being resurrected; despite His raising to life a few dead already; and despite His promise, "I will see you again" (John 16:22), they had no expectation of anything other than finding Jesus as they had last seen Him—a linen-wrapped corpse interred in a tomb. And their words to each other on the way, "Who will roll away the stone from the door of the tomb for us?" (Mark 16:3), only reinforce the evidence that, whatever they were thinking, it wasn't that Jesus was going to be resurrected.

In fact, when Mary got there and found the empty tomb, she didn't say, *Yes, Jesus has been resurrected! Yes! He is risen! Hallelujah, prophecy has been fulfilled, and Christ is raised from the dead!* Instead, she ran to some disciples and said, "They have taken away the Lord out of the tomb, and we do not know where they have laid Him" (John 20:2).

So far from their minds was the Resurrection that, at first, even an empty tomb wasn't enough to convince them that He had been raised from the dead.

What happened after, however, certainly did.

A t first glance, confusion can arise on the question of who came to the tomb and when. But again, that's only because some Bible writers focused on different things from different angles than did other Bible writers, or some ignored what others emphasized. However differing their perspectives and emphases, the synoptic Gospels—Matthew, Mark, and Luke—all state that women were first to the tomb.

> Now after the Sabbath, as the first day of the week began to dawn, Mary Magdalene and the other Mary came to see the tomb (Matthew 28:1).

> Now when the Sabbath was past, Mary Magdalene, Mary the mother of James, and Salome bought spices, that they might come and anoint Him. Very early in the morning, on the first day of the week, they came to the tomb when the sun had risen (Mark 16:1).

> Now on the first day of the week, very early in the morning, they, and certain other women with them, came to the tomb bringing the spices which they had prepared (Luke 24:1).

These accounts, taken together, could go something like this: early in the morning on the first day of the week, some women, including Mary Magdalene, went to the tomb of Jesus.

Now, let's apply this basic idea to another setting: early Tuesday night, some guys, including George, went to a vegan restaurant.

What's the immediate implication—the first image evoked by this sentence about George and others going to scarf down soy burgers and beet-juice smoothies? Probably something like this: George and the others piling into someone's car and driving to the restaurant.

But that's not what the sentence describes. George could have walked to the restaurant and arrived ten minutes before all the others, who arrived together in one car. Or they all could have come in different cars, or all walked from different directions and arrived at different times. It says nothing about when, from which direction, how they got there, and who came with whom. Nor does it absolutely imply that they were all there at the same time. George could have arrived, eaten, and left before the others came.

The sentence—early Tuesday night, some guys, including George, went to a vegan restaurant—means only that early Tuesday night George and the others went to a vegan restaurant. It says nothing definitive about when they went, how they went, or whether or not they were all there together.

It's the same with the verses about the women going to the tomb of Jesus. Nothing in the Synoptics demands that they all arrived at the same time and from the same direction. Read these verses again, with the idea that they didn't all necessarily arrive simultaneously or from the same direction:

> Now after the Sabbath, as the first day of the week began to dawn, Mary Magdalene and the other Mary came to see the tomb (Matthew 28:1).

> Now when the Sabbath was past, Mary Magdalene, Mary the mother of James, and Salome bought spices, that they might come and anoint Him. Very early in the morning, on the first day of the week, they came to the tomb when the sun had risen (Mark 16:1).

> Now on the first day of the week, very early in the morning, they, and certain other women with them, came to the tomb bringing the spices which they had prepared (Luke 24:1).

These texts don't necessarily mean that they all arrived at the same time and from the same direction. It means only that different women at some point came to the tomb of Jesus and found it empty. If, as many believe, the Gospels were written years after the event, then the authors, from a distance of years, perhaps, even decades, could have simply telescoped what happened. After Jesus' death, these various women came to the tomb. Who came exactly when, with whom, and in what order were specific details that the Bible writers weren't then addressing.

With this understanding that the women didn't all come at the same time, we can better understand what the Bible teaches about the empty tomb—an event that has changed human history so greatly that, chances are, none of us would be here, at least as us. Were Christ not raised, we might be other people in different places under different circumstances but not who we are now, not where we are now, and not in the circumstances that we are in now.

That's how world changing the Resurrection was.

The question of when Mary Magdalene arrived at the tomb is addressed in the Gospel of John. "Now the first day of the week Mary Magdalene went to the tomb early, while it was still dark, and saw that the stone had been taken away from the tomb" (John 20:1).

Though not absolute that she arrived alone or first, the text could be read that way and, when harmonized with the other accounts, makes the most sense. Again, the Synoptics don't describe all the women arriving at the tomb at the same time or from the same direction. However, John's description could be read as teaching that Mary came alone—and first too.

So Mary came by herself and saw that the stone was taken away from the entrance. Though the text itself says nothing else, we can infer that she must have looked inside the tomb. Some of the women, those not with Mary at that time, worried specifically about that stone before they arrived at the tomb: "And they said among themselves, 'Who will roll away the stone from the door of the tomb for us?' " (Mark 16:3). The stone, which the group of women knew was too large for them to move in order to get inside the tomb, had been moved before Mary got there. It's hard to imagine that she didn't look in and see the empty tomb.

So Mary gets there, sees the stone has been moved, and looking in, knows only that Jesus was gone.

What happened next?

"Then she ran and came to Simon Peter, and to the other disciple, whom Jesus loved, and said to them, 'They have taken away the Lord out of the tomb, and we do not know where they have laid Him' " (John 20:2).

Her words show that, yes, she looked in and saw the empty tomb.

The irony is outrageous here too. Though the scribes and Pharisees at first were afraid (supposedly) that the body would be stolen, they later wanted people to believe that, yes, the body had been stolen—by Jesus' own followers. And yet here's one of His followers who, finding the tomb empty, thinks that the body, in fact, had been stolen. Who stole it, she didn't say, except that they, whoever "they" were (she must have assumed the work of moving the stone and getting the body would have required more than one person), had taken Jesus, and she didn't know where "they have laid Him."

Again, despite all that Jesus had said about His own resurrection and despite the resurrection of Lazarus, she was so clueless that instead of thinking that He might have been raised as He had said, she, by default, assumed that someone took the body.

We see, again, just how alien the idea of the Messiah being resurrected was for the people of that time. On seeing the empty tomb, Mary defaults to what anyone might think: If you bury Cousin Joey and then return to the grave and the body is gone, what will your first thought be? Cousin Joey was resurrected? No, but that someone had removed him.

What her words and the subsequent initial disbelief of Jesus' followers show is that the idea of a resurrected Messiah was not anything that first-century Jews assumed (a point that becomes important in Resurrection apologetics). Nothing in the actions of Christ's followers after His death indicated that they had any expectation of Him coming back from the dead. On the contrary, every account of the Resurrection story shows just how unexpected that Resurrection was.

M ary arrived at the tomb first, alone, and saw that Jesus was not there. "Then she ran and came to Simon Peter, and to the other disciple, whom Jesus loved, and said to them, 'They have taken away the Lord out of the tomb, and we do not know where they have laid Him' " (John 20:2).

That's what we know from the texts. What we don't know is how long it took for Mary to find the disciples, and then, how long it took for the two to make it back to the tomb.

Twenty minutes? Forty minutes? Two hours? Four hours?

In the reconstruction depicted here, based on these and other texts, Mary leaves to tell the disciples. While she is gone and before the two disciples made it to the tomb, the other women get there:

> And entering the tomb, they saw a young man clothed in a long white robe sitting on the right side; and they were alarmed.
>
> But he said to them, "Do not be alarmed. You seek Jesus of Nazareth, who was crucified. He is risen! He is not here. See the place where they laid Him. But go, tell His disciples—and Peter—that He is going before you into Galilee; there you will see Him, as He said to you" (Mark 16:5–7).

Not much detail is given about the "young man clothed in a long white robe," but Luke explains that the garment was shining, which would explain their fear.*
Some other things might have already been a bit unnerving as well.

First, expecting a sealed tomb, the women find it open, and the rock—the rock whose presence had worried them—had been moved. That alone might have alarmed them. *What happened to the rock? Who moved it? Why is Jesus' tomb open?*

Second, they come and see that the body of Jesus is gone. "Then they went in and did not find the body of the Lord Jesus. And it happened, as they were greatly perplexed about this" (Luke 24:3, 4). The missing body was disconcerting, especially because they came to anoint Him. *What happened to Jesus? Who took Jesus' body? Where is He now?*

Third, the appearance of the man in the shining white robe is what the text specifies as having alarmed them. Nevertheless, the man (and in the Bible, angels can be referred to as men; see Daniel 9:21) says what angels in the Bible often first say when appearing to humans: "Don't be afraid."†

Seeing that the women were afraid, the angel seeks to calm them: "Do not be alarmed. You seek Jesus of Nazareth, who was crucified. He is risen! He is not

---

* "And it happened, as they were greatly perplexed about this, that behold, two men stood by them in shining garments" (Luke 24:4). Mark, for whatever reason, dealt with only one angel; Luke, in contrast, talked about both.

† Just two examples: when an angel appeared to the shepherds, they were afraid, and the angel said to them: "Do not be afraid" (Luke 2:10). When the angel appeared to Zacharias in the temple, he said: "Do not be afraid" (Luke 1:13).

here. See the place where they laid Him. But go, tell His disciples—and Peter—that He is going before you into Galilee; there you will see Him, as He said to you" (Mark 16:6, 7). The missing body had perplexed them, which would explain his immediate words to them: Don't be afraid. The reason He's not here is because He's been resurrected, just as He told you.

These women, then, are the first people, at least as depicted in Scripture, to hear that "He is risen!" Again, the soldiers must have seen Jesus rise from the dead, but here, in this account, we have the first "official" declaration, even from heaven, of the Resurrection. Unlike Mary, who just assumed that someone had taken Him, these women now know what the empty tomb meant.

Then, apparently, another angel is there as well, a second one, who gives them the same wonderful news: "Why do you seek the living among the dead? He is not here, but is risen! Remember how He spoke to you when He was still in Galilee, saying, 'The Son of Man must be delivered into the hands of sinful men, and be crucified, and the third day rise again' " (Luke 24:5–7).

They're told, twice, why the tomb is empty, not because someone robbed it but because Jesus, as He had said, had been raised to life. The angel reminded them of Christ's words: "The Son of Man must be delivered into the hands of sinful men, and be crucified, and the third day rise again" (verse 7). Upon hearing the angel repeat what Jesus said, the women "remembered His words" (verse 8).

So what happened next?

"So they went out quickly from the tomb with fear and great joy, and ran to bring His disciples word" (Matthew 28:8). Bring them "word"—word not just that the tomb was empty, which Mary was going to tell them, but more importantly, word about *why* it was.

So Mary came to the empty tomb and left. While she's gone, the other women arrive and are told by the angels that Christ has been raised. These women left, intending to tell the good news to the disciples. Again, how long it took for all this to unfold, we aren't told.

Meanwhile, Mary, the first one at the tomb, left and told two disciples that the tomb was empty. What happened next?

> Then she ran and came to Simon Peter, and to the other disciple, whom Jesus loved, and said to them, "They have taken away the Lord out of the tomb, and we do not know where they have laid Him."
>
> Peter therefore went out, and the other disciple, and were going to the tomb. So they both ran together, and the other disciple outran Peter and came to the tomb first. And he, stooping down and looking in, saw the linen cloths lying there; yet he did not go in. Then Simon Peter came, following him, and went into the tomb; and he saw the linen cloths lying there, and the handkerchief that had been around His head, not lying with the linen cloths, but folded together in a place by itself. Then the other disciple, who came to the tomb first, went in also; and he saw and believed. For as yet they did not know the Scripture, that He must rise again from the dead. Then the disciples went away again to their own homes (John 20:2–10).

These two disciples, Peter and (most likely) John, hear from Mary that someone had taken the corpse. Where they were when she told them, and why she told only those two, the text does not say. But they must have believed her because they ran to the tomb; otherwise, they could have just laughed her off or just meandered over whenever.

John got there first and saw that the body was gone but that the linen cloths remained. He didn't enter; arriving after John, Peter did enter and, like John, saw "the linen cloths lying there, and the handkerchief that had been around His head, not lying with the linen cloths, but folded together in a place by itself" (verses 6, 7).

Then the text says something about John after he saw the empty tomb and the cloths. "Then the other disciple, who came to the tomb first, went in also; and he saw and believed" (verse 8).

Believed what? That the body was gone? Obviously. Instead, he believed that Jesus had been resurrected. Probably because of the linen cloth lying there and the handkerchief that had been around His head folded as it was.

Why?

Because if someone had stolen the body, why waste time stripping Jesus of His graveclothes and then arranging them? They would have taken the body and run—as quickly as they could, especially with the Romans who were supposed to have been guarding the tomb being around somewhere.

What John saw in the open sepulcher convinced him that Jesus had risen, even though "as yet they did not know the Scripture, that He must rise again from the dead" (verse 9). That is, though ignorant of the texts concerning Jesus' resurrection, for John, the empty tomb, the remaining cloths, and the folded handkerchief were enough. Perhaps, too, he now remembered, as did the women, that Jesus said He would be killed and then resurrected? The text says nothing about what Peter thought, other than Luke writing that he had been "marveling to himself at what had happened" (Luke 24:12), but the implication is that, unlike John, he didn't understand anything other than, as Mary had said, the tomb was empty.

Peter and John, as did Mary and then the other women, left the empty tomb, and so, at this point, no one's there.

Mary, the women, the disciples—all came to the tomb and left. (Notice how the sentence "Mary, the women, the disciples—all came to the tomb and left" could easily be read as if they all came to the tomb *together* and left *together*, which they didn't.)

A quick summary of events, up to this time, was given by Cleopas on the road to Emmaus. After talking about Jesus being crucified, he said: "Yes, and certain women of our company, who arrived at the tomb early, astonished us. When they did not find His body, they came saying that they had also seen a vision of angels who said He was alive. And certain of those who were with us went to the tomb and found it just as the women had said; but Him they did not see" (verses 22–24).

When Mary first told Peter and John about the missing body, they ran to the grave. Mary, apparently, wasn't with them when they got there. (Maybe she couldn't keep up?) If she was there, no one mentioned it, focusing on the two disciples instead. The next time Mary appears is after "the disciples went away again to their own homes" (John 20:10).

Either way, Mary is back at the empty tomb, alone. What happens next?

But Mary stood outside by the tomb weeping, and as she wept she stooped down and looked into the tomb. And she saw two angels in white sitting, one at the head and the other at the feet, where the body of Jesus had lain. Then they said to her, "Woman, why are you weeping?"

She said to them, "Because they have taken away my Lord, and I do not know where they have laid Him."

Now when she had said this, she turned around and saw Jesus standing there, and did not know that it was Jesus. Jesus said to her, "Woman, why are you weeping? Whom are you seeking?"

She, supposing Him to be the gardener, said to Him, "Sir, if You have carried Him away, tell me where You have laid Him, and I will take Him away."

Jesus said to her, "Mary!"

She turned and said to Him, "Rabboni!" (which is to say, Teacher).

Jesus said to her, "Do not cling to Me, for I have not yet ascended to My Father; but go to My brethren and say to them, 'I am ascending to My Father and your Father, and to My God and your God.'"

Mary Magdalene came and told the disciples that she had seen the Lord, and that He had spoken these things to her (verses 11–18).

In contrast to other accounts of the angels in the tomb, Mary doesn't seem afraid, nor is she told not to be. Perhaps, she had been crying so much that she didn't realize that they were angels. Her words, in response to the angels' question about why she was crying, prove that Mary still believed Christ's corpse had been pilfered, unlike the other women who had heard the good news.

Something then caused her to turn around and see a man, who she thought was the gardener. Her eyes must have been clogged with tears for her not to recognize Jesus; plus, she thought Jesus was dead and, thus, didn't expect Him to be standing there. Thinking the gardener might have taken Him away for some reason, she asked for the body so that she could put Him somewhere else, maybe in Lazarus's empty tomb.

Then, one word from Jesus, "Mary!" and Mary recognized the voice and knew that it was Him. His words—"Do not cling to Me"—reveal that she must have rushed forward to hug Him. Why He told her not to touch Him is another matter.

But for now, we have the first recorded appearance of the resurrected Jesus. And it was to Mary. "Now when He rose early on the first day of the week, He appeared first to Mary Magdalene, out of whom He had cast seven demons" (Mark 16:9).

After forbidding Mary to cling to Him, Jesus tells her to "go to My brethren." *Brothers?* He is the risen Lord, the glorified Lord, and yet Jesus refers to the disciples who abandoned Him or who denied Him, or both, and who en masse didn't believe His words about His death and resurrection—*as brothers?* What a powerful indication of the loving bond that Christ had with them, despite their failure.

To the first women at the tomb, the angels said that He had risen, and they told the women to bring that news to the disciples. Jesus Himself now appears to Mary and commands her to do the same: tell the disciples. Only now, instead of telling them, as the first women did, that angels said He had been raised, Mary could tell them that she saw the risen Lord herself—no doubt a more powerful testimony than just hearing it secondhand, even from angels.

And yet they still didn't believe.

Why didn't Jesus just appear in person to them right away, and that would be that? We don't know, but, as we will see, the disciples' initial disbelief—despite the empty tomb, despite the testimony of the women, and despite Christ's own words beforehand about what would happen to Him—would provide more evidence for those who haven't seen Him risen from the dead that He, indeed, did rise from the dead.

Thus far, in a span of—thirty minutes, one hour, six hours?—Mary, the women, Peter and John, and then Mary (again) came and left the tomb. Up to this point, none of the original eleven had seen the resurrected Jesus, and only one, John, not having yet seen Him, believed that He had been raised. For John, the empty tomb was, apparently, enough.

Mary alone had seen the resurrected Christ.

Christ, then, made another early appearance—this time to the women who came to the tomb after Mary had left. Sometime after the women had first come and after the angels told them what happened, the women had departed and went "to bring His disciples word" (Matthew 28:8); that is, tell them what the angels had said not only about Jesus being risen but also that they should go to Galilee and see Him there.

Jesus Himself then appeared to these women, even before they got to the disciples to tell them the good news.

"And as they went to tell His disciples, behold, Jesus met them, saying, 'Rejoice!' So they came and held Him by the feet and worshiped Him. Then Jesus said to them, 'Do not be afraid. Go and tell My brethren to go to Galilee, and there they will see Me' " (verses 9, 10). (Notice, again, the phrase "My brethren"—another indication of Christ's enduring love for the disciple despite their gross failure in His hour of need.)

We haven't been told how much time passed between the women's departure and their encounter with the risen Jesus. How long after they left to the time when this meeting happened, we haven't been told. In contrast to when He stopped Mary from touching Him, Jesus didn't stop the women when they "held Him by the feet," which shows that this encounter must have been *after* He had appeared to Mary and after He had ascended to the Father.

Jesus said to the women, "Rejoice!" That is to say, *Yes, what the angels told you about Me is true. I have been raised from the dead!* Then, after they held His feet and worshiped Him, Jesus told them not to be afraid, perhaps because the thought of Him resurrected, though good news, was still somewhat fearful for them. He next repeated what the angels said about going to Galilee and seeing Him there.

Thus, three times now, Heaven had given messages to be delivered to Christ's followers about His resurrection: first, from the angels to the women; then, from Jesus Himself to Mary; and finally, from Jesus to these women. Here, too, as with Mary, Jesus calls the disciples "My brethren." Tell *My brothers* that I will meet them—another affirmation of His love despite their fleeing the ship like wet rats.

No doubt, they could have used encouragement too.

Despite all that Christ had said to the disciples, which should have disabused them of their false ideas of His purpose in coming, they still harbored hopes that He would, somehow, establish a reign of hegemony as the Messiah, the Prince of Israel. As one disciple later expressed it, "But we were hoping that it was He who was going to redeem Israel" (Luke 24:21).

Thus, whatever they were expecting to happen, Jesus being killed, crucified like the worst of criminals, was not on their agenda, no matter how often He had told them that this is exactly what would happen. What a catastrophe His death must have seemed. Not just rejected by the leaders, which would have been hard enough for them to accept, but to see their beloved Master condemned and killed by those leaders as well?

Just when the disciples probably figured that things couldn't get worse, they did. Christ's body was missing, and the religious leaders accused them of having stolen it as part of some deception involving the dead Jesus. Grave robbing was a serious offense, and who knows what they could face next, not just from the leaders but from the crowds who, perhaps, were starting to believe what their leaders said about the disciples and Jesus? After all, many in the masses had put their hopes in Him as well, and people don't like being disappointed, so might they want to take out that disappointment on the hides of Christ's closest followers?

Too bad that the disciples hadn't believed what the women told them after the angels had said, "He is risen!" And that they hadn't really listened when Jesus had told them that "He will be delivered to the Gentiles and will be mocked and insulted and spit upon. They will scourge Him and kill Him. And the third day He will rise again" (Luke 18:32, 33).

However, before long, they would not only see the resurrected Jesus but also become convincing witnesses whose testimony would give evidence to billions, not only that Jesus had been resurrected but also that, because He had been, they could be too.

So far, the Gospels depict the risen Christ twice, appearing to Mary, then to the other women. The next appearance revealed in Scripture, and the first depiction of Him appearing to males of the species (other than the Roman guards), occurs in Luke. The account begins with the two travelers, believers in Jesus, who, late on Sunday afternoon, were walking to a village outside Jerusalem and discussing all "that had happened" (Luke 24:14, NIV)—that is, all that had happened with Jesus.

So it was, while they conversed and reasoned, that Jesus Himself drew near and went with them. But their eyes were restrained, so that they did not know Him.

And He said to them, "What kind of conversation is this that you have with one another as you walk and are sad?"

Then the one whose name was Cleopas answered and said to Him, "Are You the only stranger in Jerusalem, and have You not known the things which happened there in these days?"

And He said to them, "What things?"

So they said to Him, "The things concerning Jesus of Nazareth, who was a Prophet mighty in deed and word before God and all the people, and how the chief priests and our rulers delivered Him to be condemned to death, and crucified Him. But we were hoping that it was He who was going to redeem Israel. Indeed, besides all this, today is the third day since these things happened. Yes, and certain women of our company, who arrived at the tomb early, astonished us. When they did not find His body, they came saying that they had also seen a vision of angels who said He was alive. And certain of those who were with us went to the tomb and found it just as the women had said; but Him they did not see" (verses 15–24).

Who were these travelers, other than believers in Jesus? They were not of the original crew. One, Cleopas, never appears again in Scripture; the other isn't even named. Why the first time the post-Resurrection Christ is depicted as appearing to men, it's to these two nobodies—as opposed to James, John, Philip, Andrew, or any of Christ's inner circle—we haven't been told. (Perhaps a subtle rebuke for their actions?)

Their words to the "stranger" reveal how much of what happened was known in Jerusalem, at least regarding Christ's death. The question "Are you the only stranger in Jerusalem . . . ?" implies that most everyone must have heard about Jesus, "a Prophet mighty in deed and word before God and all the people" (verses 18, 19), which is a powerful testimony to Christ's influence among the people and their belief in Him as from God.

This testimony makes their words about "the chief priests and our rulers" (verse 20) delivering Jesus to death an implicit condemnation of the leaders. If He were a prophet of God, why would the leaders have had Him killed? Already, there are inklings of the impending (and tragic) separation between Jews who believed in Jesus and Jews who didn't.

These disciples had also set their hopes on Jesus, that He was "going to redeem Israel" (verse 21), which must have meant, if nothing else, ejecting the hated Romans. Along with the others, these two missed the point of Christ's first coming, and as did everyone else—even if Cleopas and his companion had heard what Jesus said about these things having to happen—they hadn't listened.

At the time of this encounter, word of the empty tomb must have spread among Christ's followers. Cleopas and the other had heard about the women who, having come to the tomb, found it empty, had seen angels "who said He was alive" (verse 23), and had told the men, who then came and found it "just as the women had said" (verse 24). Thus, word of Christ's appearance to Mary and then to the others hadn't yet reached these two disciples.

Though still confused about "the things which happened there [in Jerusalem] in these days" (verse 18) and what they all meant, these disciples were about to get the first known Bible study on the meaning of Christ's death and resurrection— a study given by Christ Himself.

All through His ministry, Jesus referred to the Old Testament, not only in general but in regard to Himself and to events in His life in particular. He often said something like, "How then could the Scriptures be fulfilled, that it must happen thus?" (Matthew 26:54; see also verse 56; Mark 14:21; Luke 4:21; John 17:12).

In other words, before events happened, or as they were about to happen, Jesus pointed to them as predicted in the Scriptures. Then, after all of these events had happened, Jesus returns to Scripture in order to show these disciples that all that had happened, especially His death and resurrection, had been predicted in the Bible.

Jesus must have wanted them to see in the Word of God itself His life, death, and resurrection because the Word would remain long after He had returned to heaven. It would also, for future generations, testify to His resurrection and the hope that it offers us, for whom death is as real and as inevitable as life.

B efore showing Himself to these disciples or doing a miracle before them, which would have proven to them that He had been resurrected, Jesus wanted to ground them in the Word of God. Therefore, after they told Him what the fuss was all about, the story continues: "Then He said to them, 'O foolish ones, and slow of heart to believe in all that the prophets have spoken! Ought not the Christ to have suffered these things and to enter into His glory?' And beginning at Moses and all the Prophets, He expounded to them in all the Scriptures the things concerning Himself" (Luke 24:25–27).

Jesus starts out pretty hard on them, as if they, Jews conversant in the Bible, should have known these truths already. Using Moses (Genesis, Exodus, Leviticus, Numbers, and Deuteronomy) and "all the Prophets" (Isaiah, Jeremiah, Daniel, Hosea, etc.; verse 27), He must have set out how the events surrounding the Messiah, especially His suffering, death, and resurrection, were predicted in Scripture. Most telling are His words that the Christ had to "have suffered these things" (verse 26), most likely to disabuse them of the error that the Messiah would set up a new kingdom in which, among other things, the Romans would be overthrown. (The people conflated the two comings of Jesus, thinking that many of the promises of the Second Coming would occur at the first.)

Instead, He showed them how the things that Christ "suffered" were what "Moses and all the Prophets" had said would happen to the Messiah but at His first coming. According to Luke, all the things in the prophets and Moses that referred to Jesus and His first coming were explained to them.

How long this study took, Scripture doesn't say. The text next picks up with the following:

> Then they drew near to the village where they were going, and He indicated that He would have gone farther. But they constrained Him, saying, "Abide with us, for it is toward evening, and the day is far spent." And He went in to stay with them.
>
> Now it came to pass, as He sat at the table with them, that He took bread, blessed and broke it, and gave it to them. Then their eyes were opened and they knew Him; and He vanished from their sight.
>
> And they said to one another, "Did not our heart burn within us while He talked with us on the road, and while He opened the Scriptures to us?" (verses 28–32).

Only after the Bible study, only after building the case for Himself from Scripture as the crucified and risen Messiah, did Christ appear before them as the crucified and risen Messiah. And then He miraculously vanished. However powerful and effective Jesus' appearance and then disappearance would have been, that's not what Christ wanted them to base their faith on.

It worked. "And they said to one another, 'Did not our heart burn within us while He talked with us on the road, and while He opened the Scriptures to us?' " (verse 32). Rather than focus on the miracles (His appearance and disappearance), they talked about how their "heart burn[ed]" when Jesus *opened the Scriptures to them.* It was the power of the Word of God, manifested in the life, death, and resurrection of Jesus, that made the deepest impression on them.

W hat happened next? The two returned to Jerusalem, obviously to tell others what happened. However, when entering the room where "the eleven and those who were with them gathered" (verse 33), before opening their own mouths to recount the good news, they were told: "The Lord is risen indeed, and has appeared to Simon!" (verse 34).

The disciples didn't say, *The Lord is risen because we have been with Him!* Or *The Lord is risen because we have seen Him ourselves!* Instead, they said that they knew the Lord had risen because Simon had seen Him. In other words, even though they hadn't seen Him, Peter's claim that Jesus had appeared to him was enough, even though these same people rejected, as "idle tales" (verse 11), the testimony of the women. This point becomes very important in Resurrection apologetics.

In 1 Corinthians 15, Paul, in his own Resurrection apologetic, specifically mentions that after Jesus rose on the third day, "He was seen by Cephas" (verse 4).* But unlike with the women or later with other disciples, no description is given in the Gospels regarding the meeting with Peter, though one could imagine, considering Peter's open betrayal and abandonment of Jesus, it must have been moving and affirming for Peter to be the disciple to whom Christ first appeared.

Even Peter never wrote about this specific appearance of Christ to him, at least in any of the letters we have in the New Testament canon. Peter later wrote about the things that he had personally witnessed, such as when he heard God the Father speak: "For we did not follow cunningly devised fables when we made known to you the power and coming of our Lord Jesus Christ, but were eyewitnesses of His majesty. For He received from God the Father honor and glory when such a voice came to Him from the Excellent Glory: 'This is My beloved Son, in whom I am well pleased.' And we heard this voice which came from heaven when we were with Him on the holy mountain" (2 Peter 1:16–18). However, he never once mentioned in his epistles his first meeting with the risen Christ or any later meeting with Him either.

After being told that the Lord appeared to Simon, these two disciples started giving their own account of the resurrected Christ. As they were speaking, "Jesus Himself stood in the midst of them, and said to them, 'Peace to you' " (Luke 24:36).

According to the text, they were scared, afraid that it was some kind of occult experience. After hearing Peter's testimony (and whatever impact the testimony of the two disciples had on the others), they professed belief in His resurrection; however, Christ's appearance still frightened them. Jesus then showed them His hands and His feet, obviously the wounds from the Crucifixion. Yet they "still did not believe for joy" (verse 41), and so He ate before them, all in order to convince them that it was a real body, not some occult entity.

Obviously, a crucified and resurrected Messiah was not what they had expected.

---

* Simon and Cephas are both names for Peter.

Which is why He told them that all that happened was, yes, what He had already told them would happen because all that had happened had been predicted by Moses, the prophets, and the Psalms.

> And He opened their understanding, that they might comprehend the Scriptures.
> Then He said to them, "Thus it is written, and thus it was necessary for the Christ to suffer and to rise from the dead the third day, and that repentance and remission of sins should be preached in His name to all nations, beginning at Jerusalem. And you are witnesses of these things. Behold, I send the Promise of My Father upon you; but tarry in the city of Jerusalem until you are endued with power from on high" (verses 45–49).

In contrast to Cleopas and his companion, to whom Jesus appeared first and afterward gave a Bible study, Jesus first appears to the others, reveals Himself as the risen Christ, and then, only afterward, does He give them a Bible study that affirms all that had happened.

Why the reverse order, we don't know, but we do know that for Jesus, the scriptural foundation—that is, the scriptural foundation from the Old Testament—was crucial for proving who He was and what He had accomplished. He knew how important it was for His fellow Jews, especially as they witnessed to the world but "beginning in Jerusalem," to understand how this was all predicted in the Old Testament.

Jesus was going away; the disciples would have their eyewitness testimony, which would be powerful. But even that might not have always been enough to convince others (after all, they could be lying), which is why they needed Scripture as the foundation. Jesus needed them to understand that His death and resurrection had been predicted in the Old Testament. Though they had the privilege of seeing Him, what about all of those who would never have the opportunity and yet whose eternal destiny depended upon believing that it happened?

They would need more, and Jesus was providing it. After all, one day, all those who had seen Him in the flesh would be gone, and all who had heard directly from them and their eyewitness accounts would be gone, and even those who heard from those who had heard their eyewitness accounts would be gone. Eventually, all that would be left to testify to the things of Jesus would be the Word of God, which remains, to this day, the most powerful witness of the resurrection of Jesus and of the hope that it offers to all who come to Christ by faith.

Yet that upper room story wasn't done. If it was hard, at first, to convince those in the room who had seen Jesus appear mystically amid them and even eat before them, and for them to believe that it was really Him (apparently, only after the Bible study He gave did they finally believe), what about Thomas, who had not been there in the room to begin with? "Now Thomas, called the Twin, one of the twelve, was not with them when Jesus came" (John 20:24).

Even when the disciples who had seen Jesus had told Thomas, he seemed determined not to believe, declaring: "Unless I see in His hands the print of the nails, and put my finger into the print of the nails, and put my hand into His side, I will not believe" (verse 25). (Perhaps his attitude arose out of sheer stubbornness or being miffed that Christ appeared to everyone else—even women—and not to him.)

It must have been a long, brooding week for him. But then, what happened? "And after eight days His disciples were again inside, and Thomas with them. Jesus came, the doors being shut, and stood in the midst, and said, 'Peace to you!' " (verse 26). Jesus miraculously appears in the midst of them and then says to Thomas, "Reach your finger here, and look at My hands; and reach your hand here, and put it into My side. Do not be unbelieving, but believing" (verse 27).

What a powerful expression of God's grace. The Lord could have easily just written off Thomas, something like, *This man has been told by so many people that I am alive—people whom he can trust, and he had heard Me say that all of this would happen to Me. And then there are all the Bible texts as well. And yet He still refuses to believe? Too bad about him.*

Instead, the supernaturally risen Jesus supernaturally entered the closed room and appeared supernaturally to the disciples again, this time with Thomas present. In response to Thomas's own words, which he had spoken when Jesus wasn't there, Jesus gave Thomas exactly what he said that he needed in order to believe: the chance to look at His hands and put his fingers in the wounds.

After seeing the nail prints in Jesus' hands, Thomas could have then put his fingers in Jesus' side. Jesus told him to look at His hands and to touch His side, which Thomas had said that he needed to believe, but the text never says that Thomas touched Christ. Instead, Thomas says, "My Lord and my God!" (verse 28).

Merely seeing Jesus in person was, apparently, enough. "Thomas, because you have seen Me, you have believed. Blessed are those who have not seen and yet have believed" (verse 29). Jesus didn't say, *Thomas, because you have seen and touched Me, you have believed.*

However, Christ's statement "blessed are those who have not seen and yet have believed" (verse 29) is significant. According to the New Testament, before Christ finally ascended to heaven, many other people (besides the ones we've looked at) encountered the risen Jesus, including James and then, much later, Paul himself.

Paul would later write that the resurrected Christ "was seen by over five hundred brethren at once, of whom the greater part remain to the present, but some have fallen asleep" (1 Corinthians 15:6).

Yet this number, even if totaling a few thousand, is nothing compared to the billions who would be born centuries after Jesus ascended to the Father—the billions who would never see the resurrected Christ in the way that these others had. People who had firsthand eyewitness accounts of those who had seen Him resurrected had trouble believing; even those who saw Him in person struggled, at first, with belief.

And yet billions who have never seen with their own eyes the risen Christ are to believe in Him as their only hope of being, long term, nothing more than roadkill?

Yes, and that's because they have good reasons to believe in Him.

The risen Jesus had told His followers that He would see them in Galilee. "Do not be afraid. Go and tell my brothers to go to Galilee; there they will see me" (Matthew 28:10, NIV). Even before His death, Jesus said, "But after I have risen, I will go ahead of you into Galilee" (Matthew 26:32; Mark 14:28, NIV). Even the angels said the same thing after Christ had been raised: "But go, tell his disciples and Peter, 'He is going ahead of you into Galilee. There you will see him, just as he told you' " (Mark 16:7, NIV).

Besides appearing to the women, to Peter, and to the disciples in the upper room, the resurrected Christ was also going to meet them later in Galilee—His last biblically depicted appearance to the disciples as a group.

The scene picks up by the Sea of Galilee. Who knows the memories that must have seeped through the minds of the disciples at this time? On this same water, Jesus, by uttering a few words, had stilled the fierce storm. Perhaps, in sight, was the nearby beach where thousands had been fed from a few fish and loaves. And not too far away was Capernaum, the place where Jesus did many of His miracles.

The scene began with Peter deciding to go fishing, and six other disciples joined him. Perhaps, since their lives had been disrupted by the gospel (which is how it should be), they needed income, food, clothing, and shelter. Catching some fish could help provide for that.

However, "that night they caught nothing" (John 21:3, NIV). The story, then, goes as follows:

> But when the morning had now come, Jesus stood on the shore; yet the disciples did not know that it was Jesus. Then Jesus said to them, "Children, have you any food?"
>
> They answered Him, "No."
>
> And He said to them, "Cast the net on the right side of the boat, and you will find some." So they cast, and now they were not able to draw it in because of the multitude of fish.
>
> Therefore that disciple whom Jesus loved said to Peter, "It is the Lord!" Now when Simon Peter heard that it was the Lord, he put on his outer garment (for he had removed it), and plunged into the sea (verses 4–7).

Notice, He called them "children"—an endearing term that represented His Fatherly love for them. (Earlier, the resurrected Christ had called them "brethren.") Once they realized who it was, Peter immediately threw himself into the water. Peter's lack of hesitancy, even after his great betrayal, lends credence to that earlier claim that Jesus had already appeared to Peter, and perhaps at that meeting, they had first worked through that betrayal, and Peter now knew that Christ had forgiven him.

"This is now the third time that Jesus showed Himself to His disciples after

He was raised from the dead" (verse 14)—that is, the third time He appeared to them as a group, the first two being in the upper room. Jesus then goes through the now-famous question-and-answer game with Peter, though each time ending with the phrase "Feed My lambs," "Tend My sheep," or "Feed My sheep" (verses 15–17); He did it publicly, before the other disciples. Jesus appeared to them again, not only affirming them more in their faith in Him as the resurrected Christ but also showing the other disciples that Peter, despite his failure, still was to have a prominent role in the new movement. Grace is available, even for such a heinous sellout.

John then ends not only this chapter but also his Gospel with these words:

This is the disciple who testifies of these things, and wrote these things; and we know that his testimony is true.

And there are also many other things that Jesus did, which if they were written one by one, I suppose that even the world itself could not contain the books that would be written. Amen (verses 24, 25).

Whatever the hyperbole, Jesus was the Messiah, and He did many things that proved it, including—and, surely, most importantly—rising from the tomb.

However, from the religious leaders who bribed the guards to deny the resurrection of Jesus within hours of it happening to almost two thousand years later, with skeptics, atheists, and some Christians denying the Resurrection, why should anyone—especially the billions who never saw Him raised from the dead nor knew anyone who did—believe in such an extraordinary claim?

"An extraordinary claim," wrote Marcello Truzzi, "requires extraordinary proof."[2]

Fair enough.

---

1. John Lennox, *Gunning for God: Why the New Atheists Are Missing the Target* (Oxford, UK: Lion, 2011), 209.
2. Marcello Truzzi, "On the Extraordinary: An Attempt at Clarification," *Zetetic Scholar* 1, no. 1 (1978): 11, http://tricksterbook.com/truzzi/ZS-Issues-PDFs/ZeteticScholarNo1.pdf.

Why Live If You Can Be Buried for Ten Dollars?

A man in India sued his parents. As a follower of antinatalism,* which teaches that it's morally wrong for people to procreate because to be born means to suffer, he claimed that his parents had selfishly brought him into the world and were, therefore, obligated to take care of him for the rest of his life.

"I want everyone in India and the world to realize one thing that they are born without their consent. I want them to understand that they do not owe their parents anything," he said. "If we are born without our consent, we should be maintained for our life. We should be paid by our parents to live."[1]

In *A Horse Walks Into a Bar*, author David Grossman has a stand-up comedian say: "Exactly at this minute, more or less, in the old Hadassah Hospital in Jerusalem, my mother, Sarah Greenstein, went into labor! Unbelievable, isn't it? A woman who claimed to want only the best for me, and yet she gave birth to me! I mean, think about how many trials and prisons and investigations and crime series there are because of murder, but I've yet to hear a single case involving birth! Nothing about premeditated birth, negligent birth, accidental birth, not even incitement to birth! And don't forget we're talking about a crime where the victim is a minor!"[2]

Herodotus (fifth century BC) wrote about a tribe that began a period of mourning after a birth (sitting shiva† in reverse) because they anticipated the suffering that the infant, if it lived to adulthood, would face. However alien the ritual may seem to us, its logic works like geometry.

An advertisement in America that fascinated Sigmund Freud and his obsession with death read, "Why live, if you can be buried for ten dollars?"[3]

Something's obviously amok in God's world, where to be born can, indeed, be a bummer. Something is. It's called sin, and from inception, it has been the foundation of every moral and physical evil, which have for so long seeped into existence that the creation itself is in the "bondage of corruption" (Romans 8:21). All we know is suffering and death, which is why we take them for granted, even to the point where many assume that suffering and death were the means (not the antithesis) of creation itself.

But suffering, evil, and death are unnatural acts—intruders, never part of the original creation—no matter how firmly entrenched in that creation they are now.

And they arose but only because God created humanity with the ability to love, and for love to be love, it must be freely given. Otherwise, God could have created us to be like AIBO, a robot dog that, Sony claims, "has emotions and instincts programmed into his brain." He "acts to fulfill the desires created by his instincts."[4]

Emotions? Instincts? Desires? Robot dogs have no more emotions, instincts,

---

* For more information, see the Antinatalism Facebook page at https://www.facebook.com/Antinatalism/.

† A Jewish ritual mourning the dead.

and desires than a toilet has vertigo when flushed. To claim that AIBO is "also a fully cognizant, sensing, loving and communicative companion"[5] is to attribute traits of intelligent life to plastic and metal. Just make sure that the batteries are charged, and love, joy, and affection will flow out of the circuit boards, silicon chips, and plastic like photons from a light source.

But God obviously wanted to give more and get more. Rather than create us like robot dogs, He created us as moral beings with the capacity to love both Him and others, and this capacity included the freedom inherent in the kind of love that only a moral being could give, even if that capacity contained the potential to do wrong, which humanity, unfortunately, did. In contrast, robot dogs can't manifest even puppy love—much less the love that a flesh-and-fur dog expresses—which is a smoky phantom compared to the love humans can give and receive because we are human and not cold, sterile machines.

If a robot dog's "love" doesn't do much for you, you can understand, somewhat, why God created us as He did, even at the cost of the Cross for Himself, for the Cross is what it took for God to one day restore the world to what He had first created.

But the death of Jesus on the cross still wasn't enough; it took the Resurrection as well. Only in Christ's resurrection do we have the hope that our burial (even if it costs a lot more than ten dollars) isn't the end of the script. If the grave is the final line of our story, it's a fruitless, hopeless, and meaningless tale.

And somehow, someway, we sense that our meaninglessness just can't be what defines our lives, not only because we don't want it to be but because there's too much to our lives for them to total up to meaninglessness. That makes no more sense than adding up positive integers and getting zero.

There has to be more.

There is, and it's found in the resurrection of Jesus.

How ironic that the sad precursor to World War II, at least in Europe, unfolded in a land that, for the most part, stayed out of World War II: Spain. After the devastation of the Spanish Civil War (1936–1939), the Spaniards didn't need the carnage that its neighbors faced.

Nevertheless, one incident in the Spanish Civil War set a precedent for that carnage. In April 1937, while aiding General Francisco Franco, German warplanes flown by pilots eager to test their killing skills leveled Guernica, whose seven thousand people were now distinguished as history's first deliberate civilian targets of an aerial bombardment.

Enraged by the atrocity, Pablo Picasso painted one of his most famous works: *Guernica*, an eleven-foot-tall by twenty-five-foot-long oil painting that depicted, in Picasso's unique style, the town's anguish. Supposedly, a German officer saw the painting and said to Picasso, "Did you do this?"

Picasso replied, "No, you did!"

When it came to Spaniards killing Spaniards, neither side was atrocity immune, however. The Republicans, fighting Franco, spilled lots of (relatively) innocent blood too.

"As in the French Revolution," wrote Adam Hochschild, "the Catholic clergy was also a prime target: radical workers murdered priests, flaunted bishops' robes, assembled a firing squad to 'execute' a famous statue of Christ, and dug up clerical graves and displayed opened coffins full of bones to mock the Church's promise of eternal life."[6]

However graphic and gruesome, the exhumation of these bones proved nothing in regard to the "promise of eternal life" found in Jesus. Until the resurrection, all that remains are the bones of the dead, if even that much. Atheist Peter Atkins wrote about "the impossibility of being able to restore a cadaver to working condition, even one quite freshly dead. There is little point in emphasizing the almost infinitely greater impossibility, if impossibilities can be magnified, of assembling the bits and pieces of all past, present, and future Mankind, some scattered to the winds, some digested by maggots, some dispersed, some blasted into fragments, some gone up in smoke, some dissolved in acid, and some gone, literally, to the dogs."[7] How he, a chemist, knows that the resurrection of the dead is impossible, Dr. Atkins doesn't specify. It certainly seems impossible, at least from the standpoint of his expertise, which is chemistry, and even from any conceivable perspective of what humanity could do.

But to constrain all potential reality to human potentiality seems painfully narrow-minded. To limit all that could be done to only what humans can or could do is shallow, like assuming that because humans couldn't fly for most of human history, human flight was impossible, or because we don't know how information can travel faster than light, it, therefore, cannot.* Drifting amid a

---

* In fact, quantum physics seems to indicate that it can.

big cosmos, we occupy and traverse minuscule scribbles of space, nothing more. We don't begin to know what's out there (scientists speculate that a vast majority of the universe is dark matter and dark energy; *dark* as in we can't see it), so to constrain what's possible by God to only what's understandable by man is to intellectually incarcerate ourselves within a reality no broader and deeper than what chemistry and physics theories allow. Which is silly because those theories often change or are superseded or refuted even.

The whole point of the Resurrection is that *it is supernatural.* It's beyond chemistry and physics. It couldn't be anything else but. All one has to do is believe that God created the universe, and the existence of the supernatural becomes the most obvious and logical truth possible because the natural world arose from something beyond itself; that is, it arose from something *super* natural, from what is above and beyond the natural.

"Causes that are physical or that are subject to scientific law presuppose time, space, and matter to exist," wrote J. P. Moreland. "But since we are asking what *caused* time, space, and matter, the cause itself must be something other than each of these. In other words, it must be *timeless* in order to cause time; it must be *nonspatial* in order to cause space; it must be *immaterial* in order to cause matter; it must, therefore, be *supernatural,* capable of existing without the natural world and without being subject to the ultimate laws of nature."[8]

And so, whether humans be "quite freshly dead. . . . Scattered to the winds, . . . digested by maggots, . . . blasted into fragments, . . . dissolved in acid," the God who supernaturally created the world can supernaturally resurrect the dead.

He did, with Jesus.

But the question remains: Why should anyone believe it?

F or Christians, the answer is easy: The Bible says that Christ was resurrected. Over and over in the Gospels and in the epistles, the resurrection of Jesus forms a crucial, if not *the* crucial, event upon which the faith rests. Books could be filled with nothing but one-line quotes from Christian scholars on how central the resurrection of Christ is. But just a single one-line quote from Paul expresses it best: "And if Christ is not risen, your faith is futile; you are still in your sins!" (1 Corinthians 15:17).

Again, it's not that hard to believe that a Jew, Jesus of Nazareth, had been crucified by the Romans. Rome crucified Jews all the time, and most scholars don't question the reality of Christ's death on the cross. But for no other victim of Roman crucifixion has the claim been made, and by so many different sources, too, that one of those crucified Jews rose from the dead and then appeared, numerous times, to different people. And yet that's precisely what the New Testament teaches, emphasizes, even makes foundational to the faith.

But that's fine for Christians who believe in the resurrection of Jesus because they believe in the Bible. But what about people who don't believe in the Bible, at least as the Word of God? However many hundreds of people, thousands maybe, who supposedly saw the resurrected Jesus, and the smaller number who ate with Him, who touched Him, who were with Him for weeks on end after the Resurrection—what are they in contrast to the billions who weren't there, who never saw Him resurrected, and who never knew anyone who claimed to have seen Him resurrected?

Why should they believe?

Because of the powerful and convincing historical evidence for the resurrection of Jesus Christ. Even if one were to look at the New Testament, not as divinely inspired but as a historical record, the logical and rational evidence for the resurrection of Jesus remains compelling.

Christian apologist C. S. Lewis wrote the following about one of the steps along the way toward his conversion:

> Early in 1926 the hardest boiled of all the atheists I ever knew sat in my room . . . and remarked that the evidence for the historicity of the Gospels was really surprisingly good. . . . To understand the shattering impact of it [the man's admission about the "surprisingly good" evidence for the historicity of the Gospels], you would need to know the man (who has certainly never since shown any interest in Christianity). If he, the cynic of cynics, the toughest of the toughs, were not—as I would still have put it—'safe', where could I turn? Was there then no escape?[9]

Lewis, apparently, was cursed with a logical mind. If there was "surprisingly good" evidence for the historicity of the Gospels and the Gospels included the resurrection of Jesus, then, well, perhaps, the Resurrection happened?

What was this "surprisingly good" evidence, particularly for the one event in the "historicity of the Gospels" upon which the faith rests? The apostle Paul, in seeking to reach the infamously philosophical Athenians, said to them about God: "For he has set a day when he will judge the world with justice by the man he has appointed. He has given proof of this to everyone by raising him from the dead" (Acts 17:31, NIV).

Proof? And to all men too? Sure, if Jesus were raised from the dead, it would all but prove the truth of Christianity, but how can someone not there know that Jesus was resurrected?

The historical record. That's all we have been given, actually. If there is a God and He wants people, all humankind, to believe in the resurrection of Jesus, but the only evidence for it, at least for most of humanity, is the historical record, which is pretty much (but not exclusively) the New Testament, then the New Testament must contain the "proof" that Paul talked about.

For argument's sake, one can look at the New Testament, as many historians have, as a secular account of historical events—some not particularly controversial, such as Christ's crucifixion by the Romans. But this historical record also includes the empty tomb, Jesus' resurrection, and His multiple appearances. If one wants to look at the New Testament as a secular account of what are claimed to be supernatural events, how do those claims fare historically?

For those who automatically rule out the supernatural, then regardless of whatever the New Testament says, regardless of whether the resurrected Jesus appeared to them even now, they will not believe. On the other hand, for those who might not necessarily believe in the Resurrection but are open to the possibility, the claim is that the New Testament accounts provide powerfully rational and logical reasons for the Resurrection. So logical and rational that the resurrection of Jesus becomes the *only* logical explanation for what historians agree on: that, after the death of Jesus, many people claimed to have seen Him risen from the dead.

1. Lukas Mikelionis, "Indian Man to Sue His Parents for Giving Birth to Him 'Without His Consent,' Wants to Be Paid for His Life," Fox News, February 7, 2019, https://www.foxnews.com/world/indian-man-to-sue-his-parents-for-giving-birth-to-him-without-his-consent-wants-to-be-paid-for-his-life.

2. David Grossman, *A Horse Walks Into a Bar*, trans. Jessica Cohen (New York: Vintage International, 2017), 11.

3. Jamieson Webster, "The Psychopharmacology of Everyday Life," NYR Daily, November 19, 2018, https://www.nybooks.com/daily/2018/11/19/the-psychopharmacology-of-everyday-life/.

4. "Sony AIBO Robot Dog," Robot Books, accessed August 23, 2020, http://www.robotbooks.com/sony_aibo.htm.

5. "Sony AIBO Robot Dog."

6. Adam Hochschild, *Spain in Our Hearts: Americans in the Spanish Civil War, 1936–1939* (New York: Houghton Mifflin Harcourt, 2016), 63.

7. Peter Atkins, *On Being: A Scientist's Exploration of the Great Questions of Existence* (New York: Oxford University Press, 2011), 91.

8. J. P. Moreland, *Scientism and Secularism* (Wheaton, IL: Crossway, 2018), 138; emphasis in the original.

9. C. S. Lewis, *Surprised by Joy: The Shape of My Early Life* (New York: HarperCollins, 2017), 273.

The Frankenstein Factor

In his Holocaust memoir, Viktor Frankl recounted an old tale:

> A rich and mighty Persian once walked in his garden with one of his servants. The servant cried that he had just encountered Death, who had threatened him. He begged his master to give him his fastest horse so that he could make haste and flee to Teheran, which he could reach that same evening. The master consented and the servant galloped off on the horse. On returning to his house the master himself met Death, and questioned him, "Why did you terrify and threaten my servant?" "I did not threaten him; I only showed surprise in still finding him here when I planned to meet him tonight in Teheran," said Death.[1]

Death does meet us, and not just in Tehran either. Or, perhaps, we carry death around in us—a part of us more tightly wired in our cells than DNA is and only awaiting something internal (cancer?) or external (Nazis?) to bring it out. Whatever the metaphor, death wins.

That is, unless Christ was resurrected, because in that resurrection, the biblical promise that "the last enemy that will be destroyed is death" (1 Corinthians 15:26) will finally be realized.

That's the hope anyway.

"There is nothing so cruel," wrote Haruki Murakami, "in this world as the desolation of having nothing to hope for."[2] And yet the New Testament exudes hope—the hope that arises from the resurrection of Jesus.

And for good reasons too. According to the New Testament (we're taking the New Testament books and letters as, at minimum, historical documents), hundreds either saw the resurrected Jesus themselves or had enough evidence from those who did to convince them of it.

The list, chronologically, goes something like this:

The Roman guards at the tomb. Implicit in the account is that the guards must have seen the Resurrection itself, which explains why the religious leaders bribed them to lie about it. After all, a mere empty tomb wouldn't have been a big deal because maybe the disciples did steal the corpse after the angel came down, or maybe the angel himself swiped it? A missing corpse does not a resurrection prove.

Meanwhile, the actions of the religious leaders reveal that they, too, believed that Jesus had risen; again, why bribe the guards otherwise? How ironic that the first to see the resurrection of Jesus and to believe it were Christ's enemies.

Next were the women who went to the tomb, found it empty, and were told by angels that Christ had been resurrected (Mark 16:5–7).

Mary, who knew only that the tomb was empty, told Peter and John, who came to the tomb, where John "saw and believed" (John 20:8).

Mary is back at the tomb when Jesus appeared to her (verses 11–18).

Jesus later appeared to the other women (Matthew 28:9, 10).

The next time the biblical texts have Jesus manifesting Himself to people is with the two on the road to Emmaus (Luke 24:13–34).

These two then go to Jerusalem, where they are told that "the Lord is risen indeed, and has appeared to Simon!" (verse 34). These words reveal that, though Jesus hadn't appeared to these others, they believe that He had risen because He had appeared to Simon (Peter). Then Jesus manifests Himself to them all (verse 36) and eight days later again to them but now with Thomas present (John 20:26–28).

Finally, Jesus comes to them in Galilee (John 21:1–14).

According to Paul, Jesus was also "seen by over five hundred brethren at once, of whom the greater part remain to the present, but some have fallen asleep" (1 Corinthians 15:6). Though Paul doesn't say where this event happened, it must have been when the resurrected Jesus gave them, said Luke, "many infallible proofs, being seen by them during forty days and speaking of the things pertaining to the kingdom of God" (Acts 1:3).

Not long after Christ's death, when the disciples needed to replace Judas, they needed someone who

"must become a witness with us of His resurrection."

And they proposed two: Joseph called Barsabas, who was surnamed Justus, and Matthias (verses 21–23).

Thus, there were at least these two more witnesses.

Paul also says that Jesus then appeared to James (1 Corinthians 15:7), to all the apostles, and finally to Paul himself (verse 8).

We don't know how many guards were at the tomb when He rose, nor how many chief priests and other leaders they told what had happened. But they constitute more who believed it happened. Paul said that Jesus appeared to five hundred "at once" in a single meeting.* Because Jesus remained for forty days after His resurrection, it's not hard to imagine that He had appeared to many others as well. After all, if the point were to get people to believe, it's hard to imagine Him *not* appearing to others.

Thus, the resurrected Christ showed Himself to hundreds of people, and who knows how many more, perhaps thousands, then believed based on the eyewitness testimonies of those who had seen Him.

Though we have written accounts *about* the hundreds who had seen the resurrected Jesus or who had believed it to be Him because of the witness of those who did claim to see Him, we don't have written accounts *by* those hundreds but, instead, only by a handful.

Is that enough?

---

* Also, the phrase "five hundred brethren" could mean that there were women and children as well, though they weren't counted. If that's the case, then even more people saw Him.

The New Testament, as a historical document, has numerous references to Christ's resurrection, all written after the purported event, even though some texts referred to Jesus Himself, before His resurrection, forewarning that it would happen.

- All four Gospels (Matthew, Mark, Luke, and John) unambiguously depict the resurrected Christ.
- Though writing little about the life and ministry of Jesus, the apostle Paul wrote extensively about His death and resurrection.
- Peter, so involved in the death and resurrection of Jesus, wrote about them as well.

Six biblical sources aren't hundreds, but, as far as ancient history goes, six sources—some claiming to be eyewitnesses—are a lot, especially for something as limited in time and place as what, according to the New Testament, unfolded right after Christ's death.

Contrast those events with a major historical occurrence in the same century: the explosion of Mount Vesuvius along the Italian coast in AD 79. Considered one of the most catastrophic eruptions ever, it killed about thirty thousand people and buried in ash, mud, and rocks the cities of Pompeii and Herculaneum. The force of the explosion was estimated as "100,00 times the thermal energy released by the atomic bombings of Hiroshima and Nagasaki."[3] It sent columns of ash and pumice up to ninety-eight thousand feet into the atmosphere.

A modern depiction described it like this: "Shortly after midnight, a wall of volcanic mud engulfed the town of Herculaneum, obliterating the town as its citizens fled toward Pompeii. About 6:30 a.m. on the following morning, a glowing cloud of volcanic gases and debris rolled down Vesuvius' slopes and enveloped the city of Pompeii. Most victims died instantly as the superheated air burned their lungs and contracted their muscles, leaving the bodies in a semi-curled position to be quickly buried in ash and thus preserved in detail for hundreds of years."[4]

Compared to the events that unfolded after the death of Jesus—that is, scattered people in Jerusalem and later in Galilee meeting together, sometimes in small furtive groups inside buildings or along a seashore or larger groups elsewhere—the Mount Vesuvius explosion was a major public event that must have been witnessed by untold numbers who survived it.

Yet, historically, only one eyewitness account exists. One! A Roman, Pliny the Younger, recorded the event in two letters to the Roman historian Tacitus.[5] Thus, if a major natural disaster such as the AD 79 eruption of Mount Vesuvius had only one historical real-time written eyewitness, then the events regarding the resurrection of Jesus, as far as historical sources are concerned, are doing pretty well.

So well, in fact, that many of the accounts regarding Jesus are, today, accepted as historical facts even by those who aren't Christians or who don't believe in the supernatural.

From a purely historical perspective, many scholars will concede the following: Jesus, of course, would have had to have existed to have been crucified, and though some have doubted His existence, most scholars and historians, even atheist scholars and historians, don't. Hence, the presence of a Jew named Jesus of Nazareth in first-century Judea doesn't demand anything supernatural.

His death on the cross, from a historical perspective, doesn't demand a great leap of faith either. Just another Jew crucified by the Romans in the first century.

And the empty tomb? Here, too, most scholars will accept that, somehow, the body of Christ was removed from the tomb. Many non-supernatural theories have been promulgated to explain how. After all, it doesn't necessitate a resurrection to empty a tomb. And among those theories is that the disciples, as part of a ploy to salvage their new movement after the unexpected death of Jesus, simply made the whole thing up.

If you reject even the possibility of the Resurrection, this fraud theory certainly sounds like a viable explanation.

The story unfolds as follows:

An idealist young man living in the eighteenth century wanted to change the world and bring about good. (Don't they all?) He sought, through the marvels of science and technology, to defeat sickness, suffering, and death. He thought, "If I could bestow animation upon lifeless matter, I might in process of time . . . renew life where death had apparently devoted the body to corruption."[6]

And so he toiled, pursuing "nature to her hiding places"[7] until he reached his goal: creating life from nonlife.

"It was on a dreary night of November, that I beheld the accomplishment of my toils," he bemoaned as the "lifeless thing" at his feet came alive. "I saw the dull yellow eye of the creature open; it breathed hard, and a convulsive motion agitated its limbs."[8] Though working hard and long, he was horrified by the monster that he had made.

"How can I describe my emotions as this catastrophe, or how delineate the wretch whom with such infinite pains and care I had endeavored to form?"[9]

Hating what he had formed, the scientist abandoned it, only later to discover that his creation had murdered the scientist's brother as revenge for the scientist having made him such a lonely and despicable being. Eventually, the scientist and his creation meet in the Swiss mountains, and the creature demands that the scientist make him a female partner. The scientist agrees but then, realizing that he was about to create another monster, abandons the project, angering the creation, who then kills not only the scientist's best friend but also, later, his wife.

Eventually, the scientist dies, and the monster disappears into history.

This is the guts of the gothic-horror, science-fiction story *Frankenstein*, published in 1818. Written by Mary Shelley in response to a bet over who could write the best ghost story, *Frankenstein* has endured through the years, often the subject of much critical and popular review.

Some have seen in Shelley's story a critique of the French Revolution (still rocking Europe when she wrote it); others saw *Frankenstein* as an attack on slavery. Some as a warning about the dangers of technology. Others derived from it a commentary on the meaning of human life (Who are we? Where did we come from? Why are we here?).

And it's been the subject of feminist critiques as well, sparking such essays as "Mary Shelley, *Frankenstein*, and the Spectacle of Masculinity,"[10] "Here Comes the Bride: Wedding Gender and Race in *Bride of Frankenstein*,"[11] and " 'An Issue of Monstrous Desire': *Frankenstein* and Obstetrics."[12]

The story has been big in cinematic culture, inspiring such classics as *Abbott and Costello Meet Frankenstein* (1948) and *Frankenstein and the Monster From Hell* (1974). Why, a Frankenstein derivative even made an appearance in a 2003 episode of *The Simpsons*.

What does Mary Shelley's *Frankenstein* have to do with the resurrection of Jesus? A lot—at least if, as some critics have claimed, the resurrection of Jesus no more happened than did the young Victor Frankenstein create his monster.

The idea that the New Testament writers promoted as true what they knew was false—Christ's resurrection—has been called the conspiracy theory or the fraud theory. That is, though Jesus had never been raised from the dead, the Bible writers who wrote about it pushed, hard, the story that He had.

After all, look at what the disciples had invested in Jesus. Here they were when, suddenly, Jesus of Nazareth appeared, and nothing for them was the same. They became devoted followers, forsaking everything for Him. "And Jesus, walking by the Sea of Galilee, saw two brothers, Simon called Peter, and Andrew his brother, casting a net into the sea; for they were fishermen. Then He said to them, 'Follow Me, and I will make you fishers of men.' They immediately left their nets and followed Him" (Matthew 4:18, 19).

And what did Jesus say about the cost of following Him? "If anyone comes to Me and does not hate his father and mother, wife and children, brothers and sisters, yes, and his own life also, he cannot be My disciple" (Luke 14:26). "If anyone desires to come after Me, let him deny himself, and take up his cross daily, and follow Me" (Luke 9:23).

If that's not total commitment, what is?

When many of Christ's disciples pulled away, Jesus asked His inner twelve if they would too. "But Simon Peter answered Him, 'Lord, to whom shall we go? You have the words of eternal life. Also we have come to believe and know that You are the Christ, the Son of the living God' " (John 6:68).

To whom shall we go other than You? And then to confess that He was the Christ, the Son of the Living God? These words reflect a powerful commitment to Jesus.

And some had big plans built upon that commitment.

Then James and John, the sons of Zebedee, came to Him, saying, "Teacher, we want You to do for us whatever we ask."

And He said to them, "What do you want Me to do for you?"

They said to Him, "Grant us that we may sit, one on Your right hand and the other on Your left, in Your glory" (Mark 10:35–37).

Their mother, too, had the same dream for them:

Then the mother of Zebedee's sons came to Him with her sons, kneeling down and asking something from Him.

And He said to her, "What do you wish?"

She said to Him, "Grant that these two sons of mine may sit, one on Your right hand and the other on the left, in Your kingdom" (Matthew 20:20, 21).

To sit next to Jesus, one on the right and the other on the left, in His glory?

These boys wanted to be (to use modern parlance) masters of the universe!

Meanwhile, the two disciples on the road to Emmaus expressed their hope that Jesus was going "to redeem Israel" (Luke 24:21). Exactly what they expected to happen when Jesus did "redeem Israel" they didn't say, but many Jews at that time believed that the Messiah would overthrow the Romans and rule the world from Jerusalem. With crowds certain that Jesus was the Messiah, which is why they shouted, "The King of Israel!" (John 12:13) when He rode into Jerusalem, we can be sure that whatever the two men on the road to Emmaus expected "the King of Israel" to do, it wasn't to be arrested, tried as a criminal, and crucified.

With all of their hopes, plans, and ambitions nailed to the cross, these men, rather than give it all up, made it all up. Because His followers expected Jesus to be crowned, not crucified, to be hailed as the King, not vilified as a criminal, they concocted the Resurrection story.

The entire Christian faith, then, from Eastern Orthodox, Roman Catholic, and Protestant—the foundation of much of Western history in the past two thousand years—was built upon an ad hoc fabrication concocted by a handful of disgruntled disciples of a failed itinerant rabbi in Roman-occupied Judea?

That's the theory anyway.

The conspiracy theory notion has the longest history of the numerous debunk-the-bodily-resurrection-of-Jesus schemes that have surfaced over almost two millennia. And the first of these conspiracy theories dates not only to before the first written account of the Resurrection but also before any of His followers had even seen the risen Christ. In fact, it started even before they believed in His resurrection.

It started the Sunday morning of the Resurrection. No sooner was Jesus out of the tomb than the lies about it began.

> Now while they were going, behold, some of the guard came into the city and reported to the chief priests all the things that had happened. When they had assembled with the elders and consulted together, they gave a large sum of money to the soldiers, saying, "Tell them, 'His disciples came at night and stole Him away while we slept.' And if this comes to the governor's ears, we will appease him and make you secure." So they took the money and did as they were instructed; and this saying is commonly reported among the Jews until this day (Matthew 28:11–15).

The guard told them "all the things that had happened" (verse 11). What had happened? An earthquake, the angel from heaven who moved the stone from the tomb and then sat on it (verse 2).

That's it?

Obviously not, because after first telling the chief priests what happened, the chief priests "had assembled with the elders and consulted together" (verse 12), implying that whatever the guards had reported was disturbing enough to the chief priests that they got more counsel. Or maybe they just wanted to drag more people into their deception?

Whatever the reason for pulling the elders in, together, they decided to bribe the guards with a "large sum of money" in order to get them to say that the disciples "stole Him away while we slept" (verses 12, 13). (Maybe they needed the elders to get the requisite money?) Hence, the first reaction of the first ones to hear about the resurrection of Jesus is to get the first people to see the resurrection of Jesus to lie about it.

Unlike Christ's followers, who, when told by the faithful women, *didn't* believe the first reports of His resurrection, these religious leaders, when told by enemies of Jesus, *did* believe. This is why, though first posting the guard in order to stop the disciples from stealing Jesus' corpse, in an amazing reversal, they now paid the guard to say that the disciples *did* steal it. Wanting to make sure that Christ stayed in the tomb, these leaders now had to concoct a story to explain why Christ didn't stay in the tomb—a story that at every level strains credulity and common sense.

For starters, if sleeping, how would the guards have known that the disciples stole the body? How deeply had they (all?) nodded off, which enabled the disciples to sneak up, break the seal, move the large stone, snatch Christ's "embalmed" corpse from the tomb, and then leave—without a guard waking?

Meanwhile, the only way that the sleeping guards could have known (and found out so quickly) what had happened to Christ's body would have been had someone told them. Who? The disciples? Not likely. And because it was supposed to be a hoax, a conspiracy, the disciples wouldn't have been bantering about their body-snatching escapade, would they?

Also, why would the disciples have tried something so reckless and risky? They could have been struck dead, right there, if caught. *To slip past the guards, break a seal, move a rock, and rob a grave—all while the guard had been posted there precisely to stop them from slipping past them, breaking the seal, moving the rock, and robbing the grave?*

It was a ploy destined to fail.

How would the disciples have known that all the guards were sleeping? Standing with one's eyes closed, or even sitting with closed eyes, doesn't necessarily mean that someone is snoozing. Were the guards all stretched out on the ground, snoring away? All it would have taken would be one awake guard or one guard to awaken, and it would have been curtains. The audacity of the attempt makes the idea of it preposterous.

Then, assuming that the disciples did steal the body before the entire sleeping guard, why didn't the guards immediately try to get the body back, especially because their lives were in danger for having slacked off during guard duty? Grave robbing was a crime. How easily the Roman leaders, with the backing of the high priests, could have ordered the soldiers: "Find those grave robbers, and get the body back!" That would have been the most logical response to the story that they were promoting. Yet that's not what happened. Nothing was recorded about the guards, at the urging of the Jewish leaders and Pilate, trying to retrieve the body of Jesus, which makes sense only if the story was fake to begin with.

Also, if the guard had said that the disciples had stolen the body, then why hadn't they simply arrested the culprits? Why did the Romans and the Jewish leaders not pursue them? Instead, the powers-that-be just let them go. Grave robbing was bad enough. But when the leaders had more reasons to arrest the tomb raiders, *they did nothing*? The inaction of the religious leaders and the Romans would make sense only if they all knew all along that the story was a lie.

Finally, wouldn't the people have wondered why the chief priests and elders didn't complain to Pilate about such a blatant dereliction of duty? When Paul and others were in a Roman prison, their jailer, afraid that they had escaped, was ready to kill himself. "And the keeper of the prison, awaking from sleep and seeing the prison doors open, supposing the prisoners had fled, drew his sword and was about to kill himself" (Acts 16:27). Why? Most likely, that would have been an easier way to die than being publicly executed for messing up on the job. Thus, if the disciples stole the body, people surely would have wondered why the guards never got in trouble for letting the body be pilfered.

The first conspiracy theory unravels right after it starts, even if the unraveling has only just begun.

The first and earliest confrontation (at least depicted in Scripture) between the religious leaders and the disciples after the resurrection of Jesus occurred in Acts 3, which unfolded after Peter had, in the name of Jesus, healed a beggar lame from birth:

> And a certain man lame from his mother's womb was carried, whom they laid daily at the gate of the temple which is called Beautiful, to ask alms from those who entered the temple; who, seeing Peter and John about to go into the temple, asked for alms. And fixing his eyes on him, with John, Peter said, "Look at us." So he gave them his attention, expecting to receive something from them. Then Peter said, "Silver and gold I do not have, but what I do have I give you: In the name of Jesus Christ of Nazareth, rise up and walk." And he took him by the right hand and lifted him up, and immediately his feet and ankle bones received strength. So he, leaping up, stood and walked and entered the temple with them—walking, leaping, and praising God. And all the people saw him walking and praising God (Acts 3:2–9).

The leaders, when confronting the disciples, wanted to know, "By what power or by what name have you done this?" (Acts 4:7). The disciples answered, "By the name of Jesus Christ of Nazareth, whom you crucified, whom God raised from the dead, by Him this man stands here before you whole" (verse 10).

How did the leaders respond?

Jesus of Nazareth? Yeah, right. The Man whom the Romans crucified but whose body you stole from the grave and have gone around telling everyone that He was resurrected? This Jesus? In His name, this man was healed? Whom are you trying to kid?

That, of course, was not their response.

Why not? After all, this notion had been their immediate argument a few months earlier when they needed to explain the empty tomb. But now, in front of the disciples, they weren't going to try that lie because the disciples knew better.

But even if other people were listening, why didn't the religious leaders just continue the lie for their sake? Perhaps, it was because, in Jerusalem, where the resurrected Jesus had appeared to many people, they knew that this lie wasn't going to fly, as it would over the later years and when all the eyewitnesses would scatter and die. That is, maybe too many people in that region had seen the risen Christ, and they weren't going to make it easy for the leaders, at least this early on, to promulgate the story of the disciples stealing Christ's corpse.

Also, even the religious leaders acknowledged the miraculous healing. "For, indeed, that a notable miracle has been done through them is evident to all who dwell in Jerusalem, and we cannot deny it" (verse 16). Thus, how silly it would have been to have pushed the lie, then and there, before the crowd.

Well, yes, we acknowledge the miracle done in the name of the dead Jesus. But that still doesn't change the fact you disciples stole His corpse from the tomb as part of an elaborate hoax to get people to believe that He is the Messiah, or something like that.

Because of the presence of the crowd, the leaders, who had seen the miraculous healing done in the name of Jesus, whose corpse supposedly had been pilfered by the disciples and then secretly disposed of (it would have long been rotted), had to let the disciples go (verse 23).

This makes no sense in the context of the fraud theory but a lot of sense if, yes, Christ had been raised from the dead.

Another problem exists with this, the world's first fraud theory regarding Jesus' resurrection. On the Sabbath after Jesus had died, the chief priests and the Pharisees had asked Pilate to seal the tomb because Jesus had said, "After three days I will rise" (Matthew 27:63). They, therefore, wanted the tomb sealed so that the disciples wouldn't steal the body and declare: "He has risen from the dead" (verse 64).

One slight chronological difficulty: the disciples on that same Sabbath morning had not expected Jesus to be resurrected. Far from anticipating His resurrection, Christ's disciples *the next evening* were still mourning: "Then, the same day at evening, being the first day of the week, when the doors were shut where the disciples were assembled, for fear of the Jews" (John 20:19).

On Sunday evening, they were shut away and fearful, which hardly sounded as if these men were in expectation of Christ's glorious resurrection.

When Jesus met the two men on the road to Emmaus, their words showed that, even when they had heard what the women told them the angel had said and even when they had heard that Christ's tomb was empty, they were stymied. Jesus being resurrected didn't even come up until He later explained it to them, proof that they were not anticipating it.

Even when the women told the disciples about the empty tomb and what the angels had said, what was their response? *Hallelujah! Just as Jesus had said to us. He is resurrected! Our Lord is risen!* Not quite. "And their words seemed to them like idle tales, and they did not believe them" (Luke 24:11). "And when they heard that He was alive and had been seen by her, they did not believe" (Mark 16:11).

When Mary told Peter and John that someone had taken the body, they ran to the tomb to see for themselves. At this point, Peter "saw the linen cloths lying by themselves; and he departed, marveling to himself at what had happened" (Luke 24:12). Even with the empty tomb, Peter hadn't yet connected it to Christ's resurrection.

In contrast, after entering the tomb and seeing the grave cloths neatly folded, John believed that He had been resurrected. "Then the other disciple, who came to the tomb first, went in also; and he saw and believed" (John 20:8), though John, at that point, didn't believe because of what was written in the Scriptures (verse 9).

Even before the disciples had believed in the resurrection of Jesus, the enemies of Jesus were promoting the notion that the disciples were trying to fake that resurrection. Yet even after seeing the empty tomb or hearing the words of the women, or both, none of the disciples (with the apparent exception of John) thought that He had been resurrected. Only after Jesus had appeared to them in the flesh did they, finally, believe.

Thus, the chief priests had concocted the fake-the-Resurrection narrative even before the followers of Christ believed in the Resurrection. For these reasons, the lie of the chief priests and elders, who concocted the world's first fraud theory regarding Christ's resurrection, falls dead almost as soon as it left their lips. And this fall leads to another problem with all the fraud theories, from this first one to all the rest that have followed.

After the death of Lazarus, when Jesus told Martha, Lazarus's sister, that her brother would rise again, she replied, "I know that he will rise again in the resurrection at the last day" (John 11:24). What's fascinating isn't her belief in an end-time resurrection but the certainty with which she said it: *I know* that he will rise again.

Her words also express the Jewish belief at that time of the resurrection of the dead en masse "at the last day," which dovetails nicely with much Christian theology regarding the resurrection of the dead en masse "at the last day" as well.*

Not all Jews, however, believed. The New Testament referred to the contrast between the Pharisees, who believed in the resurrection of the dead, and the Sadducees, who didn't. "For Sadducees say that there is no resurrection—and no angel or spirit; but the Pharisees confess both" (Acts 23:8; see also verse 6; Matthew 22:23).

Disagreeing over theology? Jews? (Say it ain't so!)

Exactly what the Jews believed regarding the resurrection of the dead hasn't been easy to pin down because, much like today, the Jews back then had many different beliefs, not only on what happened immediately to the dead but on their ultimate fate. Though later Jewish theology, at least among the more religious Jews, accepted the resurrection of the dead, even regarded it as foundational to their faith,[13] scholars and students would often retrodict these current views onto earlier times, when this teaching might not have been so explicitly believed and promoted.

The Old Testament itself doesn't have a lot to say about the resurrection of the dead, though what it says seems explicit.

"And many of those who sleep in the dust of the earth shall awake, some to everlasting life, and some to shame and everlasting contempt" (Daniel 12:2).

Your dead shall live;
Together with my dead body they shall arise.
Awake and sing, you who dwell in dust;
For your dew is like the dew of herbs,
And the earth shall cast out the dead (Isaiah 26:19).

Over the centuries, these few texts, along with many noncanonical sources, influenced Jewish thinking regarding the dead. Their views included everything from the immortality of the soul, reincarnation, belief in a physical, bodily resurrection, to denial of any afterlife—all reflective (somewhat) of the diversity of Jewish belief today on death and the afterlife. N. T. Wright observes,

* Many Christians see their great hope, not in some ascent of the soul to heaven at death, which is not a New Testament teaching, but in the resurrection of the dead at the end of time.

Jews, it used to be said, believed in resurrection, while Greeks believed in immortality. Like most half-truths, this one is as misleading as it is informative, if not more so. . . . The second-Temple period provides something more like an artist's palette: dozens of options, with different ways of describing similar positions and similar ways of describing different ones. The more texts and tombstones we study, the more there seem to be. Almost any position one can imagine on the subject appears to have been espoused by some Jews somewhere in the period between the Maccabean crisis and the writing of the Mishnah, roughly 200 BC to AD 200.[14]

Even through the thick fog of centuries, one point is certain: whatever the Jews at the time of Jesus believed about the Messiah and about resurrection, it wasn't that the Messiah was going to be killed and then resurrected. That idea seemed to have been so alien to their minds that, even though Jesus had told His disciples that it would happen, they didn't expect it, and when He first appeared to them, they *still* had trouble believing it.

On the contrary, some Jews (at least now) believe that the Messiah will resurrect the dead, not Himself be resurrected from it.*

---

* With the exception, as we have seen, of some devotees of Menachem Schneerson and of Messianic Jews—that is, Jews who believe in Jesus and who believe not only that the Messiah was resurrected from death but that He will resurrect the dead as well.

One has to be careful about projecting present Jewish belief about the Messiah and what Jews often now call the "Messianic Age" onto the past, especially two thousand years past. Yet parallels exist, including the idea of a Messianic king who ushers in a Messianic era.

At the birth announcement of Jesus, what did the angel Gabriel say to Mary? "And behold, you will conceive in your womb and bring forth a Son, and shall call His name Jesus. He will be great, and will be called the Son of the Highest; and the Lord God will give Him the throne of His father David. And He will reign over the house of Jacob forever, and of His kingdom there will be no end" (Luke 1:31–33).

Though Gabriel obviously was looking long term, as were many Old Testament Messianic texts (see below), these words do reflect the Jewish expectation that the Messiah would usher in a political kingdom.

After Jesus performed some astonishing miracles, such as feeding about five thousand people with five loaves of bread and two fish, the people wanted to "take Him by force to make Him king" (John 6:15). The implication of the words *by force* is that Jesus wasn't cooperating with their plans, which surely included Messianic ideas of a king who would make Israel a great power.

It's not hard to imagine their thinking: *If Jesus can do these miracles, what can't He do? Can He be the One to make Judea an earthly paradise again, breaking the power of the hated Romans and deliver Judah and Jerusalem from our enemies? Surely, after all that He has done with healing the sick, He could heal soldiers wounded in battle. And after this miracle of the food, He could supply whole armies. Yes, with His power, He can conquer the nations and give Israel its long-sought dominion. Indeed, the Lord will, as the angel told Mary, "give Him the throne of His father David."*

When Jesus entered Jerusalem, the crowd worshiped Him, proclaiming, "Hosanna! Blessed is He who comes in the name of the Lord! The King of Israel!" (John 12:13).

The King of Israel? That's whom they were expecting, and it was a king whom they wanted, a King who "will reign over the house of Jacob forever, and of His kingdom there will be no end." And John then quoted a Messianic text:

"Fear not, daughter of Zion;
Behold, your King is coming,
Sitting on a donkey's colt" (verse 15).

Behold, your King is coming!
Clearly, the people's understanding of the Messiah included Him reigning as a king (which, ultimately, He will do but just not at that coming).

The mother of James and John wanted her boys to sit "one on Your right hand and the other on the left, in Your kingdom" (Matthew 20:20, 21). *Kingdom;* that is, Jesus would be King on His throne in His earthly kingdom, and they would rule with Him.

Even after Jesus had been resurrected and lived among them for forty days, what did His disciples ask just before His ascension? "Therefore, when they had come together, they asked Him, saying, 'Lord, will You at this time restore the kingdom to Israel?' " (Acts 1:6). So strongly did the Jews, His own disciples even, hold this view that they were still expecting it to happen—and "at this time" too.

Why?

Though differences abound among Jews today anticipating the Messiah, or *Moshiach*, who will usher in the Messianic age, many believe that He will, as the Jews in Christ's day believed, reign as King. And during His reign, various things are supposed to unfold, at least according to their interpretation of Scripture. Here are some of the biblical texts that they use to promote that belief.

First, He will build the third temple; obviously, a notion that came *after* the destruction of the second in AD 70: "Moreover I will make a covenant of peace with them, and it shall be an everlasting covenant with them; I will establish them and multiply them, and I will set My sanctuary in their midst forevermore. My tabernacle also shall be with them; indeed I will be their God, and they shall be My people. The nations also will know that I, the LORD, sanctify Israel, when My sanctuary is in their midst forevermore" (Ezekiel 37:26–28).

They believe, too, that the Messiah will gather all the Jews back to the land of Israel:

"Fear not, for I am with you;
I will bring your descendants from the east,
And gather you from the west;
I will say to the north, 'Give them up!'
And to the south, 'Do not keep them back!'
Bring My sons from afar,
And My daughters from the ends of the earth" (Isaiah 43:5, 6).

The Messiah will usher in a period of global peace and harmony:

They shall beat their swords into plowshares,
And their spears into pruning hooks;
Nation shall not lift up sword against nation,
Neither shall they learn war anymore (Isaiah 2:4).

"The wolf also shall dwell with the lamb,
The leopard shall lie down with the young goat,
The calf and the young lion and the fatling together;
And a little child shall lead them.
The cow and the bear shall graze;
Their young ones shall lie down together;
And the lion shall eat straw like the ox.
The nursing child shall play by the cobra's hole,
And the weaned child shall put his hand in the viper's den.
They shall not hurt nor destroy in all My holy mountain,
For the earth shall be full of the knowledge of the LORD

As the waters cover the sea" (Isaiah 11:6–9).

Finally, *Moshiach* will spread universal knowledge of the God of Israel, which will unite humanity as one:

And the LORD shall be King over all the earth.
In that day it shall be—
"The LORD is one,"
And His name one (Zechariah 14:9).

Without closely analyzing these texts or what they are talking about specifically, many Christians recognize the Second Coming in some of them. Though the Old Testament points to Christ's first coming, it also points to His second, and it wasn't always easy—at least before the establishment of the Christian church and the writing of the New Testament—to distinguish between which advent of Christ the prophets or Moses or David was referring to.

This helps to explain why many were confused about the role of the Messiah when Jesus came. Throughout Christ's ministry, the Jews, even His followers, had conflated first and second coming ideas about the Messiah, which is why they were looking for a Messianic King who would subdue all of their enemies and establish an eternal kingdom—a Second Coming teaching such as found in the book of Daniel:

"Then the kingdom and dominion,
And the greatness of the kingdoms under the whole heaven,
Shall be given to the people, the saints of the Most High.
His kingdom is an everlasting kingdom,
And all dominions shall serve and obey Him" (Daniel 7:27).

There's another teaching, too, that some Jews associate with the Messiah and the Messianic age: the resurrection of the dead.

For many Jews today, even religious Jews expecting the Messiah and the Messianic era, the resurrection of the dead is a bit much. However utopian their Messianic hopes, those hopes don't go that far. (Ultimately, though, how utopian can their hopes then be?)

Others do cling to the promised resurrection, such as the Lubavitch. Based on sources other than the few biblical resurrection texts, their resurrection eschatology goes something like this:

The Messiah comes and rebuilds the temple in Jerusalem, and the exiles return to the land of Israel. Then, about forty years later, the dead will be resurrected, though the *tzaddikim* (righteous men and women through the ages) will be resurrected immediately when the Messiah returns.

"First the dead who are buried in Israel will rise from their graves, they will be followed by the dead of the Diaspora, followed by the generation that left Egypt and died in the desert. Last of all will rise the Patriarchs and Matriarchs. Their resurrection is postponed so that they should have the *nachas** of waking to find all their children alive, well, and happy."[15]

Things, then, get stranger.

"All the dead will be resurrected in the land of Israel. Those who are buried outside the Holy Land, their bodies will burrow through the earth until they reach Israel, and there their souls will be reinstated into their bodies. For *tzaddikim*, special tunnels will form beneath the ground, in order to make the journey easier and more dignified. Avoiding this laborious process is one of the reasons why so many choose to be buried in the soil of the Holy Land."[16]

Modern historian Simon Sebag Montefiore wrote that "Jews who lived far away wanted to be buried close to the Temple so that they would be the first to rise again on Judgement Day. Thus began the Jewish cemetery on the Mount of Olives."[17]

Many of these traditions were established long after the second temple period. That's why they shouldn't be projected back to the time of Jesus, as if the Jews then believed this, even if they assumed some linkage between the Messiah and the resurrection.

However, and this is important, nothing in the life, death, and resurrection of Jesus Christ was what the Jews believed about the Messiah, especially if some were expecting the Messiah to raise the dead and not be resurrected from it Himself.

* Yiddish for pride in their children.

B ecause the Jews were not expecting a resurrected Messiah, that leads to another problem with any fraud theory.

If attempting to deceive the Jews, why would Christ's disciples come up with a story of the Messiah being resurrected if no Jews (themselves included) expected the Messiah to be resurrected? After their hopes of a Messianic kingdom failed, they conjured up an idea alien to everyone's thinking and did so in hopes that they could keep their movement alive? If they were so determined to lie, why not make the lie about something that the masses were expecting or (at least) somewhat anticipating?

But the idea of the disciples announcing, in an attempt to deceive, a resurrected Messiah made about as much sense back then as the notion of a company today announcing, in an attempt to dupe customers, that its new smartphone, instead of being cheaper, faster, and smaller (as would be expected), will, rather, make chocolate-chip pancakes, and then expecting the masses to line up and buy it.

And how was the disciples' ploy supposed to work again?

Jesus was killed, and His corpse was put in the tomb. His followers, on the first Sunday after His Friday death, immediately concoct an elaborate plan to fake His resurrection. That is, amid the shock of His death, while still mourning that death, and despite their fear for their own safety (after all, they were His closest followers), they quickly devise this new story about a resurrected Jesus—a story that nobody had anticipated?

And to pull it off, they would have to, despite all odds, slip past the Romans and steal the corpse. Then after managing that slick feat, they must dispose of the body, hiding it so well that no one would find it. Then they go around telling everyone that Jesus had been raised from the dead, which, they now claim, was what the Messiah was supposed to have done all along, even though there's no resurrected Jesus around to verify this new and astonishing claim, which, until then, no one had ever heard of or anticipated.

And people were supposed to believe it? Wouldn't the logical questions that they would have asked be things such as, *The tomb is empty, yes, but an empty tomb doesn't prove He was resurrected, especially because our leaders are saying that you guys stole His body, right?*

Wouldn't it be nice if we, who are supposed to believe in Him being so newly resurrected, could actually see Him resurrected?

What is the most logical explanation for the vacated tomb, then? You stole His corpse, or He was resurrected from the dead?

And now you guys come up with stuff about a dead and resurrected Messiah, which we have never heard before and is not what our religion, as we have traditionally understood it, teaches. Why should we believe you?

The idea that an empty tomb alone would prove His resurrection would have been such a foolish and incredulously stupid move that it's hard to imagine how the disciples would have thought anyone would have believed it. And yet a powerful movement in Jerusalem was started, even built, on this foolish deception?

"Then the word of God spread, and the number of the disciples multiplied greatly in Jerusalem, and a great many of the priests were obedient to the faith" (Acts 6:7).

Priests even? A "great many" too? Why would they believe? Because of an empty tomb and a handful of people making a preposterous claim that they can't back with anything more than, *Well, just trust us, He did rise from the dead,* or the like?

All of these people believing an outlandish lie founded on an empty tomb, which, in and of itself, could mean nothing other than, as the leaders said, the disciples stole away His body? That, and the word of some disgruntled, disappointed disciples who can't produce the Jesus whom they claim was just resurrected?

This was the foundation of Christianity?

On the other hand, according to the New Testament, the resurrected Christ had been seen by hundreds, perhaps more, which explains how the Jesus movement could have spread so quickly. And that's because it wasn't resting on a far-fetched lie whose only evidence was an empty tomb and the false testimony of a handful of followers who claimed that He had risen from the dead and who appeared just to them but to no one else.

Instead, according to the New Testament, the resurrected Jesus was there, among them for weeks, preaching and teaching as He had done before—His physical presence surely all the proof that they needed of His resurrection. Said Scripture about Jesus at this time: "He presented himself alive to them after his suffering by many proofs, appearing to them during forty days and speaking about the kingdom of God" (Acts 1:3, ESV).

The word translated "proofs" has also been translated as "infallible proofs" (verse 3, KJV), which comes from the Greek word *tekmeriois*, which is defined as "that which causes someth[ing] to be known in a convincing and decisive manner, proof."[18] Exactly what these *tekmeriois* were, the text doesn't say. But it's not hard to imagine that the mere presence of the resurrected Jesus, among them for almost six weeks, was pretty powerful *tekmeriois*. Whatever else these proofs consisted of, they were enough to turn the frightened, weeping, mourning disciples into bold witnesses for Christ and His resurrection.

Within weeks of Christ's death, Peter stood before a crowd at Pentecost and loudly proclaimed not only Christ crucified but Christ resurrected.

> "Men and brethren, let me speak freely to you of the patriarch David, that he is both dead and buried, and his tomb is with us to this day. Therefore, being a prophet, and knowing that God had sworn with an oath to him that of the fruit of his body, according to the flesh, He would raise up the Christ to sit on his throne, he, foreseeing this, spoke concerning the resurrection of the Christ, that His soul was not left in Hades, nor did His flesh see corruption. This Jesus God has raised up, of which we are all witnesses" (Acts 2:29–32).

Peter could have been lying, yes, even though he said to the crowd that "we are all witnesses" to it—that is, we all were witnesses of the Resurrection. He specifically emphasizes that they *all* saw it.

Who were all of these witnesses who saw it? Only the original eleven as well as Matthias, the new one who replaced Judas, and was "numbered with the eleven apostles" (Acts 1:26)? Or was Peter referring also to the "hundred and twenty" (Acts 1:15) disciples now among them? Or also to any one of the hundreds of others who had seen Christ alive?

Peter said this, about those who had seen the risen Christ, at Pentecost, when hordes of Jews were in Jerusalem, which most likely included some who had seen the resurrected Christ. Peter was basically saying to the crowd: *Don't just take my word for it. We have these other witnesses as well. Ask them.*

And what was the reaction?

"Now when they heard this, they were cut to the heart, and said to Peter and the rest of the apostles, 'Men and brethren, what shall we do?' " (Acts 2:37). Many were powerfully convicted of what Peter said, cut to the heart even.

What convinced them? Peter's preaching alone? The empty tomb alone, which anyone in the crowd could have seen but by itself meant little? Or did they have the testimony of all of these other witnesses? That is, among them at Pentecost were those who had seen the resurrected Jesus and perhaps had already been telling others about it. And then Peter stood before them and, with power from on high, started explaining what it all meant.

Otherwise, Peter's lie and the lies of the other disciples were so convincing that all of these Jews started to believe, despite no physical evidence other than an empty tomb? That was supposed to prove the Messiah was resurrected from the dead? Were all of these witnesses, then, part of this elaborate plot to dupe the masses, and it worked so well that, early on, thousands of Jews in Jerusalem started believing something that their religion, at least as they then understood it, never taught—that is, a crucified and then risen Messiah?

One undisputed historical fact remains: the movement that became the Christian church took off quickly from Jerusalem, where the death and alleged resurrection of Christ happened and where, perhaps more than any other place, it could have been most easily refuted, such as if one of the disciples changed his mind, admitted the lie, and even led people to the body of Jesus.

But that never happened, did it?

What accounts, then, for the remarkably swift growth of the early church, which started among so many Jews who believed in Jesus? A lie, so flimsy and silly, it's hard to believe that anyone, much less thousands, including the educated priestly class in Jerusalem (Acts 6:7), would have believed it? Yet they did anyway despite the objections of the leadership, who, having opposed Jesus, even violently, most likely didn't feel as though they could change their minds now. (In actuality, they could have and would have been forgiven as well. That's the power of the gospel.)

Instead, the message took hold in Jerusalem so quickly because these early believers were confronted with powerful evidence of the Resurrection, not just the empty tomb but the eyewitness testimony of those who had seen, touched, talked to, and eaten with the risen Christ. And thus, they not only believed in Him but, as the New Testament explains, also became evangelists, teachers, and promoters of the gospel, with the crowd at Pentecost some of the first to believe based on their testimony—a testimony that soon spread all through the ancient world.

These arguments make sense but only on a presupposition, unproven too. (Though isn't the point of a presupposition not to be proven? If proven, it wouldn't be a presupposition.) And that presupposition is that what's written in the Gospels, Acts, Paul's letters, and Peter's epistles about the resurrection is true.

But the argument of the fraud theory or the conspiracy theory is that what's written in the Gospels, Acts, Paul's letters, and Peter's epistles about the resurrection is *not* true: it's a fraud—it's a conspiracy. In other words, to assume the validity of these texts in order to disprove the fraud theory is to assume what you set out to prove. If you assume the texts to be true and use that assumption to reject the fraud theory, you have assumed the truth of what is being challenged to begin with: the veracity of the claims of Matthew, Mark, Luke, John, Paul, and Peter about Christ's resurrection.*

That's a fair criticism; one that can't be utterly and absolutely refuted, as with most challenges to ancient history. Events that far back in antiquity don't lend themselves to the level of scrutiny that more recent ones do. If people today will challenge the reality of the Holocaust or the moon landings or the roundness of the earth, then one certainly could challenge New Testament accounts of Christ's resurrection almost two thousand years ago.

Nevertheless, the challenge itself faces numerous problems besides what we've looked at—one being motives.

Why did the early apostles make up this story, an outrageous lie, and then run with it? Either Jesus Christ was resurrected, or He wasn't. And if He wasn't, then the New Testament accounts of that resurrection are outright lies perpetrated by charlatans and hucksters.

But for what purpose?

Christ's immediate inner circle, the remaining eleven, yes, had high hopes for themselves when Jesus was to establish, they believed, His Messianic kingdom. But when it all collapsed, their hopes evaporated in the stench of Christ's rotting corpse. That's why they concocted this Resurrection story in order to keep their dying movement alive. (Obviously, it worked too—probably better than they could have ever imagined, with billions around the world claiming to be Christians.)

---

* Then, too, how do we know that Matthew, Mark, Luke, John, Paul, and Peter were the authors of these texts anyway? Though much scholarly work has been done on this topic, on one level, it's not crucial. Critics, for instance, have challenged Homer's authorship of *The Iliad* and *The Odyssey*. One answer is that if these works were not written in the ninth (some say twelfth) century BC by the blind poet named Homer, then they were written in the ninth or twelfth century BC by another blind poet named Homer. Though not quite the same thing here with the New Testament accounts of the Resurrection, the point is that these books and letters in the New Testament were written by people who were promoting beliefs that, at that time, led to persecution and death. So even if one were to take seriously the challenge to the exact authorship, the question remains the same: What motives did these authors, whoever they were, have when such beliefs could lead to so much suffering and hardship for themselves and for many of those who accepted them?

But for any immediate purpose, their lie makes no sense. What did they gain? Everything we know about the apostles is that they suffered persecution, rejection, and eventually, jail and death for their faith. They were rejected not only by their own people, the Jews, but also by the Romans, the masters of the world at that time. The idea gets even more preposterous because, in the Gospels, they record Jesus, more than once, telling them that, by believing in and following Him, they were going to face hardship, rejection, and persecution.

Oh, yes, let's make up the story about Jesus, His life, death, miracles, and resurrection. And let's go with the lie, even though it will bring upon us, and those who believe our lie, prison, stoning, torture, exile, and death by the Romans. Sure, we know it's a fraud, but so what? We have everything to gain by promoting, fervently, even to the end our lives, the lie of the resurrected Christ.

What source tells of Peter getting rich and powerful for his belief in the Resurrection? What honors did the Jewish leadership bestow on John for his dedication to the risen Jesus? What high office did Thomas receive for belief in the Nazarene as the living Messiah? Whatever the veracity (or lack thereof) of extrabiblical traditions regarding the lives and deaths of these men, nothing indicates that they received anything other than hatred, violence, and rejection for their promotion of the resurrected Jesus.

The idea, then, that they made up Christ's resurrection for some kind of personal gain is a nonstarter.

Some have argued that they made it up, at first, just to save immediate face and then simply walked away from it over time.

Nice theory, except the Gospels were produced a few decades after the events that they depict. Without Facebook, Twitter, or Instagram, the original group could have quietly moved on, leaving the fiasco behind and starting life anew somewhere else. Instead, as far as we know, none ever changed their mind about the resurrected Jesus or announced the story as a fraud; instead, the men stuck with it until death. Indeed, it was their sticking to the story that, in many cases, led to their death.

Besides, the idea of saving face or of keeping the movement going, however unfeasible as motives for the original eleven, cannot begin to explain the intrusion of Saul of Tarsus into the equation. Something else (but what?) turned this enemy of the Jesus movement, despite the threat of persecution, even death, into its greatest evangelist.

C ome on!

Religious people facing persecution or death for their faith? Never happens, does it?

Religious history is blood soaked with the faithful willing to suffer and die for their beliefs. Catholics were tortured, jailed, and killed rather than renounce their belief in the pope and Roman Catholicism, while their Protestant neighbors, in much greater numbers, were tortured, jailed, and killed rather than profess belief in the pope and Roman Catholicism.

And those nineteen hijackers on 9/11 had to believe the promises of Paradise, didn't they? Otherwise, what? Willingly blow themselves up for a promise that they knew all along was a lie? And what about the Jews who chose to be drowned rather than be baptized into Roman Catholicism? Or the Falun Gong religion in China, where adherents have faced persecution rather than give up their beliefs?

One would be hard-pressed to find any enduring faith where people, at one time or another, weren't willing to suffer and die for it. Dying for a belief hardly makes that belief true because so many have died for a belief that contradicts the belief that many others have just as willingly died for. And not just religious belief either. How many Communists in the last century gave their lives for the promise of a Marxist utopia?

Which means, of course, that those willing to die for their belief in the resurrection of Jesus no more proves that resurrection true than the 9/11 hijackers' willingness to die for Islam proves it true.

Yet, with the resurrection of Christ, the parallel with these other beliefs falls apart because of the "Frankenstein factor."

The what?

Imagine that, after the publication of *Frankenstein*, Mary Shelley and her husband, Percy Bysshe Shelley, and some friends involved in the writing of the book began promoting *Frankenstein* as true. They insisted that, yes, a young Victor Frankenstein really did—in a well-meaning attempt to do good—create life from nonlife but ended up making a violent monster whom he hated. Suppose they not only insisted that the story were true but also attempted to find adherents and even start a new version of Christianity based on the *Frankenstein* story.

Then, suppose that the religious leaders of the time worked feverishly against the Shelleys and their friends, labeling them apostates and heretics, and then persecuted them. Suppose, too, the political authorities became concerned about the dangers of this Frankenstein movement and began a vicious attack on the Shelleys and their cohorts, threatening them with arrest, imprisonment, torture, and death.

And yet the Shelleys and their small group were willing to face jail, imprisonment, torture, and death for a story that they all knew, from the start, was a lie?

In the history of fiction, what author, even if basing his or her characters on real people and events, not only insisted that the characters and the story were true but also was ready to face violence and punishment rather than deny the truth of his or her story and the existence of the characters? Imagine Mark Twain facing the gallows for claiming that the *Adventures of Huckleberry Finn* were true. Or Leo Tolstoy standing before a firing squad rather than deny the veracity of *Anna Karenina*. Or Herman Melville ready to be jailed, insisting that *Moby Dick* were a true story.

Something similar challenges the conspiracy theory proponents. It's one thing to suffer and die for a false belief that you sincerely, even passionately, believe. History is filled with people like that. But to suffer and die for a lie that you know is a lie—a lie that you concocted yourself?

Even more problematic is that we would have to believe that these men not only were willing to suffer and die for what they knew was a lie but also were willing to let others, many others, suffer and die for what they knew was a lie. That is, the persecution of the church began while they were alive, which means that they themselves willfully watched others—perhaps family, friends, or whoever—face hatred, calumny, jail, torture, even death for a story that they, for whatever reason, had fabricated? If true, these men were not only liars but exceedingly evil as well.

To accept this theory, one has to believe "(1) that twelve poor fishermen were able to change the world through a plot laid so deep that no one has ever been able to discern where the cheat lay, (2) that these men gave up the pursuit of happiness and ventured into poverty, torments, and persecutions for nothing, (3) that depressed and fearful men would have suddenly grown so brave as to break into the tomb and steal the body, and (4) that these imposters would furnish the world with the greatest system of morality that ever was."[19]

And they did this all based on a lie that they had made up but adhered to at the cost of their lives?

Makes no sense.

What makes better sense is that the God who created the world and its natural laws, and who not only sustains these laws but, at times, transcends them, had transcended them on the Sunday morning after Christ's death and raised Him from the dead, and the New Testament is the official account of that resurrection.

lso, imagine seeking to start a movement—political, religious, social, or whatever. And you base that movement upon a miracle, such as what the disciples did with the resurrection of Christ, which, alone, transformed the tragedy of the cross into the triumph and victory of Christ over death and darkness.

That's the spin at least:

> "O Death, where is your sting?
> O Hades, where is your victory?"

The sting of death is sin, and the strength of sin is the law. But thanks be to God, who gives us the victory through our Lord Jesus Christ (1 Corinthians 15:55–57).

Now, because most of the people whom you want to convince of this seminal event, this miracle upon which your movement rests, weren't witnesses to it, you create a document or, in the case of the Resurrection, documents that tell about it.

However, suppose that you were basing your new movement upon a lie—a lie that you know is a lie; a lie that you want others to believe—in this case, a miracle that never happened. This is exactly what the fraud-theory people assert about the resurrection of Jesus.

So you create your documents, and in them, you make up eyewitnesses to the "miracle"—that is, people whom you claim saw the miracle. And whom do you make up as these eyewitnesses? Mafiosi? Politicians? Gang members? Child pornographers? Fraudsters and hucksters?

Why would you do that?

Instead, if making the whole thing up, wouldn't you make your first eyewitnesses the highly trusted, the highly regarded, and those whose word others would be likely to accept? Why not depict, as the first witnesses to the key event, not criminals and con men but those whose testimony would be deemed credible for people who weren't there and whose only knowledge of the event was the bogus account that you had written?

The point?

The Gospels—Matthew, Mark, Luke, and John—all have women as the first ones to see the empty tomb, the first ones to hear about the Resurrection, and the first ones to whom the resurrected Jesus appeared (again, not counting the Roman guards).

Sure, in our society today, that wouldn't be a big deal. Women, men—what difference would it make, at least in terms of credibility? But that's our society, a radically different universe and social reality from first-century Judea, where women were, generally, deemed such untrustworthy and capricious witnesses that their testimony was often not even allowed in court. Yet these were the first ones to see the empty tomb, hear from angels of Christ's resurrection, and see Him resurrected?

This fact makes little sense; that is, it makes little sense if the Gospels were concocted. If the writers wanted to be more relevant, more politically correct, and more culturally attuned to their times, they would have had Peter, John, Andrew, or even better, Nicodemus or Joseph of Arimathea, not a handful of women (including, perhaps, a former prostitute), be the first ones to see the empty tomb, hear about the resurrected Jesus, and be the ones to whom Jesus first appeared. Again, from our perspective today, it seems like no big deal, but in that society, in that culture, it was a big deal.

How big? Here's how Paul, years later, depicted the Resurrection appearances:

For I delivered to you first of all that which I also received: that Christ died for our sins according to the Scriptures, and that He was buried, and that He rose again the third day according to the Scriptures, and that He was seen by Cephas, then by the twelve. After that He was seen by over five hundred brethren at once, of whom the greater part remain to the present, but some have fallen asleep. After that He was seen by James, then by all the apostles. Then last of all He was seen by me also, as by one born out of due time (verses 3–8).

Without exception, in all four Gospels, women were the first ones to have encountered the risen Christ. And yet Paul, in recounting the Resurrection appearances, *never mentions the women*. Why? The obvious answer, however repugnant to our sensibilities, is that he knew that in this culture, the testimony of women wouldn't have mattered to his readers, so he just skipped it.

When the women first reported what they had seen and heard, what was the response of the men? "And their words seemed to them like idle tales, and they did not believe them" (Luke 24:11). "And when they heard that He was alive and had been seen by her, they did not believe" (Mark 16:11). In contrast, when the two men on the road to Emmaus told the disciples in Jerusalem what happened to them, what did they hear? "The Lord is risen indeed, and has appeared to Simon!" (Luke 24:34). Though the woman had already told them, they didn't believe; when Simon (Peter) told them, they believed.

The scholar William Lane Craig wrote:

Their low rung on the Jewish social ladder is more than evident in such texts as these: "Sooner let the words of the law be burnt than delivered to women." "Happy is he whose children are male, and alas for him whose children are female." When one considers these facts, it becomes very remarkable that women should be named as the witnesses to the important events of Jesus' death, burial, and empty tomb. If one were going to invent witnesses to these events, then why not use the male disciples? The testimony of women was not only worthless, but actually embarrassing.[20]

Why, then, would the Gospel writers have depicted women in such a prominent early role? Because, far from making up the story, they were simply recounting what had happened, however politically incorrect it might have been at that time.

When in control of the narrative, the story, people tend to make their leaders into, if not gods, then the closest thing to them—especially when they have a goal in mind.

Such was the cult of personality that surrounded Joseph Stalin when he ruled the Soviet Union (1922–1953). Stalin was described as "Great," "Beloved," "Bold," "Wise," and "Genius." Stalin was called the "Father of Nations" as well as "Our Best Collective Farm Worker," "Our Darling, Our Guiding Star," and the "Gardener of Human Happiness." In 1935, the phrase "Thank You Dear Comrade Stalin for a Happy Childhood!" appeared above the entrances to nurseries, orphanages, and schools.

One song, called "Hymn to Stalin," went like this:

Thank you, Stalin. Thank you because I am joyful. Thank you because I am well. No matter how old I become, I shall never forget how we received Stalin two days ago. Centuries will pass, and the generations still to come will regard us as the happiest of mortals, as the most fortunate of men, because we lived in the century of centuries, because we were privileged to see Stalin, our inspired leader. . . . Everything belongs to thee, chief of our great country. And when the woman I love presents me with a child the first word it shall utter will be: Stalin.[21]

We get the point, which leads to another point about the fraud theory: the idea is that the Bible writers concocted the Resurrection story in an attempt to salvage their movement after the unexpected death of their Rabbi, Jesus, but with them now installed as the new leaders.

Fine. But why would they have depicted themselves and each other as such skeptical and disbelieving buffoons? The Gospel stories in general, and the death and resurrection accounts of Jesus in particular, don't portray the early followers of Jesus, the first leaders of "the Way" (Acts 9:2), in particularly glowing terms.

From Peter's denial of Jesus—three times (Matthew 26:69–75)—to the disciples fleeing when He was arrested (Matthew 25:56), these men are not presented as would be expected if they were creating a cult of personality around themselves as the Soviets did with "Our Best Collective Farm Worker," "Our Darling, Our Guiding Star," and the "Gardener of Human Happiness." In this case, they could have been called "Our Bumbling, Disbelieving Skeptics" or "The Unfaithful, Wavering Gang."

In all the Resurrection accounts, the original group was portrayed as fearful (John 20:19) and disbelieving (Luke 24:11). Mark has Jesus rebuking them for their unbelief: "Later He appeared to the eleven as they sat at the table; and He rebuked their unbelief and hardness of heart, because they did not believe those who had seen Him after He had risen" (Mark 16:14). Jesus, too, rebuked the two on the road to Emmaus: "O foolish ones, and slow of heart to believe in all that the prophets have spoken!" (Luke 24:25). And even when Jesus appeared to them in the flesh, how did they respond?

> But they were terrified and frightened, and supposed they had seen a spirit. And He said to them, "Why are you troubled? And why do doubts arise in your hearts? Behold My hands and My feet, that it is I Myself. Handle Me and see, for a spirit does not have flesh and bones as you see I have."
>
> When He had said this, He showed them His hands and His feet. But while they still did not believe for joy, and marveled, He said to them, "Have you any food here?" So they gave Him a piece of a broiled fish and some honeycomb. And He took it and ate in their presence (verses 37–43).

If this story were made up, why would they have written about themselves in such an unflattering light? Why not portray themselves as men full of faith, firm in truth, and bold with assurance. Why not write, *And when He appeared to them, they, Peter, John, Thomas, and the others, His faithful and loyal followers, immediately understood who He was, and they thus rejoiced in their resurrected Lord. For they saw, instantly, that, yes, all this was in fulfillment of prophecy, and Jesus was, indeed, the long-awaited Messiah,* or something, anything, to that effect? Instead, they are depicted—in some cases, depicted by themselves—as full of fear and doubt, hardly the way anyone making up a story would have depicted themselves, especially if the whole reason they were doing it was to start a new movement with themselves as the head.

Worth mentioning, too, is the idea that, as opposed to outright frauds, the Gospels were later legends that simply evolved over time. If legends, which tend to make their heroes into, well, legends or even heroes, why did these accounts portray their "heroes," which, in some cases, were the writers themselves, in such unflattering light? That's not the way legends and myths usually grow.

Meanwhile, who were the ones who attended to Jesus' corpse? Peter? John? Andrew? Instead, two Jewish leaders, from the body of men who had been their biggest opponents, are depicted as not only getting Jesus down from the cross but also preparing Him for burial and, thus, sparing the corpse from being thrown in some common grave with a bunch of other criminals. Instead, they put Him in a new tomb:

> After this, Joseph of Arimathea, being a disciple of Jesus, but secretly, for fear of the Jews, asked Pilate that he might take away the body of Jesus; and Pilate gave him permission. So he came and took the body of Jesus. And Nicodemus, who at first came to Jesus by night, also came, bringing a mixture of myrrh and aloes, about a hundred pounds. Then they took the body of Jesus, and bound it in strips of linen with the spices, as the custom of the Jews is to bury. Now in the place where He was crucified there was a garden, and in the garden a new tomb in which no one had yet been laid.

So there they laid Jesus, because of the Jews' Preparation Day, for the tomb was nearby (John 19:38–42).

If they had followed the model of Stalin, it would have been more likely to have read like this: *And our heroes of faith, Peter and John, full of hope and trust despite the great personal danger to themselves, dared to go right into the camp of their enemy, Pilate, and courageously and selflessly got permission to retrieve the body of their Lord, whom they gave a great burial.* That is, if they were making the whole thing up.

If not, and they were simply telling the truth, that truth included their doubts and fears, which is why the Gospels expose all the weakness and foibles of the men who would, despite those weaknesses and because of God's grace, become the earliest leaders of the Christian church.

A nd, finally, if the Resurrection story were fabricated by disgruntled followers of Christ who tried to salvage something from their few years with Jesus after He had the temerity to get Himself crucified, then why no systematic explanation, or any explanation at all, in the Gospels about what Christ's resurrection meant? This was the event upon which everything rested and the event which proved (they claimed) that Jesus was the promised Messiah and His death and resurrection were the fulfillment of Old Testament prophecies.

And yet nothing in the Gospels explains the theology of that resurrection?

Instead, we read in Paul's writings, not in the Gospels, the great truth about how Christ's resurrection is inseparably linked to ours. "But if there is no resurrection of the dead, then Christ is not risen. And if Christ is not risen, then our preaching is empty and your faith is also empty. Yes, and we are found false witnesses of God, because we have testified of God that He raised up Christ, whom He did not raise up—if in fact the dead do not rise" (1 Corinthians 15:13–15).

Why, in none of the Gospels—where the resurrection of the dead was often referred to, even by Jesus Himself (Matthew 22:30, 31; Mark 12:24–27; Luke 20:35, 36; John 5:29)— does anything link Christ's resurrection to the promised resurrection of the dead? Again, Matthew, Mark, Luke, and John were, supposedly, fabrications created in order to justify belief in Jesus, with His resurrection the key event that kept the movement together after His death. *And yet none explain the meaning of this central truth?*

As we have seen, some Jews at that time believed in the resurrection of the dead at the end of days. "I know," said Martha about her dead brother, "that he will rise again in the resurrection at the last day" (John 11:24). And, yes, John records Jesus' response: "I am the resurrection and the life. He who believes in Me, though he may die, he shall live" (verse 25). This sentence was, perhaps, the closest thing in the Gospels relating Christ's resurrection to ours. But even then, it was the perfect place for John, looking back, to have inserted this central theme into their hoax; however, nothing there links this hope to Christ's resurrection.

And though they recorded Jesus Himself, in other contexts, talking about the resurrection of the dead (Matthew 22:30, 31; Luke 14:14; 20:35, 36; John 5:25, 26), they never record Him talking about it in the context of His own death and resurrection, which is strange if they had made the whole thing up decades after the purported events. Again, these would have been perfect places to have enhanced their narratives with theological explanations of what Christ's resurrection was supposed to mean. Instead, there's powerful evidence that they were recording what Jesus had said, as opposed to making up stories to promote what they knew all along was a lie.

Why do we have to go to Peter's writings, not the Gospels, to read: "Blessed be the God and Father of our Lord Jesus Christ, who according to His abundant mercy has begotten us again to a living hope through the resurrection of Jesus Christ from the dead, to an inheritance incorruptible and undefiled and that does not fade away, reserved in heaven for you, who are kept by the power of God through faith for salvation ready to be revealed in the last time" (1 Peter 1:3–5)?

Where do we learn the central truth that "God demonstrates His own love toward us, in that while we were still sinners, Christ died for us. Much more then, having now been justified by His blood, we shall be saved from wrath through Him. For if when we were enemies we were reconciled to God through the death of His Son, much more, having been reconciled, we shall be saved by His life" (Romans 5:8–10)? Not from the Gospels but Paul in Romans.

How strange that not one of the Gospel writers, in talking about the resurrected Christ, says anything about a central theme in the New Testament: through Christ's resurrection, our hope of eternal life is found.

Instead, the Gospels have Jesus, after His resurrection, appearing at various times to the disciples and seeking to alleviate their doubts, even rebuking them for "their unbelief and hardness of heart" (Mark 16:14), or showing them that His death and resurrection had fulfilled Scripture: "And He opened their understanding, that they might comprehend the Scriptures" (Luke 24:45). Wouldn't that time, with Jesus explaining the Scriptures regarding His death and resurrection, have been a perfect place to have easily tied Christ's resurrection to the hope of ours—that is, if they had been making the whole thing up all along? Why not stick this key truth in right then and there?

What about the Great Commission? "All authority has been given to Me in heaven and on earth. Go therefore and make disciples of all the nations, baptizing them in the name of the Father and of the Son and of the Holy Spirit, teaching them to observe all things that I have commanded you; and lo, I am with you always, even to the end of the age" (Matthew 28:18–20). Not a word, however, about the meaning of His resurrection and why it was so central to the faith that they were to preach to the world.

What's even stranger about the silence is that early on, the disciples were preaching Christ's resurrection as the foundation of ours. Acts 4 records that the Sadducees, who didn't believe in the resurrection of the dead, were "greatly disturbed that they taught the people and preached in Jesus the resurrection from the dead" (verse 2).

They preached, *in Jesus*, the resurrection of the dead? That is, they were teaching that because of Christ, because of His death and resurrection, these people had the hope of their own resurrection. What else could preaching "in Jesus the resurrection from the dead" mean?

Early on, then, within a few months after His death, the disciples had tied Jesus to the resurrection of the dead—a central theme of the New Testament. They were preaching it at Pentecost. They knew what His death and resurrection meant.

And yet, when they wrote their Gospels many years later and were fabricating their stories about His resurrection, they left that *small* theological detail out?

That lack makes no sense; that is, it makes no sense if the Gospel accounts of Christ's resurrection were a hoax. It's another reason why the fraud theory fails to explain the assertion, so central to the Christian faith, that Christ was raised from the dead.

This lack also debunks the idea that the Gospels were later legends, as opposed to purposeful frauds. If legends, which slowly evolved over time in order to promote the theological agenda of their writers (i.e., that Jesus was the Messiah, risen from the dead according to Old Testament prophecies), the legends surely would have included—in fact, *emphasized*—the theological meaning of the resurrection of Christ. But they don't; all of them tell about His resurrection and appearances afterward and then move on, never explaining what this seminal event, the foundation of their faith, meant. Rather strange, isn't it?

If Christ were not resurrected, and they did not make it all up, then what else could explain the claim that He was?

1. Viktor E. Frankl, *Man's Search for Meaning* (Boston: Beacon, 2006), 56.

2. Haruki Murakami, *The Wind-up Bird Chronicle: A Novel* (New York: Vintage Books, 1997), 346.

3. Wikipedia, s.v. "Mount Vesuvius," last modified September 16, 2020, https://en.wikipedia.org/wiki/Mount_Vesuvius.

4. Mary Bagley, "Mount Vesuvius & Pompeii: Facts and History," *LiveScience*, December 20, 2017, https://www.livescience.com/27871-mount-vesuvius-pompeii.html.

5. *Pliny: Letters and Panegyrics in Two Volumes* (Cambridge, MA: Harvard University Press, 1969).

6. Mary Shelley, *Frankenstein* (Boston: Sever, Francis, 1869), 42.

7. Shelley, 42.

8. Shelley, 44, 45.

9. Shelley, 45.

10. Bette London, "Mary Shelley, *Frankenstein*, and the Spectacle of Masculinity," *PMLA* 108, no. 2 (March 1993): 253–267.

11. Elizabeth Young, "Here Comes the Bride: Wedding Gender and Race in *Bride of Frankenstein*," *Feminist Studies* 17, no. 3 (Autumn 1991): 403–437.

12. Alan Bewell, " 'An Issue of Monstrous Desire': *Frankenstein* and Obstetrics," *Yale Journal of Criticism* 2, no. 1 (Fall 1988): 105–128.

13. The twelfth-century Jewish philosopher Moses Maimonides named the resurrection of the dead as one of the thirteen articles of faith for Jews, which has been called "the fundamental truths of our religion and its very foundations." It included "the belief in the resurrection of the dead." For more information, see Maimonides, "The Thirteen Principles of Jewish Faith," Chabad.org, accessed September 29, 2020, https://www.chabad.org/library/article_cdo/aid/332555/jewish/Maimonides-13-Principles-of-Faith.htm.

14. N. T. Wright, *The Resurrection of the Son of God*, Christian Origins and the Question of God, vol. 3 (Minneapolis, MN: Fortress, 2003), 129. See also Shailer Mathews, "The Jewish Messianic Expectation in the Time of Jesus," *Biblical World* 12, no. 6 (December 1898): 437–443.

15. Naftali Silberberg, "The Resurrection Process," Chabad.org, accessed August 23, 2020, https://www.chabad.org/library/article_cdo/aid/1127503/jewish/The-Resurrection-Process.htm.

16. Silberberg, "Resurrection Process."

17. Simon Sebag Montefiore, *Jerusalem: The Biography* (New York: Vintage Books, 2011), 145.

18. Frederick W. Danker, Walter Bauer, William F. Arndt, and F. Wilbur Gingrich, *A Greek-

English Lexicon of the New Testament and Other Early Christian Literature, 3rd ed. (Chicago: University of Chicago Press, 2000), 994.

19. William Lane Craig, *The Son Rises: The Historical Evidence for the Resurrection of Jesus* (Eugene, OR: Wipf and Stock, 1981), 27, 28.

20. Craig, 60, 61.

21. Wikipedia, s.v. "Stalin's Cult of Personality," last modified September 25, 2020, https://en.wikipedia.org/wiki/Stalin%27s_cult_of_personality.

Deceived, Not Deceivers

A n ancient Chinese emperor had prohibited all mention of death in his presence; violation guaranteed execution. Instead, those in the court had to
create and sing odes to his immortality. "On once hearing that graffiti suggesting
he would soon die had been found in a distant part of the empire, the emperor
sent officials to find the culprit; when they failed, he had all the people living
in the district put to death. He was not a man to take intimations of mortality
lightly."[1]

Most of us don't either. We shouldn't. *But killing people to stamp out the idea
of death?*

Yet the good news of the gospel is that because of the resurrection of Jesus
—that is, because of His victory over death—believers will share in that victory
as well. They close their eyes in death, and the next thing they know, "in the
twinkling of an eye," at the second coming of Jesus, they "will be raised incorruptible, and we shall be changed" (1 Corinthians 15:52)—that is, changed into
immortality.

Christ's resurrection, then, wasn't merely what kept the fledgling movement
of His followers, after the shock of His death, from dissolving into the ether of
time. If it were that alone, big deal.

Instead, from the start, the Jewish believers in Jesus were preaching the promise
of eternal life (that is, the resurrection of the dead) based on His resurrection.
The answer to the human dilemma of not just death but our anticipation of
death—this ugly shadow that covers the earth more consistently than does night,
taints all that we do, and is at the bottom of our deepest fears—the answer, they
claimed, was Christ's resurrection.

From the dead at Cannae to the dying young woman, Kim, who wanted
to upload her brain to a computer, to all humanity for all ages, the promise
exists—whether they ever heard of it or not—that because of Christ's resurrection,
the specter of death, this simple rearrangement of key molecules, doesn't have
to eternally end our existence but can be, rather, only an unfortunate interlude
before the divine gift of immortality.

That promise is not just a big deal; it's the biggest of all deals; try to envision
one bigger.

In the earliest days of the new movement, after Peter had healed (through
the power of God) the lame man, he proclaimed Christ's resurrection: "But you
denied the Holy One and the Just, and asked for a murderer to be granted to
you, and killed the Prince of life, whom God raised from the dead, of which we
are witnesses" (Acts 3:14). Peter then gives them evidence, the healed man, the
truth of His words, and the power of the God whom they served and who had
raised Jesus from the dead. Based on that event, Peter follows with an appeal to
repent and turn away from their iniquities—a basic gospel sermon.

Then, "the Sadducees came upon them, being greatly disturbed that they taught the people and preached in Jesus the resurrection from the dead" (Acts 4:1, 2). Whatever else the disciples were preaching, what disturbed them the most was that these followers of Jesus were preaching, in Jesus, a doctrine that they rejected: "the resurrection from the dead."

Yet this promise—the promise of our resurrection and of eternal life in Jesus—is a foundational theme all through the New Testament. Yes, we can love Jesus; we can love His moral teaching; and we can seek, by faith, to emulate Him and His selfless love, and by so doing, make the world around us, to whatever degree possible, a better place. Yes, we can minister to the hurting, the needy, and the downtrodden. Yes, we can, by faith, follow Paul's words: "Let nothing be done through selfish ambition or conceit, but in lowliness of mind let each esteem others better than himself. Let each of you look out not only for his own interests, but also for the interests of others" (Philippians 2:3, 4).

But what ultimate long-term good does it all do if, in the end, we die, everyone we helped dies, and all people who ever lived die and die forever?

Wrote Friedrich Hölderlin about two hundred years ago: "Oh, you wretches who feel all this, who, even as I, cannot allow yourselves to speak of man's being here for a purpose, who, even as I, are so utterly in the clutch of the Nothing that governs us, so profoundly aware that we are born for nothing, that we love a nothing, believe in nothing, work ourselves to death for nothing only that little by little we may pass over into nothing—how can I help it if your knees collapse when you think of it seriously?"[2] Alfred Döblin mused about ninety years ago: "If the sun rises, and we are pleased, we should really be depressed, because what does that make us, the sun is some 300,000 times as big as the earth, and there are lots and lots of other numbers and zeroes that go to tell us how null and void we are."[3]

And then we die, so what does any of it matter anyway?

Unless . . . unless the resurrection of Jesus points to ours, and then everything about us and the meaning of our lives change as well. Because the fraud theory obviously doesn't work, what then explains those extraordinary claims that Jesus of Nazareth rose from the dead and, even more extraordinarily, that His victory over death will lead to ours as well?

I t's easy to explain these claims about Jesus' resurrection: the disciples were hallucinating; they were suffering from post-traumatic stress disorder (PTSD), and that trauma, the emotional distress brought about by Christ's death, caused the disciples to believe that Jesus had been resurrected. Unable to cope with the reality that their beloved Leader, upon whom they placed so many of their hopes, had died, these poor men simply imagined Him resurrected.

Once you discard the fraud theory, what explains the claims that Christ was resurrected? The evidence for the disciples' belief in Jesus' resurrection is hard to dispute historically. Even atheist critics or those who, because of philosophical views, reject the possibility of the Resurrection admit that the historical evidence confirms that the early Christians certainly believed it.

Their belief, however, has to be attributed to something other than Jesus being raised from death. Some natural phenomenon had to explain why all of these people believed in Christ's resurrection so strongly that, as far as we know, to the end of their lives, they were willing to suffer, even die, for a belief that the skeptics claim *must* be mistaken.

Why must it be mistaken?

Because, if miracles cannot happen, then Jesus couldn't have been raised from the dead. Hence, the idea that the disciples were suffering from hallucinations or some other psychological trauma becomes another naturalistic explanation. They weren't deceivers; they were deceived.

"It was similarly the case that, about 100 years ago, the hallucination hypothesis was also the most popular critical position until it passed out of scholarly favor," wrote scholar Gary Habermas. "Then, based on my recent survey of more than five hundred publications on the subject of Jesus' resurrection published between 1975 and the present, we will document the increased popularity of this hypothesis in the present, chiefly from scholars during the last decade or two."[4]

In an online article, Resurrection skeptic Gary Whittenberger wrote: "This hypothesis may be simply stated: *After Jesus died from crucifixion and was placed in the tomb, his corpse was removed from the tomb by unknown persons who placed it in an unknown location. Furthermore, after the women discovered the tomb to be empty, one or more of the intimate disciples of Jesus had an auditory-visual vision or hallucination of Jesus, which he or they interpreted as the 'risen Jesus,' which became the basis of the Gospel stories and the spreading resurrection belief."* Whittenberger then explains why he believes in that theory. "The purpose of this essay is to demonstrate that the hallucination hypothesis is a plausible explanation of the post-crucifixion 'appearances' of Jesus, and to defend it against some of the current criticisms of Christian apologists."[5]

What, then, of this hallucination theory? How well does it work, and is it a plausible naturalistic explanation for the claim that Jesus was never resurrected from the dead but His followers simply hallucinated that He did?

Though there are about as many variations on the hallucination theory as there are hallucination theorists, all the theories share a motif, which goes, loosely, as follows: Christ's followers, particularly His inner circle, despite His overt warnings about His impending death and resurrection—"The Son of Man must suffer many things, and be rejected by the elders and chief priests and scribes, and be killed, and be raised the third day" (Luke 9:22; see also Matthew 20:19; Mark 9:31; Luke 18:33)—never saw it coming. Instead, they had big plans, thinking that in some manner, Jesus was going to overthrow the present order, particularly the Romans, and establish His earthly kingdom. This view was based on a belief, held by some Jews even today, that the coming of the Messiah will inaugurate a new earthly existence.

Then, however, Jesus was arrested, tried, and crucified, the most degrading form of punishment in that time and place. The trauma must have been overwhelming—made even more painful by the mocking inscription that Pilate had placed over the cross:

Now Pilate wrote a title and put it on the cross. And the writing was:

JESUS OF NAZARETH, THE KING OF THE JEWS (John 19:19).

Pilate probably hadn't meant the sign that way, but what an extra slap in the face of Christ's disciples.

Even worse, Old Testament law declared that anyone executed by being hung on a tree was cursed: "If a man has committed a sin deserving of death, and he is put to death, and you hang him on a tree, his body shall not remain overnight on the tree, but you shall surely bury him that day, so that you do not defile the land which the LORD your God is giving you as an inheritance; for he who is hanged is accursed of God" (Deuteronomy 21:22, 23). Was their beloved Leader, who on the cross had cried out, "My God, My God, why have You forsaken Me?" (Mark 15:34), really cursed by God? How much worse could their disappointment be?

According to one version of the theory, after His death, someone (we don't know who) robbed Christ's grave. Perhaps, knowing that He had been buried with expensive spices (John 19:39), they robbed the grave for the spices, even though this version leaves unanswered the big question of why they pilfered a rotting corpse too. Nevertheless, when Mary first saw the empty tomb, she assumed that someone had taken the body, perhaps grave robbers. "They have taken away the Lord out of the tomb, and we do not know where they have laid Him" (John 20:2).

Whatever the reason for the supposed robbery, because of it (also problematic is the question of how someone was able to do it with the Roman guard around), the tomb was empty. Still traumatized by events and still under great psychological pressure, the followers of Jesus (the theory goes), upon hearing about the empty tomb, began to imagine, even having visual-auditory hallucinations, that Jesus had been raised from the dead. These men and women, overcome with sorrow, suffered a group delusion in which they believed that their beloved Jesus, far from being dead, had been miraculously resurrected to life.

Or, as others have suggested, a few of His followers had the delusion of seeing Jesus alive, or specifically, Peter did first, and he (or they) was so convincing that he (they) got others to think that they saw Him alive as well. Like a viral bug, this hallucination was picked up by His earlier followers and spread among them.

Not everyone had the exact same hallucination, explaining the different versions of events and why, when supposedly Jesus had appeared, there were still skeptics: "When they saw Him, they worshiped Him; but some doubted" (Matthew 28:17). How could they doubt if He were there before them in the flesh?

The Christian church was founded, then, not by deceivers but by the deceived, not by conniving charlatans by but grief-stricken survivors suffering from severe psychological trauma who, based on that trauma, started a movement that has shaped world history to this day.

In short, Christianity was based not on a lie but on a delusion. That's the theory anyway.

With the revolution in the scientific view of the world," wrote Gerd Lüdemann, "the statements about the resurrection of Jesus have irrevocably lost their literal meaning."[6] This sentence comes near the end of *What Really Happened to Jesus*—a Lüdemann book promoting the hallucination theory.* Yet the sentence itself reflects a rabid philosophical error that forms the heart and soul of much modern (the past few hundred years) skepticism, or outright rejection, of Christ's bodily resurrection. The sentiment could be expressed like this: *In an era of smartphones, nuclear submarines, and genetic editing, who still can believe in miracles?* Though, at first glance, that line might sound logical, it's a classic non sequitur—a conclusion or statement that does not logically follow from the previous argument or statement—and is about as logical as this statement: *Belinda can do advanced algebra; therefore, God does not exist.*

The scientific view of the world has, of course, greatly expanded human understanding of nature and the physical realm (however difficult the idea of the "physical" can be at times to define, especially at the quantum level). But the advances of science don't invalidate the idea of miracles because science, at least as practiced now, has nothing to say about anything other than natural phenomena, which puts miracles outside its purview.

Thanks to modern science, what some ancients might have viewed as the wrath of their gods, we now understand as electrical currents building up in clouds. Hundreds of years ago, an old widow selling herbs might have been burned at the stake as a witch, blamed for a plague that today could be better explained by unsanitary conditions at the local watering hole. And sure, the ancient Egyptians' fear that the serpent god Apep was about to devour Ra, the sun god, could today be better explained as a solar eclipse.

But these incidents, and others like them, are indicative only of human ignorance. They have nothing to do with the existence of the miraculous or of the supernatural, and to conclude that because science has explained† so much of the natural world (or that phenomena which, at one time, had been deemed supernatural can now have natural explanations) no more means that the supernatural cannot be real than does understanding the chemical composition of the words in Shakespeare's plays mean that Shakespeare's genius never existed.

Nevertheless, many in the Western world, dominated by the technological success of science, have adopted some of the unwarranted philosophical presuppositions of science as well. Even worse, many in the West have adopted some

---

* This book is a popularized version of Lüdemann's earlier one, *The Resurrection of Christ: A Historical Inquiry* (Amherst, NY: Prometheus Books, 1994). For what it's worth, and it's worth something, Prometheus Books has been publishing anti-Christian literature for decades now and is a strong proponent of atheistic materialism.

† Actually, the idea of a scientific explanation is a very complicated subject; some argue that science explains nothing; it only describes. Take, for instance, the famous formula $E = mc^2$. Though describing the relationship between matter and energy, it explains nothing about why or how matter can be converted to energy. Some see this as an across-the-board limitation of the whole scientific endeavor.

false conclusions drawn from these unwarranted presuppositions, such as the conclusion that, because of science, "statements about the resurrection of Jesus have irrevocably lost their literal meaning."[7] Without quite saying it, Lüdemann is saying science has disproved the resurrection of Jesus.

But this conclusion is false, and most scientists, even atheist-materialist scientists, would agree that it's false, not because they believe in the resurrection of Jesus or even that it could have happened but because science, they would argue, has nothing to say about the supernatural. Science, the claim is, deals only with natural phenomena, not the supernatural, which is why science must be silent on the resurrection of Jesus.*

Lüdemann, however, came to this false conclusion honestly because even without specifically claiming it, much of science has presupposed *ontological naturalism*—a fancy phrase for the claim that all reality is only materialistic. If so, then the supernatural does not exist, even though this claim contradicts the idea that science has nothing to say about the supernatural, including whether or not it exists.

Be that as it may, the overwhelming assumption, unwarranted as it is even in an era intellectually dominated by science, is that supernatural events, such as the resurrection of Jesus, cannot happen. Hence, the quest to find another explanation, such as the hallucination theory, for the disciples' belief that Jesus had been resurrected.

---

* Not all scientists, however, agree. Wrote Sean Carroll: "Science should be interested in determining the *truth*, whatever that truth may be—natural, supernatural, or otherwise. The stance known as methodological naturalism, while deployed with the best of intentions by supporters of science, amounts to assuming part of the answer ahead of time. If finding the truth is our goal, that is just about the biggest mistake we can make." Sean Carroll, *The Big Picture: On the Origins of Life, Meaning, and the Universe Itself* (New York: Dutton, 2016), 133; emphasis in the original.

A text in the book of Hebrews reads: "But without faith it is impossible to please Him, for he who comes to God must believe that He is, and that He is a rewarder of those who diligently seek Him" (Hebrews 11:6). In contrast, Gerd Lüdemann begins a chapter in his first anti-Resurrection book with this quote by the atheist evolutionist Julian Huxley: "It will soon be as impossible for an intelligent, educated man or woman to believe in a god as it is now to believe that the earth is flat, that flies can be spontaneously generated, that disease is a divine punishment, or that death is always due to witchcraft."[8] (Huxley died in 1975; his prediction has failed, obviously.)

These two quotes, however, point to something important: human subjectivity. We cannot read and interpret a text, biblical or otherwise, without bringing ourselves and all of our intellectual, cultural, historical, and even biological baggage into it. How do you step out of your own skin, your own mind, your own body, your own thoughts, and your consciousness when you read something—anything? You don't. No one does.

And because of our subjectivity, inevitable as it must be, we must take the world, including the texts that we read, with a certain amount of faith. That is, if we understand the word *faith* to mean the obvious: we believe in and accept things without fully understanding everything about them. Whether the pills you pop for a disease, a jet you fly in across the sea, or a book you read about Spartan history, to some degree or another, you do it on faith. And that's not only because you don't understand or know everything about the disease, the pill, or the doctor who prescribed it, the laws of aerodynamics (much less the mechanics of the jet engine), or many details of the Spartans whom you are reading about—but also because even those things that you do understand, or think that you do understand, you do so still filtered through your own subjectivity.

The Christian approaches the biblical text with his or her own presuppositions and subjectivity; Lüdemann came to the text with his own as well. He can no more "prove"* the anti-supernaturalism that underpinned his reading of the Resurrection texts than someone reading it from a supernaturalist perspective can "prove" his or her supernaturalist assumptions.

Both require faith. But, considering that our world does exist and that the most logical argument for this existence that an atheistic, anti-supernaturalistic worldview can muster is that nothing is the foundation of everything, one could argue that the theistic, supernaturalistic worldview is the more rational of the

---

* The concept of proof itself is exceedingly complicated and deep. How do you know your proofs are correct? How do you prove your proof? Why do proofs that supposedly work in one realm not work in another? In this case, we are using the word *proof* in a more formal sense, like pure logic, such as what has been called the law of noncontradiction, which means that something cannot be both true and false at the same time (though even that itself has come under question, in which the idea is said to be an assumption, not a law). One could argue, for instance, that Scripture gives powerful evidence for God's existence and for the supernatural, even if evidence is not "proof" in a formal sense of the term.

two. This means, then, that it takes less faith to accept the supernaturalistic view than it does the anti-supernaturalistic worldview—the one that Lüdemann brings into his reading of the New Testament texts about the Resurrection. And even if one disagrees with the argument above, Lüdemann's historical approach to the text is still as chock-full of subjectivity, assumptions, and faith as is the most devout Christian's.

One could argue, too, that reading the New Testament from a purely naturalistic perspective makes about as much sense as using a Chinese lexicon to interpret a book in French. By denying the supernatural from the start, Lüdemann was fated, destined, predestined even, to conclude that—whatever happened to Jesus Christ after He had been crucified—surprise of surprises, He was not resurrected from the dead. He couldn't be because people don't rise from the dead, at least not in his naturalistic world.

What, then, explains the belief of so many that He did? The hallucination theory.

Hence, Lüdemann's books.

I n *What Really Happened to Jesus* (notice, it's not a question, as in, What really happened to Jesus? but rather, this is what really happened to Jesus), Lüdemann—again, working from a non-supernaturalistic perspective—reconstructs in his own way the story leading up to Christ's death and then what followed. Though all but dismissing much of the Gospels' version of events, he does concede that "the fact of the death of Jesus as a consequence of crucifixion is indisputable, despite hypotheses of a pseudo-death or a deception which are sometimes put forward."[9]

But beyond Christ's death by crucifixion, which fits nicely within a naturalistic worldview, much of the Gospel narratives are, he writes, not trustworthy and certainly not historical accounts of what happened. Rather, they are later traditions, legends, and embellishments, often written by people who were not always eyewitnesses to the events that they wrote about and who were shaping the stories to fit their own theological perspectives.

In short, Lüdemann challenged or openly denied pretty much everything depicted in the Gospels regarding every event after Christ's death, such as the account of how Jesus had been buried, especially the story of Joseph of Arimathea putting Him in his own tomb. Instead, Lüdemann insists, "We can only conjecture the precise place of the burial of Jesus."[10] Besides, had Jesus' tomb location been known, "the early Christians would have venerated it."[11]

Unless, that is, the tomb was empty, which means it wouldn't be all that important to the early believers because an empty tomb, in and of itself (that is, without Christ's appearances), doesn't mean Jesus was resurrected.

According to Lüdemann, Christ's disciples didn't know where Christ had been buried. Nevertheless, they then heard some rumor that Christ's body, wherever it had been interred, had been stolen for some reason. Lüdemann doesn't assert that it had truly been stolen but only that the disciples heard the rumor that it had.

"While the story of the theft of Jesus' corpse is certainly historical, the theft itself is not. For one thing, the disciples did not know where or even whether Jesus had been buried; and for another, their grief, fear, and disappointment would have rendered them unable to perpetrate such a hoax."[12] The disciples themselves were not the source of the rumor but, instead, were victims of it. Lüdemann states that the tomb wasn't really empty, but that Christ's body was there and "rotted away."[13]

Whatever really happened, according to Lüdemann, Matthew completely concocted the story of the religious leaders bribing the guards to say that the disciples stole the body. "The tradition about the bribing of the guards cannot be taken seriously." Why? Because "it too clearly has partisan features of Matthew or the Matthaean tradition."[14] The whole story, he says, had been concocted by Matthew (or whoever he thinks wrote it) to push a specific theological agenda—in this case, to make the Jewish leaders look bad and the Christians good.

Anyway, this is the kind of thinking all through the book; to help buttress his arguments in his first book, he even quotes such "authoritative" sources as the Gospel of Peter and something, written in the middle of the second century, called the Epistle of the Apostles.

Lüdemann's bottom line? Jesus was never resurrected from the tomb.

What does he say happened instead?

What happened, Lüdemann writes, was that broken, grieved, and suffering, the followers of Jesus simply hallucinated Him out of the grave and into the role of the risen Messiah. That's it. The truth wasn't supernatural but psychological, nothing divine from heaven above but from tormented psyches below.

"The critical investigation of the various resurrection appearances," Lüdemann writes, "produced a surprising result: they can all be explained as visions."[15] His use of the word *visions* is not as in Daniel's visions (Daniel 7), Ezekiel's (Ezekiel 1:1), or the apostle John's on Patmos (Revelation 9:17) but more like the visions of someone not quite with it mentally—someone perhaps ready for therapy followed by pharmacology.

It started, Lüdemann claims, with Peter, most likely because Peter felt the most guilt, the most torment, about the death of Jesus, all as a result of his shameful betrayal of Jesus after He had been arrested and, when confronted about being one of Christ's disciples, Peter openly denied it, multiple times, too.

> Now Peter sat outside in the courtyard. And a servant girl came to him, saying, "You also were with Jesus of Galilee."
>
> But he denied it before them all, saying, "I do not know what you are saying."
>
> And when he had gone out to the gateway, another girl saw him and said to those who were there, "This fellow also was with Jesus of Nazareth."
>
> But again he denied with an oath, "I do not know the Man!"
>
> And a little later those who stood by came up and said to Peter, "Surely you also are one of them, for your speech betrays you."
>
> Then he began to curse and swear, saying, "I do not know the Man!" (Matthew 26:69–74; see also Mark 14:66–72; Luke 22:56–62).

With this heavy background weighing on him and the guilt overwhelming him, Peter started having psychotic hallucinations of Jesus being alive, visions of the Teacher appearing to him, even though Jesus was dead, buried, and rotting away somewhere unknown to Peter.

"Peter received the first vision," wrote Lüdemann, "which is to be interpreted psychologically as failed mourning and the overcoming of a severe guilt complex. He had 'sinned' against Jesus by denying him. But under the impact of Jesus' preaching and death, through an appearance of the 'Risen Christ,' Peter once again referred to himself God's word of forgiveness which was already present in the activity of Jesus, this time in its profound clarity."[16]

Though the English translation here is a bit muddled, Lüdemann basically says that Peter, overcome with guilt, hallucinated and, in his hallucinations, saw the risen Jesus, whom he then interpreted as providing him the forgiveness that Jesus had preached about, forgiveness that he now greatly needed.

In short, Peter simply imagined that he saw the resurrected Christ, and this was the foundation of the ministry that dominated him for the rest of his life.

However, it didn't end with Peter. According to Lüdemann, others influenced by Peter's delusion were then afflicted. He writes: "This first vision became the initial spark which promoted the further series of visions mentioned by Paul in 1 Cor. 15. The subsequent appearance of Christ can be explained as mass psychoses (or mass hysteria). This phenomenon was first made possible by Peter's vision."[17]

Of course, one question does arise by Lüdemann's mentioning 1 Corinthians 15, which Paul wrote. It's one thing to argue that Peter, overcome with guilt and sadness over the death of his beloved Teacher, hallucinated the risen Christ. But that argument can't explain Paul's supposed hallucination of the risen Christ, can it? Paul certainly wasn't saddened over Christ's death; he hated Christ and thought Him a false messiah.

That, too, is easily understood, Lüdemann claims. Paul suffered a hallucination over some kind of "Christ complex" that led him to believe that the resurrected Christ appeared to him as well.

"By contrast," Lüdemann writes, "Paul's appearance did not depend on Peter's vision, since here it was not a follower but an 'enemy' of Jesus or his supporters who was affected. Here Paul's biography gives strong indications that his vision of Christ is to be explained psychologically as an overcoming of a smouldering 'Christ complex' which led to severe inner (unconscious) conflicts in him and finally released itself in this vision."[18]

According to Lüdemann, these hallucinations are the best way to explain the fact, which he concedes, that many people after the death of Jesus *believed* that they had seen the risen Christ. Their belief, however, resulted from "mass hysteria" or the like. Therefore, he writes, the "resurrection of Jesus is completely unnecessary as a presupposition to explain these phenomena. *A consistent modern view must say farewell to the resurrection of Jesus as a historical event.*"[19]

Writing nineteen hundred or so years after the events, he claims to understand better what happened than did those who either were eyewitnesses to the events or lived simultaneously with those events. Or, expressed another way, he is basically psychoanalyzing people dead for almost two thousand years.

Lüdemann isn't alone either. Another version of the hallucination theory comes from an American Protestant cleric, Bishop John Shelby "Jack" Spong (born 1931), who is a longtime critic of any literal interpretation of most everything in the Bible.

For Spong, heavily influenced by modern science and materialism, the Bible's stories are metaphors designed to teach us to be kind and compassionate, but they certainly are not accurate accounts of historical events. Perhaps his most famous quote—one that captures his thinking—is "God is not a Christian, God is not a Jew, or a Muslim, or a Hindu, or a Buddhist. All of those are human systems that human beings have created to try to help us walk into the mystery of God. I honor my tradition, I walk through my tradition, but I don't think my tradition defines God, I think it only points me to God."[20]

Who ever said that God was a Christian or a Jew or a Hindu (though Jesus was, yes, Jewish) or a member of any religion? His point is rather nonsensical, whatever it is supposed to mean. Yet, whoever the God is whom his "tradition only points" him to, that God certainly doesn't sound like the One depicted in Scripture, who declared of Himself:

"Tell and bring forth your case;
Yes, let them take counsel together.
Who has declared this from ancient time?
Who has told it from that time?
Have not I, the LORD?
And there is no other God besides Me,
A just God and a Savior;
There is none besides Me" (Isaiah 45:21).

Anyway, working from such weak, even illogical, premises, Spong, in his book *Resurrection: Myth or Reality? A Bishop's Search for the Origins of Christianity*[21] rejects many of the Gospel narratives as literal accounts of events. These stories take on a mythological, or midrashic, character instead.

What is that?

Midrash—from a Hebrew word (*drsh*) that means "to seek out, to inquire"—is a form of Jewish biblical interpretation that has a long history in the religion itself. For our purposes, Spong argued that many of the accounts in the Gospels were merely midrashic spins, or interpretations, of Old Testament stories that were placed in the context of Jesus of Nazareth.

The Sermon on the Mount, for example, was something that had been concocted, or modified, merely in order to portray Jesus as the new Moses.

The feeding of the multitudes certainly didn't happen as depicted either. Instead, these accounts were midrashic embellishment created by the Gospel writer in order to bring Elijah and Elisha motifs into the story of Jesus. "Thus," wrote Spong, "the generosity of the lad who gave up his lunch of five loaves and two fish to feed the hungry crowd inspired the others to bring out their hidden food supplies, and that's how the five thousand were actually fed. It was a feeble attempt to make believable once again what had become unbelievable."[22] In other words, nothing miraculous happened, but the story was spun that way by the Gospel writer in order to make some spiritual point or another.

Even the words of Jesus were, said Spong, in many cases concocted: "Surely Jesus never called himself the bread of life or the source of 'living water,' but when people came to know the transcendent meaning of his life as that which fed their deepest human hunger and satisfied their deepest thirst for God, it became appropriate for believers to place these words upon the lips of Jesus himself."[23]

In short, the followers of Jesus, after He had died, used Jewish interpretative principles to make up stories about Jesus or to embellish incidents that did happen.

This idea applies also, even especially, to Christ's resurrection, which, according to Spong, never happened to begin with.

"At its very core," Spong claims, "the story of Easter has nothing to do with angelic announcements or empty tombs. It has nothing to do with time periods, whether three days, forty days, or fifty days. It has nothing to do with resuscitated bodies that appear and disappear or that finally exit this world in a heavenly ascension. Those are but the human, midrashic vehicles employed to carry the transcendent meaning of Easter by those who must speak of the unspeakable and describe the indescribable because the power of the event was undeniably real."[24]

One could be excused for not totally understanding what he meant here. The actual resurrection of Jesus—as in His having been killed and then coming back to life—never happened. Yet "the power of the event [that never happened] was undeniably real" and came heavily laden with "transcendent meaning" as well? So an event that never happened was, nevertheless, "undeniably real" and filled with spiritual meaning?

OK?

Spong's point is that, though Jesus had not really been resurrected, as in having been dead and then having been brought back to life (the way the Gospels depict it), the *idea* of Him having been dead and then having been brought back to life is a powerful one, and that's what matters—that's what was "undeniably real" and filled with spiritual and transcendent meaning.

And this, according to Spong, is the foundation of the resurrection of Jesus and, essentially, the Christian faith. It was not built on an outright blatant and purposeful lie but rather on the creative imagination of early Christians who simply interpreted the person of Jesus in ways that gave His life and then death transcendent meaning.

Again, not deceivers but deceived.

How, though, did this myth, this midrash, about the resurrected Jesus happen? That's a question that Spong himself asks: "How was it that people came to believe that a crucified man had conquered death? What really happened to change despairing men and women into courageous witnesses who believed that Jesus lived and that they had seen the Lord?"[25]

Spong answers the question by following the basic hallucination-theory approach but with his own spin, which makes it not quite the psychological pathology depicted by Lüdemann but still a projection of their own minds rather than a real event.

For starters, he denies the historicity of most of the biblical elements of the Resurrection story: the angels descending, the empty tomb, the appearances (and disappearances) of Jesus, the woman at the tomb of Jesus, the intervention of Joseph of Arimathea, the darkness over the land, the splitting of the temple veil, and the profession of faith by the centurion; for him, these are all legends.

"Sacred legends, I might add, but legends nonetheless."[26]

What, then, happened?

In a subsection titled "The Crucifixion as It May Have Happened,"[27] Spong reconstructs events like this: Having threatened the power structure of the ruling elite, Jesus had, yes, been crucified and killed, but His body was thrown into a common grave and covered with dirt. And that was it, at least as far as Jesus Himself in the flesh was concerned. Dead, buried, rotting.

Christ's followers, understandably distraught, get out of Dodge; in this case, "Dodge" being Jerusalem. Spong says that Peter, James, John, and Andrew (and perhaps others) all ended up in Galilee, where they grieved.

> Together they processed their experiences and wondered what it all meant. Together they felt the void of darkness. The sense of meaninglessness was almost like a physical presence among them. The clouds did not lift with the passing of time. The intensity of one person's presence in another person's life is equaled only by the intensity of absence when that person is gone. Jesus, the intensely present one in the consciousness of this little band, was now the intensely absent one in the very being of those who tried to put their lives back together in their homes in Galilee.[28]

How Spong knows all this, he doesn't say, admitting that "no one can finally do anything other than speculate!"[29] And so he continues his speculation, supposing that amid the grieving, Peter, who had been especially close to Jesus, struggled to make sense of it all. How could Jesus, the wonderful Jesus, have been so ignominiously and unfairly executed? How could God have allowed one so precious and holy to be killed like that? It just didn't make sense; it was not right.

Then, writes Spong, it was during the time of the Feast of Tabernacles, when

Simon Peter heard the prophet Zechariah being read in the synagogue, which, says Spong, included the text "where the rulers of the temple paid thirty pieces of silver to rid themselves of one whom God had appointed to be shepherd of Israel."[30] Simon Peter talked about that text and others with his fellow travelers, the other disappointed disciples. His mind, then, began to muse, over and over, on these things.

One morning after a big catch of fish, as they sat around eating breakfast and Simon Peter said the blessing, it suddenly all came together for Peter. Christ's death wasn't a punishment; it had been planned by God all along! Simon Peter now saw the meaning of Christ's death as never before, and that must have included the idea of Him being resurrected. Thus, Christ's resurrection was, therefore, concocted in Peter's mind as something that could "open the eyes of those whose eyes could be opened in no other way to the meaning of Jesus as the sign of God's love."[31]

Jesus had never been resurrected, and none of the Gospels' accounts of the Resurrection were accurate records of the events surrounding the Resurrection because none of the events surrounding the Resurrection happened. Instead, these were later embellishments, legends, midrash—all based on Peter's imagination, which created the idea of Christ being resurrected as the only way Peter could make sense of His death.

"That was the dawn of Easter in human history," wrote Spong. "It would be fair to say that in that moment Simon felt resurrected. The clouds of his grief, confusion, and depression vanished from his mind, and in that moment he knew that Jesus was part of the very essence of God, and at that moment Simon saw Jesus alive."[32]

It was his imagination—his own "vision" of the risen Jesus—that Peter then shared with others. And they, too, caught up in the passion of the idea, began proclaiming that Jesus was risen, even though, wrote Spong, that proclamation "had nothing to do with empty tombs or feeling wounds."[33] Nevertheless, these Jews, all self-deceived, all believing a lie (however "sacred"), then returned to Jerusalem and started Christianity.

That's, at least, how John Shelby "Jack" Spong explains why the followers of Jesus all believed, even passionately, that Jesus had been raised from the dead.

Hallucinations? Overactive imaginations? PTSD? Wish fulfillment? Some kind of psychotic, delusional, and schizophrenic mania brought about by too much of one neurohormone or another or by some misfiring of the synaptic connections in the brain—this, or something like this, explains the foundation of Christianity? In this view, it's about psychology, not theology; one needs Sigmund Freud, not Philip Schaff,* to understand the origins of the Christian church.

And this notion, we are told, explains the passionate belief among these first evangelists and preachers that Jesus of Nazareth was the Messiah not just of the Jews but of all humanity, and that in Him, we have the hope of eternal life.

If this theory is correct, then one has to believe that Peter and the eleven others with him (Acts 2:14) were all sharing the same mental illness, the same hallucination, when the twelve of them stood together before the large crowd at Pentecost and Peter began to preach Jesus. And, too, as Peter preached, in the short time between then and whenever he suddenly started hallucinating, or (as Spong put it) "that moment Simon saw Jesus alive"[34]—this humble fisherman managed to find biblical texts for the idea of a resurrected Christ? In other words, their psychoses and hallucinations also just happened to square with Scripture.

How convenient!

None other than Pinchas Lapide, the rabbi who believed in Jesus' resurrection, wrote: "When this scared, frightened band of the apostles which was just about to throw away everything in order to flee in despair to Galilee; when these peasants, shepherds, and fishermen, who betrayed and denied their master and then failed him miserably, suddenly could be changed overnight into a confident mission society, convinced of salvation and able to work with much more success after Easter than before Easter, then no vision or hallucination is sufficient to explain such a revolutionary transformation."[35]

Right after preaching about Jesus to the crowd and talking about the miracles, along with the signs and wonders that were done through Jesus, which he reminds them, "You yourselves also know" (Acts 2:22), Peter goes right to the Bible in order to defend—what? A hallucination?

For David says concerning Him:

> "I foresaw the LORD always before my face,
> For He is at my right hand, that I may not be shaken.
> Therefore my heart rejoiced, and my tongue was glad;
> Moreover my flesh also will rest in hope.
> For You will not leave my soul in Hades,

---

* Philip Schaff (1819–1893) was a famous church historian.

Nor will You allow Your Holy One to see corruption.
You have made known to me the ways of life;
You will make me full of joy in Your presence" (verses 25–28).

Remember what the claim is: Peter and the other disciples had delusions of the resurrected Christ. But now, based on those delusions, they had not only numerous Bible texts to back up those delusions but had constructed the theological foundation of Christian theology in that short time as well.

After Peter had quoted those texts, he pointed out that they couldn't have been talking about David because he "is both dead and buried, and his tomb is with us to this day" (verse 29). The texts pointed, instead, to Christ, and then Peter gives them even more biblical texts that affirmed who Jesus was and what He would accomplish.

Then, in the midst of his exposition, he says, with the eleven next to him: "This Jesus God has raised up, of which we are all witnesses" (verse 32). Twelve men, twelve deluded men, suffering not only hallucinations but suffering the same hallucination, stand before this crowd of their fellow religionists and affirm Christ's resurrection from the dead? Then, with amazing boldness, Peter proclaims: "Therefore let all the house of Israel know assuredly that God has made this Jesus, whom you crucified, both Lord and Christ" (verse 36).

Working off of a fantasy, he told the Jewish people, the crowd, that they had crucified their own Messiah? That charge would have been bold enough if true. But he does it based on a delusion, a figment of Peter's overactive imagination concocted in his head just a few weeks earlier while eating breakfast? With the eleven others up there with him, might not one, or a few even, come to their senses and realize how crazy this was, backed off, especially after such a provocative and potentially dangerous charge was made to the crowd?

And how did the crowd respond?

Come on! You guys are wacked. The body of Jesus was stolen. Maybe you even stole it. Besides, who ever heard of a crucified Mashiach? *The* Mashiach *comes as a ruler, not a criminal hanging on a cross. Our leaders have told us what happened to His body. How stupid do you think we are to believe such nonsense?*

Isn't something like that the logical and reasonable response to a group of deluded men proclaiming that something happened that, in fact, never did happen, no one expected to happen, and they had no evidence to back that it did happen, other than their own words, which were based on delusions?

Instead, the presence of the twelve men, together claiming to be eyewitnesses to Jesus' resurrection, must have been persuasive because those in the crowd said to the apostles, "Men and brethren, what shall we do?" (verse 37). In other words, *we believe you! We believe what you said about the death of Jesus and His resurrection! We acknowledge our complicity!*

And then, astonishingly—considering that this was supposedly based on a recently concocted delusion—Peter gives them what is, in essence, the theological foundation of the gospel. "Then Peter said to them, 'Repent, and let every one of you be baptized in the name of Jesus Christ for the remission of sins; and you shall receive the gift of the Holy Spirit. For the promise is to you and to your children, and to all who are afar off, as many as the Lord our God will call' " (verse 38).

Right there, amid the fervor, Peter the fisherman expresses the cardinal doctrine of biblical Christianity, which is justification by faith based on Jesus as the crucified and risen Messiah. Some of the greatest expositions in the New Testament epistles, especially by Paul, basically flesh out and elaborate what Peter said here.

And even more astonishing, he tells them that even those who were complicit in Christ's death, as some in the crowd might have been, that they, too, can have the promise of salvation based on the death of the Man whom they helped kill.

Not only does Peter give them the gospel, but he also points to the universality of what happened at the Cross. That is, the gospel wasn't just for Jews, which it never was to begin with (Isaiah 51:4; Deuteronomy 7:6–8; Isaiah 43:10), even if some of the religious leaders thought so; the gospel was for all humanity—another theme powerfully expressed later by Paul.

In fact, Peter's words, and most surely the testimony of others, were so persuasive that they resulted in mass conversions: "Then those who gladly received his word were baptized; and that day about three thousand souls were added to them" (Acts 2:41).

And we're supposed to believe that all this, and so much more, arose from nothing but wish fulfillment, phantasms, and PTSD?

The hallucination theory runs into numerous problems, other than just sheer implausibility and that it appears so ad hoc—that is, created only for a specific purpose: to try to explain why so many people, after the death of Jesus, believed that He had been resurrected.

Sure, those who promote this idea have their contemporary psychiatrists and scientists to affirm their mass hallucination machinations (though those who reject it have their psychiatrists and scientists as well). But, aside from the experts, who hasn't known mentally imbalanced people or the mentally ill? Or those with a deep bipolar disorder or schizophrenia? Whatever broad commonalities, these are individuals with their own individual expressions of their sickness. Who has ever known mentally ill people, or those who hallucinate, to share the same illusions and hallucinations? Who has known even two like that, much less a group, even hundreds?

A man, deluded, believed that he was a piece of corn. After being hospitalized, he was finally released, cured of his delusion. However, on his first day out, as he was leaving the building with his doctor, he saw a chicken and got frightened, thinking it was going to eat him.

"But," his doctor said, "you know that you are not a corn kernel, right?"

"Yes," said the frightened man. "I know that, but does the chicken?"

Delusions are subjective, personal, and individual. Sure, masses can quickly believe lies, but that's not what this theory teaches. Not just Peter but dozens, hundreds, all supposedly sharing in the same hallucination of the risen Jesus?

What makes this idea even more preposterous is that, again, the notion of a crucified and risen Savior was not what anyone was expecting nor was it what anyone had been hoping for. As N. T. Wright wrote: "Nobody, after all, believed that the Messiah would be raised from the dead; nobody was expecting any such thing."[36] Thus, these people, based on some delusionary moment Peter had at breakfast (if one follows Spong's approach), all begin to hallucinate the same unknown and unexpected notion of the Messiah, who, after being crucified, rose from the dead? And what do you know? It turns out that dying and then being resurrected was what the Messiah was supposed to do all along? And they even find Bible texts to back up their mass delusion?

Wrote two historians about the idea of the early church being made up, primarily, of people deluded enough to hallucinate—hallucinations that then dominated their lives,

First, today we know that hallucinations are private occurrences, which occur in the mind of an individual. They are not collective experiences. In a group, all of the people may be in the frame of mind to hallucinate, but each experiences hallucinations on an individual basis. Nor will they experience the same hallucination. Hallucinations are like dreams in this way. Imagine that it is the middle of the night. You wake up your wife and say, "Honey, I just had a dream that we were in Hawaii. Come back to sleep and join me in my dream and we'll enjoy a free vacation together." It would be impossible for her to do so, since a dream exists only in the mind of the individual. It cannot be shared with another person. Likewise, a hallucination cannot be shared.[37]

People no more share hallucinations or psychotic delusions than they do dreams. Many remember the 2010 science-fiction thriller *Inception*, in which—through some future technological gizmos—people could share dreams, and some of those sharing the dream could influence what happened in it. But that's all it was, futuristic science fiction; even this concept seems more plausible than the idea that hundreds of people, many of whom were not of Christ's inner circle—that is, those not initially devastated by Christ's death—suddenly all shared the same delusions and hallucinations of those who were.

Again, from Pinchas Lapide, who, after examining the various claims, wrote, "If the defeated and depressed group of disciples overnight could change into a victorious movement of faith, based only on autosuggestion or self-deception—without a fundamental faith experience—then this would be a much greater miracle than the resurrection itself."[38]

If the hallucination option seems preposterous, it's because it is, and it gets only more so.

For instance, according to the hallucination theory, these people have their mass hallucinations, in which they believe that they have seen the resurrected Christ. And then these deluded souls somehow manage to convince themselves, based on their fantasies and mental mirages, that the death and resurrection of Christ was part of God's plan all along, even predicted by Moses, the prophets, and in the Psalms. What a lucky coincidence for Peter, along with the rest of those deluded souls, that Isaiah 53 reads like this:

He is despised and rejected by men,
A Man of sorrows and acquainted with grief.
And we hid, as it were, our faces from Him;
He was despised, and we did not esteem Him.

Surely He has borne our griefs
And carried our sorrows;
Yet we esteemed Him stricken,
Smitten by God, and afflicted.
But He was wounded for our transgressions,
He was bruised for our iniquities;
The chastisement for our peace was upon Him,
And by His stripes we are healed.
All we like sheep have gone astray;
We have turned, every one, to his own way;
And the Lord has laid on Him the iniquity of us all (verses 3–6).

Christ died, and afterward, they hallucinated His resurrection. Coincidentally (what else would it be?), they discovered Old Testament texts that talk about Christ's death, which did happen, and texts that talk about His resurrection, which didn't happen, but, luckily for them, fit their hallucinations.

Next, over the years, traditions, legends, and stories (midrash) were built up to buttress those hallucinations. And those traditions, legends, and midrash, none true, form the essence of the New Testament. The seminal event upon which the whole New Testament narrative is based, the whole Christian narrative actually, is nothing but fictitious stories erected upon someone's (after all, it had to start with someone, and Peter seems to be a favorite choice) delusion? In contrast to the hoax theory, which from the start was based on a lie, the hallucination theory means that Christianity is just a bunch of fairy tales ignited and then fueled by one person's mental aberration.

Pretty much everything written in the four Gospels about events after the death of Jesus was, then (how to say it nicely?), lies. Well-meaning lies, perhaps. Lies designed to teach spiritual "truths" (though using lies to teach truths seems a bit oxymoronic). Lies created to point to God and His goodness. (Does God need lies to reveal Himself or His goodness?)

Or if the word *lies* comes off as too morally heavy laden, then they were myths and legends pawning off as true what were lies. Think of Plato's "magnificent myth,"[39] in which the people in power concoct a false narrative for the masses to consume, but they do so for a higher good: the stability of the republic. For the earliest Christians, that higher good must have been salvaging something from the fiasco of Christ's death; for later Christians, it was, perhaps, to teach lessons about God's goodness and love.

Whatever the motives of those who, even if done sincerely, created the legends, myths, and midrash about the Resurrection, what does this theory say, then, about the Gospel accounts regarding that same resurrection?

For instance, what about the account of Joseph and Nicodemus taking Jesus from the cross and putting Him in Joseph's tomb (John 19:38–40)? The answer? It never happened; it was a later concoction designed to promote someone's theological agenda.

The story of the angel coming down while the soldiers were guarding the tomb (Matthew 28:2)? A midrash created to promote the notion that God and heaven were behind the events.

The religious leaders bribing the guards to keep silent (verse 15)? A legend devised to make the Jews look bad.

Jesus meeting the women and saying to them, "Rejoice!" (verse 9)? Another story, this time to embellish the Resurrection fantasy and give it some "meat."

Jesus appearing to Mary (Mark 16:9)? A fabricated account designed to buttress the idea that He had been resurrected.

Peter and John running to the tomb and finding it empty (Luke 24:12; John 20:1–8)? More midrash, this time to help promote the empty-tomb idea, so crucial to the Resurrection narrative.

Christ's Bible study with the two disciples on the road to Emmaus? A later story made up by those who wanted to convince others that Christ's death and resurrection were predicted in the Old Testament.

In short, the accounts in the Gospels as well as in Acts that purported to show the resurrected Christ were merely embellishments designed to promote the Christian faith.

That's the theory anyway.

If the accounts of Christ's resurrection were either outright lies (the hoax theory), later embellishments (the hallucination theory), or legends, then why did none of them ever depict, in real time, the actual Resurrection itself? Instead, all we get is this, from Matthew: "And behold, there was a great earthquake; for an angel of the Lord descended from heaven, and came and rolled back the stone from the door, and sat on it. His countenance was like lightning, and his clothing as white as snow. And the guards shook for fear of him, and became like dead men" (Matthew 28:2–4).

Obviously, from the story line that followed, Christ had been resurrected during this time. This account, and this one alone, is all that was written in the Gospels about the actual resurrection of Jesus as it happened. But if the whole thing were a hoax or a later embellishment based on previous hallucinations, why did the disciples portray it like that? If everything else were fabrications or midrash or whatever, those conjuring up the Resurrection itself certainly could have, if making it all up, depicted the Resurrection in real time. If they fabricated everything else, why not specific Resurrection details too? If this invention were no more real than the others about the events after His resurrection—the resurrected Christ appearing to Mary, the other woman, the two disciples on the road, and other appearances—couldn't they have done a more graphic and explicit job in regard to the actual Resurrection event? If what Matthew wrote was a legend, a myth, all based on something as subjective as a hallucination, why not depict Jesus' resurrection as, for instance, something that all the disciples had actually seen take place?

Instead, the legend, the myth, that they created came with no description of His resurrection; that is, no description of His coming out of the tomb. Rather, all we get is the angel coming down, the guard collapsing, and then later, the angel telling the women who had come to the tomb afterward: "Do not be afraid, for I know that you seek Jesus who was crucified. He is not here; for He is risen, as He said. Come, see the place where the Lord lay. And go quickly and tell His disciples that He is risen from the dead, and indeed He is going before you into Galilee; there you will see Him. Behold, I have told you" (verses 5–7).

Another fatal flaw exists with this hallucination speculation—a flaw that parallels the hoax theory as well—and this has to do with how the "heroes" of the Resurrection narratives were portrayed in the very myths that they supposedly created about themselves.

Again, especially as Spong spun it, they hallucinated the Resurrection. It was wish fulfillment, mass hysteria, or PTSD. Whatever the actual psychological diagnoses, these dozens, even hundreds, of people had somehow convinced themselves that they had all actually seen the resurrected Jesus, numerous times, over many weeks, too, even though Christ's body was rotting away wherever He had been ignominiously dumped.

Then, over the years, the early church leaders—Peter, John, the others who shared his hallucination, and maybe even those who believed the Resurrection story based on those hallucinations—they all what? They began to make up events about what followed the Resurrection in order (one guesses) to create a new faith centered on their concocted idea of Jesus as the crucified and risen Messiah.

Even if one buys this painfully far-fetched spin, why would the legends that they made up, the embellishments, and the stories—none true, at least as depicted in the Gospels—portray the founders of the faith as lame and as faithless and unbelieving as depicted in the Gospels? If all of these unflattering renderings were a problem with hoax theories, which perhaps had to be made up pretty quickly to keep their lies going, according to hallucination theories, the church had years to create whatever stories and accounts that they wanted to.

And what did they come up with? Not a Robin Hood in Sherwood Forest, who robs the rich and gives to the poor; not the warrior Beowulf, who slays the monster Grendel; not an Odysseus, the hero of the Trojan War, who did many amazing feats. Instead, in the Gospels—in these supposed tales, the legends, and the midrash—we get stories like Nicodemus and Joseph attending to the body of Jesus while those of Christ's inner circle are nowhere to be seen (John 19:38–42).

As with the hoax theory, numerous other accounts after the Resurrection make no sense as mere hallucinations that were then embellished into legends. This would include the appearance of Jesus in the room with the disciples, as depicted in Luke:

> Now as they said these things, Jesus Himself stood in the midst of them, and said to them, "Peace to you." But they were terrified and frightened, and supposed they had seen a spirit. And He said to them, "Why are you troubled? And why do doubts arise in your hearts? Behold My hands and My feet, that it is I Myself. Handle Me and see, for a spirit does not have flesh and bones as you see I have."
>
> When He had said this, He showed them His hands and His feet. But while they still did not believe for joy, and marveled, He said to them, "Have

you any food here?" So they gave Him a piece of a broiled fish and some honeycomb. And He took it and ate in their presence (Luke 24:36–43).

What are the options to explain this account—that is, if one accepts the hallucination theory? First, they hallucinated the whole story? We are to believe that a number of them in this room hallucinated the appearance of Jesus, who spoke with them all? He then told them, in their common hallucination, to feel His "flesh and bones," and He showed them, in their common hallucination, the scars on His hands and feet? And then, in their same hallucination, He ate fish and honeycomb before them?

Can anyone with a straight face accept that explanation for what was written here?

The other option is that, no, they didn't hallucinate that account per se, but rather, after they started hallucinating or having visions of the resurrected Jesus, then over the years, they created the legend about Him being resurrected, which included this story in Luke.

If so, why make up an account like the one here, in which they depict themselves as terrified and frightened and thought they were seeing an apparition or the like—an account in which "they still did not believe for joy"? Why make that up? Why make up Jesus rebuking them, "Why are you troubled? And why do doubts arise in your hearts?" (verse 38). Remember, this is all supposedly later legends, later midrash—myths that the followers of Jesus had created. But again, why create stories that portray themselves in such a skeptical light? It makes no sense, not as a myth.

On the other hand, if that's what really happened, and the Gospels are true renditions of what actually happened, these accounts, as unflattering as they are, make perfect sense.

Also, as legends, as midrash, these accounts of the resurrected Jesus teach almost nothing about the theology of the Cross, nothing about justification by faith, nothing about substitutionary atonement, and nothing about Christ's righteousness covering sinners, both Jews and Gentiles—all foundational teachings of the new faith that they started.

With the hoax theory, one might argue that the disciples had to conjure up something quickly to explain the death of their beloved Leader in order to salvage the movement, and so they just didn't have time to create a sophisticated theological basis for a hoax. But according to the hallucination theory, these legends, these myths, were created years, maybe even decades, after the events that they purported to depict. Why, as they evolved and embellished these stories, did they not come up with any explanation for the meaning of Christ's death as a substitution and atonement for the sins of all humanity, as so clearly expressed in Paul?

Instead, the Gospels, especially after the Resurrection stories, say almost nothing about the real significance not only of His death but also of His resurrection. Even the Gospel of John, the one deemed the most evangelistic in the sense of seeking to get people to believe in Jesus as the Messiah—"And truly Jesus did many other signs in the presence of His disciples, which are not written in this book; but these are written that you may believe that Jesus is the Christ, the Son of God, and that believing you may have life in His name" (John 20:30, 31)—said nothing about the theological meaning of Christ's resurrection, after depicting, numerous times, the resurrected Jesus. This is kind of strange for something so apologetic in nature as a whole.

Yes, Jesus died, but He was resurrected; yes, His followers were to tell the world about it; yes, "repentance and remission of sins should be preached in His name to all nations, beginning at Jerusalem" (Luke 24:47); yes, they should "go therefore and make disciples of all the nations, baptizing them in the name of the Father and of the Son and of the Holy Spirit" (Matthew 28:19); and yes, they should "go into all the world and preach the gospel to every creature. He who believes and is baptized will be saved; but he who does not believe will be condemned" (Mark 16:15).

But why do the disciples not say much of anything about *why* He died; *why* He was resurrected; *why* they must preach repentance, even to the Gentiles; *why* they should baptize; and why those who believe will be saved and those who don't will be condemned?

It's just rather strange that with all of those years, those decades, of preaching Jesus, of studying, of learning more to defend their mass hallucinations, they didn't come up with a more defined theology, especially because, according to this theory, it was all myths and legends anyway. Which meant, therefore, that they could have shaped the narrative and the explanations for the narrative in any way that they wanted.

In contrast, if one accepts the Bible as the Word of God and, ergo, the four Gospels as divine revelation, then their silence is better understood. The Lord simply wanted to use these men to tell the story, the narrative, of the birth, life, death, and resurrection of Jesus. Meanwhile, He later raised up Paul, who would provide most (but not all) of the theological explanation of what Christ's death and resurrection meant. In short, the Gospels told the story of Christ's death and resurrection; Paul (and others) explained their theological significance.

It's obvious that the hallucination theory doesn't explain, at least with any plausibility, why all of these people, perhaps hundreds, believed, in the first days after the death of Christ, that they had seen Jesus risen from the grave—a belief that many certainly took with them to their own graves.

Because both the hoax and hallucination schemes can't explain the disciples' belief, and if one rejects the possibility of Jesus being bodily resurrected, based on a philosophical bias, what, then, does explain why all of those people, hundreds even, believed that they had seen the resurrected Savior when, in fact, He was probably "dead as a boot"[40] in some unmarked and unknown grave, perhaps even, as John Dominic Crossan suggested, eaten by "scavenging animals"?

O ne should (or perhaps, not even bother to) deal with John Dominic Crossan's "revolutionary biography"[41] of Jesus, though nothing's revolutionary
about the book itself. Crossan's work is just another secular, materialistic interpretation of the New Testament, especially the Gospels and Paul's writings; it's
about as sensible as using a PET scan to interpret "The Star-Spangled Banner."
This self-proclaimed "revolutionary biography" all but makes Spong look plausible
(well, not really, but almost).

Using what he calls "three independent vectors"[42]—(1) cross-cultural anthro-
pology, (2) Greco-Roman and especially Jewish history, and (3) the textual or
literary vector—Crossan pretty much does what most higher critics like Spong
and Lüdemann do: choose what he deems in the Gospels as true (not much)
and what he considers as later myth or legend, created to promote a theological,
social, and/or political agenda.

For instance, according to the esteemed scholar, the account in Luke 2:1–7 of
Joseph taking Mary to Bethlehem, where she gave birth to Jesus, never happened.
"It is a little sad," he informs his readers, "to have to say so, because it has always
been such a captivating story, but the journey to and from Nazareth for census
and tax registration is a pure fiction, a creation of Luke's own imagination, providing a way of getting Jesus' parents to Bethlehem for his birth."[43]

Of the biblical accounts of Christ's birth and earliest years, what has Dr.
Crossan's "three independent vectors" approach yielded in terms of discerning the
truth about Jesus' early years? "Jesus was not born of a virgin, not born of David's
lineage, not born in Bethlehem, that there was no stable, no shepherds, no star,
no Magi, no massacre of the infants, and no flight into Egypt."[44]

Crossan's "revolutionary" insights don't end here, however. Another deals with
Christ's miraculous healing of the lepers, as in Mark, when, after Jesus had spoken
and touched the sick man, "the leprosy left him" (Mark 1:42). Coming up with
the nebulous distinction "between *curing a disease* and *healing an illness*,"[45] Crossan
claims that what really happened was not a miraculous cure but a social healing.
"Jesus heals him, in other words, by taking him into a community of the margin-
alized and disenfranchised—into, in fact, the Kingdom of God."[46]

Or here is this all-time classic of New Testament historiography. The account
of the young Jesus in the temple grounds, astonishing the elders with "His
understanding and answers" (Luke 2:47), or years later, when Jesus in the synagogue in Nazareth was quoting Isaiah (Luke 4:16–21)—both were mere "Lukan
propaganda."[47] How does Crossan know? He writes, "Since between 95 and 97
percent of the Jewish state was illiterate at the time of Jesus, it must be presumed
that Jesus also was illiterate."[48]

What is Crossan doing?

Suppose the Holocaust had occurred about two thousand years ago. Sources
would have been much more limited (to say the least) than we have today. Now

imagine someone unearthing a partial text from a biography of Hitler, written by German author Volker Ullrich, which read:

> On 23 December, the day of Klara Hitler's [Adolf's mother] funeral, the 18-year-old Hitler appeared in Bloch's office and declared, "I will be forever grateful to you, Doctor." And he did not forget his gratitude in his later years. In 1938, when he celebrated Austria's incorporation into the German Reich with a triumphant march into his "home city" of Linz, he is said to have asked: "Tell me, is good old Dr. Bloch still alive?" Alone among Linz's Jews, Bloch was put under the special protection of the Gestapo. In late 1940, he and his wife were able to flee to the United States via Portugal.[49]

Following Crossan's hermeneutic, one could argue, based on this text (remember, other sources are limited), that Hitler, depicted here as so kind to these Jews—"good old Dr. Bloch" and his wife—didn't know about the Holocaust or what was happening in it. The parallel here reveals, somewhat, Crossan's methodology, so insightful that it led him also to argue that Jesus was never buried in Joseph's tomb to begin with nor, of course, resurrected from it.

Based on his three-vector approach, Crossan concluded that Jesus' "burial by his friends was totally fictional and unhistorical. He was buried, if buried at all, by his enemies, and the necessarily shallow grave would have been easy prey for scavenging animals."[50] However, that truth was superseded by this legend instead: "Moreover, far from a hurried, indifferent, and shallow grave barely covered with stones from which the scavenging dogs would easily and swiftly unbury the body, there is now a rock tomb and a heavy rolling stone for closure and defense."[51]

And all of those people who claimed to have seen the resurrected Christ? Here Crossan gets vague, mumbling about trances and apparitions that did serve a purpose: to establish a power base in the early church. For him, many of these Gospel accounts were "not about Jesus' physical power over the world but about the apostles' spiritual power over the community."[52] He writes: "Those stories, then, are primarily interested not in trance and apparition but in power and authority."[53]

Power and authority over what? A despised, persecuted, and rejected fringe group facing persecution? *Oh, yes, let's create these stories so that we can be, as leaders, prime targets of the Sanhedrin and the Romans.* Crossan is reading later sensibilities and sentiments back onto these people, a no-no in the study of history. The early years after the death of Jesus were not the years of, for instance, Innocent III's pontificate (1198–1216), the height of papal power. Crossan's guess about the motives of people two thousand years ago is just that, a guess—a particularly bad one that reflects a methodological faux pas: retrodicting the motives and beliefs of one era onto those of another.

Meanwhile, Crossan's approach comes heavily laden with the problems that all but voided the other attempts to explain the Gospel accounts of Christ's resurrection. Why create a belief, based on apparitions and trances, that no one expected: a crucified and risen Messiah? Why make up legends and mythologies that caused not only themselves but those who believed their myths and legends to be persecuted, sometimes unto death? Why make themselves look so bad? Why no theological explanation in the Gospels about the meaning of the Resurrection? If all of this Resurrection stuff were later mythological concoctions, why does Acts have, within a few months of Christ's death, the Jewish believers preaching the resurrected Jesus? Was Luke lying? If so, we're, again, back at the issue of motives and all the other problems associated with the hoax theory.

Hence, the skeptic's conundrum remains: Why did so many people believe that they had seen, talked with, or even eaten with the resurrected Jesus when He had not been resurrected?

Because, maybe, He didn't really die?

1. Stephen Cave, *Immortality: The Quest to Live Forever and How It Drives Civilization* (New York: Skyhorse, 2017), 34.

2. Friedrich Hölderlin, *Hyperion and Selected Poems*, trans. Eric L. Santer (New York: Continuum, 1990), quoted in *The Peacock and the Buffalo: The Poetry of Nietzsche* (New York: Continuum Books, 2010), 34.

3. Alfred Döblin, *Berlin Alexanderplatz*, trans. Michael Hofmann (New York: New York Review Books, 2018), 202.

4. Gary R. Habermas, "Explaining Away Jesus' Resurrection: The Recent Revival of Hallucination Theories," *Christian Research Journal* 23, no. 4 (2001), http://www.garyhabermas.com/articles/crj_explainingaway/crj_explainingaway.htm.

5. Gary J. Whittenberger, "On Visions and Resurrections," *Skeptic*, February 1, 2012, https://www.skeptic.com/eskeptic/12-02-01/; emphasis in the original.

6. Gerd Lüdemann, *What Really Happened to Jesus*, trans. John Bowden (Louisville, KY: Westminster John Knox, 1995), 135.

7. Lüdemann, 135.

8. Gerd Lüdemann, *The Resurrection of Christ: A Historical Inquiry* (Amherst, NY: Prometheus Books, 2004), 29.

9. Lüdemann, *What Really Happened*, 17.

10. Lüdemann, 23.

11. Lüdemann, 24.

12. Lüdemann, *Resurrection of Christ*, 97.

13. Lüdemann, *What Really Happened*, 135.

14. Lüdemann, 52.

15. Lüdemann, 129.

16. Lüdemann, 129, 130.

17. Lüdemann, 130.

18. Lüdemann, 130.

19. Lüdemann, 130; emphasis in the original.

20. John Shelby Spong, "God Is Not a Christian, God Is Not a Jew . . . ," *Progressive Christianity*, October 28, 2016, https://progressivechristianity.org/resources/god-is-not-a-christian-god-is-not-a-jew/.

21. John Shelby Spong, *Resurrection: Myth or Reality? A Bishop's Search for the Origins of Christianity* (New York: HarperCollins, 1994).

22. Spong, 17, 18.

23. Spong, 20.
24. Spong, 21.
25. Spong, 73.
26. Spong, 233.
27. Spong, 239.
28. Spong, 248.
29. Spong, 237.
30. Spong, 254.
31. Spong, 255.
32. Spong, 255.
33. Spong, 257.
34. Spong, 257.
35. Pinchas Lapide, *The Resurrection of Jesus: A Jewish Perspective*, trans. Wilhelm C. Linss (Eugene, OR: Wipf and Stock, 1982), 125.
36. N. T. Wright, *The Resurrection of the Son of God*, Christian Origins and the Question of God, vol. 3 (Minneapolis, MN: Fortress Press, 2003), 700.
37. Gary R. Habermas and Michael R. Licona, *The Case for the Resurrection of Jesus* (Grand Rapids, MI: Kregel, 2004), 106.
38. Lapide, *Resurrection of Jesus*, 126.
39. Plato, *The Republic*, trans. Desmond Lee (New York: Penguin, 2003), 177.
40. Tom Robbins, *Another Roadside Attraction* (New York: Bantam Books, 2003), 249.
41. John Dominic Crossan, *Jesus: A Revolutionary Biography* (New York: HarperOne, 1994).
42. Crossan, xvi.
43. Crossan, 22.
44. Crossan, 30, 31.
45. Crossan, 91; emphasis in the original.
46. Crossan, 94.
47. Crossan, 29.
48. Crossan, 25.
49. Volker Ullrich, *Hitler: Ascent, 1889–1939*, trans. Jefferson Chase (New York: Alfred A. Knopf, 2016), 28.
50. Crossan, *Jesus*, 180.
51. Crossan, 176.
52. Crossan, 191.
53. Crossan, 190.

The Elvis Sighting Society

In a novel about World War I, Ernest Hemingway depicted a hospital scene where the main character, having just learned that his child died at birth, anticipated the death of the mother as well. "Now Catherine would die. That was what you did. You died. You did not know what it was about. You never had time to learn. They threw you in and told you the rules and the first time they caught you off base they killed you. Or they killed you gratuitously like Aymo. Or gave you the syphilis like Rinaldi. But they killed you in the end. You could count on that. Stay around and they would kill you."[1]

Writing about her father, William Styron (author of *Sophie's Choice*, among other books), Alexandra Styron depicted some of the celebrated writer's last days: "For the next hour he raved about his miserable past and his sins and the waste of his life. Everything was repeated over and over. 'I love you so much. And the other children. And your mother. You'll hate me for what I'm going to do to myself. My head is exploding. I can't stand the agony anymore. It's over now. Tell the others how much I love them. I've betrayed my life. All my books have been about suicide. What a miserable waste of life. I'm dying! I'm dying!' "[2]

Pontificated Thomas Ligotti about the human predicament: "This is the tragedy: Consciousness has forced us into the paradoxical position of striving to be unselfconscious of what we are—hunks of spoiling flesh on disintegrating bones."[3]

And finally, poet Albert Goldbarth mused about "when death's demoralizing shadow slinks out of its hole and puddles across our path on its way to some engagement."[4]

Most of us, we don't die well. We shouldn't. We're not all the stoic Socrates, who easily and calmly drank the hemlock.[5] We do not "go gentle into that good night"[6] because nothing's "good" about that night other than it ends the suffering here, at least for the dead. (Those remaining above ground, amid all of their other troubles, can now add mourning and grieving as well.) Our situation is pretty pathetic when the only hope we have for relief is to die.

Death, Scripture says, is an "enemy," but it says so in the context of the resurrection of Jesus: "For as in Adam all die, even so in Christ all shall be made alive. But each one in his own order: Christ the firstfruits, afterward those who are Christ's at His coming. Then comes the end, when He delivers the kingdom to God the Father, when He puts an end to all rule and all authority and power. For He must reign till He has put all enemies under His feet. The last enemy that will be destroyed is death" (1 Corinthians 15:22–26).

In Adam, we all die, but because of the resurrection of Jesus, we can have the hope of our own resurrection as well. Death—that which leads to the destruction of our bodies, which turns our lives, breath, emotions, loves, and memories into only desiccated chemicals and scattered molecules of almost nothingness—is the enemy to be destroyed.

We tend to think of death as the crème de la crème destroyer because, in a world where death beats out every living thing, death's triumph is all that we can comprehend and imagine. It's so dominant that many believe death itself was the process by which life was created and formed to begin with.* *Death as the means of creating life?* OK.

But what the Bible teaches is that, because of Christ's resurrection, death—this alien intruder that turns the body on itself until every cell wall crumbles and all that's within drains out and decays—this process itself will be destroyed. "The last enemy that will be destroyed is death" (verse 26). Or as John, one of the witnesses of the resurrected Christ, wrote: "And God will wipe away every tear from their eyes; there shall be no more death, nor sorrow, nor crying. There shall be no more pain, for the former things have passed away" (Revelation 21:4).

But again, this hope rests upon one thing: the resurrection of Jesus. A miracle. A supernatural act. Something that goes beyond what physics, chemistry, and biology allow. Big deal! Could not the God who created the stuff of physics, chemistry, and biology do a work that transcended them, or at least our present understanding of them? How shallow to think otherwise!

However, if one doesn't believe that God exists, or that if He did, He wouldn't raise Jesus, He couldn't raise Jesus, or He didn't raise Jesus, then why did so many people immediately believe that God did raise Jesus? After all, the hoax theory is itself kind of a hoax; the hallucination theory is, itself, closer to a hallucination than to a viable explanation of the facts.

What else, then, can explain this belief that He rose from the dead? The answer some give is that the question itself presupposes part of what it claims. Christ didn't rise from the dead because, according to the swoon theory, He never died to begin with.

---

* Basically, theistic evolution, if true, means that Christ came to redeem humanity from sin, death, and destruction—*the very means God used to create life to begin with?*

T he issue with the swoon theory isn't whether Jesus of Nazareth was crucified by the Romans around AD 31 in Jerusalem under the reign of Pontius
Pilate. As we have seen, most historians, even those whose philosophical biases
and presuppositions don't allow for any resurrection, concede the historicity of
Christ's death on the cross. John Dominic Crossan, not one to take much of the
New Testament seriously, admits it: "That he [Jesus] was crucified is as sure as
anything historical can ever be, since both Josephus and Tacitus, in texts to be seen
in the final chapter, agree with the Christian accounts on at least that basic fact."[7]

For swoon theorists, the issue is that Jesus, though crucified, hadn't died. That's
it. Period. What else "logically," "rationally," "scientifically" (that is, without
recourse to the supernatural) could explain all the sightings of Jesus after His
"death" other than that He hadn't died? Isn't this theory simpler, less ad hoc, and
less far-fetched and needful of all the accoutrements, assumptions, and leaps of
faith that both the hoax and hallucination schemes require?

In short, despite all that had happened to Him—the scourging, the beating,
carrying the cross, the crucifixion, the spear in His side—Jesus of Nazareth somehow survived, was buried, and then revived. This means that those who saw Him
afterward saw a Jesus not supernaturally resurrected from the dead but naturally
revived from unconsciousness.

One source depicted an eighteenth-century advocate of the theory as explaining the events like this:

> Jesus, by uttering a loud cry and immediately afterwards bowing his head,
> shows every appearance of a sudden death. The centurion has been bribed
> not to allow any of his bones to be broken. Then comes Joseph . . . of
> Arimathea, and removes the body to the cave of the Essenes, where he
> immediately commences measures of resuscitation. . . . In the cave the
> most strengthening nutriment was supplied to him. "Since the humours of
> the body were in a thoroughly healthy condition, his wounds healed very
> rapidly, and by the third day he was able to walk, in spite of the fact that
> the wounds made by the nails were still open."[8]

In short, though crucified, Christ survived and then went about making people
think that He had risen from death.

Of course, if the swoon theory were true, it certainly would not have been the
only time that someone, mistaken for dead, revived. The English phrase "saved
by the bell" (though originally a boxing term) has been attributed to the idea of
people, hundreds of years ago, who, afraid of being erroneously deemed dead,
had special coffins built with a cord attached to an above-ground bell. Awakening
in the ground, they could pull the string, ring the bell, and be saved.

And who hasn't heard of near-death experiences (NDEs) where those deemed clinically dead come back to life? Thousands of cases have been reported.* If this happens now, why not then, but with Jesus of Nazareth on the cross?

The claim that Jesus hadn't really died is the essence of the swoon theory. Jesus *swooned*; that is, He fell into a state of temporary unconsciousness from which He later recovered. That's the theory, and it has been used throughout history, even now, as a non-supernaturalistic way to explain why so many people believed that they had seen Jesus after His burial.

How well does it work?

---

* The most famous book on the subject is Raymond Moody's *Life After Life,* which appeared in 1975 and was a phenomenon. Since then, a whole field of study has opened up on the question of NDEs.

As with other attempts to explain the belief that Jesus rose from the dead, the swoon theory comes in various versions, even if all assume the same unproven premise.

Interestingly enough, though rejecting the most basic Christian theology of the cross, Islam has its own spin (or spins) on what happened there. In contrast to the naturalistic perspective, Islam's rejection is theological.* Jesus was a prophet, and though He didn't die on the cross, Allah later brought Jesus to heaven, and He, Jesus, will one day return to the earth.

The only place in the Koran where the death of Jesus is mentioned has been variously interpreted over the centuries. It reads, "But they did not kill him, nor crucify him, but so it was made to appear to them, and those who differ therein are full of doubts, with no (certain) knowledge, but only conjecture to follow, for certain they did not kill him."[9]

Despite myriad elucidations of this text, the basic idea in Islam is that Judas Iscariot, Simon Peter, or someone else died on the cross, even though everyone thought it was Jesus. Who this replacement was and how he got there have been speculated upon through the ages, but the essential belief is whoever it was and however he got there, he wasn't Jesus of Nazareth.

In more contemporary times, some Muslim scholars—accepting that the historical evidence of Christ's crucifixion cannot be seriously denied—have adopted the swoon hypothesis instead. One example states,

> In effect, Ally admits that Jesus was *put* on the cross, but that he did not *die* on the cross, and therefore the koranic and biblical accounts are, to some degree, in harmony. He goes on to support his contention, saying: "There is a subtext, which points to the fact that Jesus could not be verified to have died on the cross. He may very well have been taken down while still alive."
>
> Ally points out that Jesus wasn't on the cross for very long, whereas crucifixion normally took days to kill a man, noting Pilate's astonishment that Jesus was apparently dead before nightfall. In this respect, Ally subscribes to the "swoon" theory of the crucifixion: that Jesus passed out on the cross, but later revived.[10]

Meanwhile, Mirza Ghulam Ahmad, the founder of the Ahmadiyya Muslim

---

* Islam rejects the whole idea of substitutionary atonement, much less the substitution of a "holy man" like Jesus. And the idea of God Himself, the Creator, dying for the sins of others is denied. For Islam, sacrifices are meant simply to show human dominion over animals, nothing more. They have nothing to do with atonement for sin. In fact, in Islam, a person is saved by works. Basically, the idea is that you need more good works than bad works. That's it. The Koran says: "Then those whose balance (of good deeds) is heavy, they will be successful. But those whose balance is light, will be those who have lost their souls; in hell will they abide" (Surah 23:102, 103). Though Islam does talk about Allah's grace, that grace is nothing like the radical, legal declaration of grace found in Christianity.

movement, proposed that Jesus not only didn't die on the cross but also, after coming down from the cross and healing, traveled to India. One Ahmadiyya apologist for the swoon view, in a book called *Death on the Cross?* argued:

> The duration of crucifixion or the period of time for which Jesus remained on the Cross was not long enough to warrant his death on the Cross. Criminals generally took several days to die a lingering death on the cross on account of the loss of blood from the wounds on hands and feet, the physical pain and the pangs of hunger and thirst. The minimum time of death on the cross ranged between 24 and 28 hours, but in some cases it took several days to die on the cross. In such cases it became necessary to break the legs of the criminals so that death may be hastened and consummated.[11]

According to the author, Jesus had been a healthy thirty-three-year-old male who just should not have died so quickly, especially if His legs had not been broken. "Jesus retained his consciousness up to the ninth hour of the day and then he fell into a swoon or lost consciousness. This is what the New Testament writers call 'giving up the ghost.' . . . The 'swoon' was taken to be 'death' and 'death on the cross' means an accursed death."[12]

Though not a typical Muslim belief, the swoon theory nevertheless promotes the idea that, whatever happened to Jesus, He didn't die on the cross.

In 1965, a British scholar named Hugh J. Schonfield wrote a book called *The Passover Plot*,[13] which claims that, from a young age, Jesus of Nazareth believed Himself to be the promised Messiah. What might have first spurred this belief was the death of His father, Joseph, when Jesus was still young. Wrote Schonfield, "The intensity with which Jesus turned to God as the Father in Heaven is eloquent of how greatly he had loved and felt the loss of his earthly parent. Today it would probably be said that he had a father fixation. The unexpected death of Joseph when Jesus was still at a most impressionable age may well have been an important factor in convincing him of his messianic destiny."[14]

Over the years, the young Jesus studiously and fervently studied the Hebrew texts, especially Messianic ones. His Davidic lineage helped convince Him, even more, that He was the Messiah—a belief no doubt fanned by the Messianic fervor of His time.

Thus, not only did Jesus think that He was the Messiah but He also started an intricate plot that, He hoped, would get others to believe as well.

> His visualization of the role of the Messiah was highly theatrical, and he played out the part like an actor with careful timing and appreciation of what every act called for. His calculated moves, his symbolic actions such as the forty days in the wilderness and the choice of twelve apostles, his staging of the triumphal entry into Jerusalem and the Last Supper, all testify to his dramatic consciousness, as do many of his gestures and declamations. Only one who possessed such a consciousness could have conceived, contrived and carried out the Passover Plot so masterfully and so superbly. But the portrayal of the Messiah's tragedy, and the anticipation of the happy ending, was utterly sincere.[15]

Though deceitful and conniving, Jesus was doing it for a good reason, says Schonfield. He wanted to give His people hope, promise, and trust in God, and what better way than for them to believe that the Messiah had come, according to the prophecies?

With the help of a few fellow plotters and the most meticulous planning, Jesus managed to stage all the events leading up to His arrest, trial, and crucifixion, even finding a way to get Judas to betray Him—and at just the right time too. Jesus had it all plotted out: He would be crucified on Friday before the Sabbath so that He would be on the cross only for a few hours, at most, before being taken down.

"Calculating," wrote Schonfield, "that it would require some hours on Friday morning for the Council to obtain his condemnation by Pilate, which could not be withheld as the charge was treason against the emperor, and knowing that in accordance with custom he would not be left on the cross over the Sabbath, but would be taken down well before sunset when the Sabbath commenced, Jesus could roughly reckon that he would experience crucifixion for not much more than three or four hours, whereas normally the agonies of the crucified lasted for as many days."[16]

Jesus, meanwhile, had prearranged for someone to bring Him a drink to quench His thirst while He was on the cross, even though it was really a potion that, rendering Him unconscious, would make everyone else think Him dead. Another cohort, Joseph of Arimathea, would then get the body down as quickly as possible and take Him off somewhere so that He could be secretly nursed back to health and finally reappear as the risen Christ.

"He plotted and schemed with the utmost skill and resourcefulness," wrote Schonfield, "sometimes making secret arrangements, taking advantage of every circumstance conducive to the attainment of his objectives. It is difficult to credit that he had neglected to do anything about the supreme crisis of his career, when it was imperative that he should outwit the forces arrayed against him and wrest victory from the very jaws of death."[17]

No matter how much this calculating Christ "plotted and schemed," the best-laid plans can go awry. And though things were, so far, going astonishingly, even amazingly, well, some Roman soldier, not following the script, ruined it all by jabbing the crucified Christ with a sword. Then, according to Schonfield, Jesus was brought down, and Joseph and whoever else were in on the Passover plot did what they could to try to revive Him. "What seems probable is that in the darkness of Saturday night when Jesus was brought out of the tomb by those concerned in the plan he regained consciousness temporarily, but finally succumbed."[18] His body then was interred in some unknown location.

However, said Schonfield, the accounts of Jesus resurrected could, perhaps, be explained because, in the little time that Jesus had lived after the cross, He used "these precious minutes to beg his friends to deliver a message to his disciples,"[19] which was that He really did rise from the dead.

But what about those early sightings of Jesus? They were, Schonfield asserted, someone else, perhaps Joseph, whom people simply mistook for Jesus, having heard that He had been resurrected.

This is, essentially, the Passover plot.

It's hard to see why *The Passover Plot* was controversial because it's hard to see why anyone—even those who reject the existence of God, the supernatural, or the resurrection of Jesus—could have taken this book seriously. Most didn't. And for good reasons too.

According to this scenario, Jesus had somehow perfectly timed each event, including the exact day, Passover, and the time of the day, a few hours before the Sabbath, when He would be crucified. And though knowing that He would be scourged and beaten before being nailed to the cross, Jesus did it anyway—all in order to try to convince people that He was the Messiah, even though the Jews were expecting the Messiah to reign as king, not to hang on a cross with a mocking sign, "JESUS OF NAZARETH, THE KING OF THE JEWS" (John 19:19) over His head.

And then, despite the hiccup in the Passover plot—that is, Jesus dying—the scheme worked, probably way beyond where Jesus' wildest imagination would have taken Him. Hundreds of Jews believed early on that they had seen Him risen. And not only that, they believed that the risen Jesus was, contrary to all common belief, the Messiah. And soon, many Gentiles believed as well.

Hence, argues Schonfield, Christianity was founded upon a deception that, going radically awry, worked anyway.

Despite its farfetchedness, *The Passover Plot* is on to something. Everything has worked out, fastidiously so, not because of some clever religious fanatic but because of God's providence.

What's more likely: that Jesus contrived things beforehand so that His legs wouldn't be broken by the Romans (suppose the potion didn't work as well as He had hoped, and the guards had broken His legs)? Or that His legs were not broken because, centuries earlier, God had said of the Passover lamb that the Israelites should "not break any of its bones" (Exodus 12:46, ESV; see also Numbers 9:12), and thus Christ the Messiah, the true Passover Lamb, could not have any of His bones broken? "For indeed Christ, our Passover, was sacrificed for us" (1 Corinthians 5:7). Because it was a fulfillment of prophecy and not a slick con job, John could write, "For these things were done that the Scripture should be fulfilled, 'Not one of His bones shall be broken' " (John 19:36).

What's more likely: that Jesus had worked it out beforehand that the Roman guards would, as He was on the cross, divide some of His clothes and cast lots for others? "Then the soldiers, when they had crucified Jesus, took His garments and made four parts, to each soldier a part, and also the tunic. Now the tunic was without seam, woven from the top in one piece. They said therefore among themselves, 'Let us not tear it, but cast lots for it, whose it shall be' " (verses 23, 24). Or instead, the guards unwittingly fulfilled a Messianic prophecy that said: "They divide My garments among them, and for My clothing they cast lots" (Psalm 22:18)? And that's why Matthew would write:

Then they crucified Him, and divided His garments, casting lots, that it might be fulfilled which was spoken by the prophet:

"They divided My garments among them,
And for My clothing they cast lots" (Matthew 27:35; see also John 19:24).

Can anyone seriously think a mere mortal Jesus somehow planned, in advance, that they would do this with His clothes?

What is more likely: that among all the other things Jesus had amazingly managed to manipulate, He also worked out that He would be crucified with two thieves just so a prophecy of Isaiah—"And He was numbered with the transgressors" (Isaiah 53:12)—would *look* divinely fulfilled? Or instead, was it God's providence that those men were crucified with Him in another fulfillment of Messianic prophecy? Hence, Mark wrote, "So the Scripture was fulfilled which says, 'And He was numbered with the transgressors' " (Mark 15:28).

The plan of salvation had been put in place long before the first advent of Jesus. Paul wrote that we had been called to Christ, "not according to our works, but according to His own purpose and grace which was given to us in Christ Jesus before time began" (2 Timothy 1:9). *"Before time began"?* When "before time began" is anyone's guess (according to the latest rendition of the big bang theory, it would have been at least thirteen billion years ago). But the point is that everything that happened to Jesus—His life, death, and resurrection—was part of God's "everlasting covenant" (Hebrews 13:20). The plan of salvation was worked out through "the Lamb slain from the foundation of the world" (Revelation 13:8)—and not a deceptive plot designed to get people to believe that Jesus of Nazareth was the Messiah when, according to Schonfield, He wasn't.

Meanwhile, most swoon theorists manage to conjure up plenty of experts who claim it medically possible that Christ could have survived the cross. Those who reject the idea have plenty of their own experts who deny the possibility. However, even if Christ did survive the cross and interment in the tomb, one important factor seems to be ignored.

New Testament theology is unambiguous about the centrality of Christ's resurrection and what it means for our own. Regardless of the various views of what happens immediately to the faithful at death, for the New Testament, the Christian's final reward is completed with the resurrection of the dead at the end of time, which itself depends upon Christ's resurrection. As we have already seen, Paul was adamant in responding to the claim that there was no resurrection of the dead by tying it directly to Christ's, his point being that Christ's resurrection is the hope and foundation of our own.

And if Christ is not risen, then our preaching is empty and your faith is also empty. Yes, and we are found false witnesses of God, because we have testified of God that He raised up Christ, whom He did not raise up—if in fact the dead do not rise. For if the dead do not rise, then Christ is not risen. And if Christ is not risen, your faith is futile; you are still in your sins! Then also those who have fallen asleep in Christ have perished. If in this life only we have hope in Christ, we are of all men the most pitiable (1 Corinthians 15:14–19).

If Christ didn't rise, we don't either, which means that Paul's preaching is "empty," from the Greek word *kenos*, which means "vain, empty-handed, purposeless." He also said that if Christ has not risen, their faith was "futile," from the Greek word *mataios*, which means "futile, useless, vain, worthless." Thus, everything depended upon Christ's resurrection.

Paul, then, continues: "But now Christ is risen from the dead, and has become the firstfruits of those who have fallen asleep. For since by man came death, by Man also came the resurrection of the dead. For as in Adam all die, even so in Christ all shall be made alive. But each one in his own order: Christ the firstfruits, afterward those who are Christ's at His coming" (verses 20–23).

Christ was resurrected as the firstfruits* of the dead, of those who have "fallen asleep" in Christ; that is, they died as converted souls. And then, these same people, "who are Christ's," shall be resurrected when He returns. As Christ was raised from the dead, His followers will be too.

Swoon theorists say that, unfortunately for us, Christ had survived the cross and burial, which means that those who saw Him afterward mistakenly thought that He had been resurrected.

After all, it certainly would not be the first time that people have claimed to have seen alive someone who had supposedly died, would it? Take Elvis, for example. Many have claimed to have seen the "King" even after his tragic demise near the "throne."† The Elvis Sighting Society, dedicated to this idea, writes about its own origins: "When the number of Elvis sightings in and around the City of Ottawa became too great to ignore, Elvis enthusiasts—Earl McRae, Moe Atallah, and Ervin Budge, met over breakfast at the Newport Restaurant on April 1, 1989 and established The Elvis Sighting Society."[20] The society's website also claims: "The three knew, of course, that contrary to popular opinion (and petty details like police and coroners' reports) the King was very much alive. They were also aware that, thanks to strenuous workouts and a healthy diet, he looks more like the 'old Elvis' we first knew and loved."[21]

---

* Paul is referring to the Jewish practice of giving the first of their harvest as a dedication to the Lord. "Speak to the children of Israel, and say to them: 'When you come into the land which I give to you, and reap its harvest, then you shall bring a sheaf of the firstfruits of your harvest to the priest' " (Leviticus 23:10).

† Presley was found in his bathroom at Graceland.

How serious these people were, or are, is anyone's guess. But notice what they wrote: having worked out and having been on a healthy diet, "Elvis" looked pretty good, even after all of those years (he died in 1977).

Which directly leads to the fatal flaw in the swoon theory.

From the time of His arrest, Jesus of Nazareth faced intense physical abuse, starting with the beatings by the guards. "Then they spat in His face and beat Him; and others struck Him with the palms of their hands" (Matthew 26:67; see also Luke 22:63, 64). Next, He was scourged, which was an exceedingly violent process that shredded the victim's flesh. "So then Pilate took Jesus and scourged Him" (John 19:1; see also Mark 15:15; Matthew 27:26). He was beaten again by the guards (Matthew 27:29, 30). And what almost no scholars deny, Jesus was then crucified. "When they had twisted a crown of thorns, they put it on His head, and a reed in His right hand. And they bowed the knee before Him and mocked Him, saying, 'Hail, King of the Jews!' Then they spat on Him, and took the reed and struck Him on the head" (verses 29, 30). Nailed through His wrists and feet on a wooden cross, He remained there for hours. "Now it was about the sixth hour, and there was darkness over all the earth until the ninth hour. Then the sun was darkened, and the veil of the temple was torn in two. And when Jesus had cried out with a loud voice, He said, 'Father, "into Your hands I commit My spirit." ' Having said this, He breathed His last" (Luke 23:44–46). And just to be sure that He was dead, a Roman shoved a spear into His side. "But one of the soldiers pierced His side with a spear, and immediately blood and water came out" (John 19:34). Finally, He was taken down, wrapped in burial cloths, and placed inside a tomb. "When Joseph had taken the body, he wrapped it in a clean linen cloth, and laid it in his new tomb which he had hewn out of the rock; and he rolled a large stone against the door of the tomb, and departed" (Matthew 27:59, 60; see also Mark 15:46; Luke 23:53).

What do swoon theorists say happened next?

Managing (somehow) to escape the tomb, get past the guard, and appear before all of those people, Jesus convinced them that He had conquered death, not merely avoided it. But how? A Jesus who had survived the cross and then the tomb would have been severely wounded; He would have been bloodied, weak, and barely able to walk (if at all). He would have been a man in need of immediate medical attention.

And yet this was Jesus, the Prince of life, the Conqueror of the grave, whose resurrection is the firstfruits of all of His followers? When "the dead in Christ . . . rise" (1 Thessalonians 4:16), are they coming out of the tomb as messed up, or worse, as when they went in? Even Elvis Presley, according to the Elvis Sighting Society, appeared as good as he ever did: "He looks more like the 'old Elvis' we first knew and loved." But what would a Jesus who had managed to survive the cross look like?

Outside of the appearances in the upper room, when Jesus showed the disciples His scars—"When He had said this, He showed them His hands and His side" (John 20:20)—not one account of the resurrected Christ hints at Him being in the physical shape that He would have to have been in had He somehow merely survived. In every account of those first days and weeks, whether Jesus was with the women, with the travelers on the road to Emmaus, or in the upper room, nothing indicated that He was greatly wounded or suffering.

In the words of Gary Habermas and Michael Licona,

So even if Jesus got off of the cross while he was still alive, the disciples would not have been convinced that he had risen from the dead, since the sight of his body and his slow and careful movements would have clearly indicated that he was a horribly hurting man. Upon seeing a swooned Jesus who was limping, bleeding, pale, and stooped over in pain, Peter would not have responded, "Wow, I can't wait to have a resurrection body just like that!" Rather the disciples would have said, "Let's get you a doctor. You need help!"[22]

But that's not what happened, not even close. This is another reason why, however critics seek to explain the belief of all of these people that they had seen the resurrected Christ, the swoon theory doesn't cut it. They need to come up with something else instead.

They have.

1. Ernest Hemingway, *A Farewell to Arms* (New York: Scribner, 2012), 279, 280.
2. Alexandra Styron, *Reading My Father: A Memoir* (New York: Scribner, 2011), 223.
3. Thomas Ligotti, *The Conspiracy Against the Human Race* (New York: Penguin Books, 2018), 11.
4. Albert Goldbarth, "What We Were Like," in *Everyday People: Poems* (Minneapolis, MN: Graywolf Press, 2012), 178.
5. Plato, *Phaedo*, in *The Collected Dialogues*, ed. Edith Hamilton and Huntington Cairns, trans. Hugh Tredennick (Princeton, NJ: Princeton University Press, 1961), 40–99.
6. Dylan Thomas, "Do Not Go Gentle Into That Good Night," in *The Poems of Dylan Thomas* (New York: New Directions, 2003), 239.
7. John Dominic Crossan, *Jesus: A Revolutionary Biography* (San Francisco: HarperSanFrancisco, 1994), 145.
8. Dr. [Albert] Schweitzer, "The Swoon Theories," *Review of Religions*, June 15, 2010, https://www.reviewofreligions.org/2323/the-swoon-theories/.
9. *The Qur'an Translation*, trans. Abdullah Yusuf Ali (Elmhurst, NY: Tahrike Tarsile Qur'an, 2009), 72; see Surah 4:157.
10. Justin Brierley, "Islam's Apologist: Why I Believe What the Koran Says About Jesus," *Premier*, accessed August 24, 2020, https://www.premier.org.uk/Topics/Society/Religion/Islam-s-apologist-Why-I-believe-what-the-Koran-says-about-Jesus; emphasis in the original.
11. Maulana Abul-Ata Jalandhri, "V—Duration of Crucifixion," in *Death on the Cross?*, 2nd ed. (Amritsar, India: Printwell, 2004), https://www.alislam.org/book/death-on-cross/v-duration-of-crucifixion/.
12. Maulana Abul-Atta Jalandhri, "Death on the Cross," *Review of Religions*, April 12, 2010, https://www.reviewofreligions.org/2183/death-on-the-cross-2/.
13. Though first published in Great Britain in 1965, a fortieth anniversary edition was published in the United States in 2005 by the Disinformation Company in New York.
14. Hugh Schonfield, *The Passover Plot*, 40th anniversary ed. (New York: Disinformation, 2005), 59, 60.
15. Schonfield, 68.

16. Schonfield, 161.
17. Schonfield, 162.
18. Schonfield, 172.
19. Schonfield, 173.
20. "Viva Elvis!!" Elvis Sighting Society, accessed July 30, 2020, http://elvissightingsociety.org.
21. "Viva Elvis!!"
22. Gary R. Habermas and Michael R. Licona, *The Case for the Resurrection of Jesus* (Grand Rapids, MI: Kregel, 2004), 102, 103.

Twins and Aliens

*D*ave was a 1993 political comedy starring Kevin Kline and Sigourney Weaver in which the hero, Dave, a startling look-alike to the president of the United States, ends up surreptitiously taking over the job when the president suffers a stroke.[1] Critics raved, and even then-president Bill Clinton registered approval for the flick, which debuted at number one in its second week.

In short, *Dave* was a success, despite its absurdity. A look-alike to the president fools the president's wife (at least at first), Congress, his cabinet, the vice president, and everyone else into thinking he's president, enabling him to run the United States' federal government for months, and even getting bills passed, without being discovered?*

Funny plot? Yes. Plausible? Not even close.

This leads to another funny but implausible plot involving a twin who was able to fool everyone into thinking that he was someone else. Not the twin of the president of the United States but of someone much more consequential: Jesus the Messiah. Called the twin theory or the substitution theory, this view teaches the reason people believed that they saw the resurrected Christ was that Jesus, though Himself dying on the cross, had an identical twin who early Christians thought was Jesus risen from the dead. Hence, all the early sightings of Jesus could be rationally and logically explained without any recourse to the supernatural. Instead, it was a case of mistaken identity, that's all, because anyone can be fooled by an identical twin.†

In other words, when Mary saw Jesus right after His death, it was really His twin brother.

> Now when she had said this, she turned around and saw Jesus standing there, and did not know that it was Jesus. Jesus said to her, "Woman, why are you weeping? Whom are you seeking?"
>
> She, supposing Him to be the gardener, said to Him, "Sir, if You have carried Him away, tell me where You have laid Him, and I will take Him away."
>
> Jesus said to her, "Mary!"
>
> She turned and said to Him, "Rabboni!" (which is to say, Teacher) (John 20:14–16).

This was not a hallucination, a deception on the part of the disciples, or a revived Jesus. No, the person she saw, and whom she didn't recognize at first, was

---

* No spoiler alert here.

† About the time of this writing, I went to some friends' house for Thanksgiving. There I saw one of their daughters, Amber, whom I knew well but who had moved away. I went up to her, hugged her, and asked where her husband was. She then pointed to a man, standing nearby, whom I didn't recognize. I was confused. Then my wife told me this was Allison, Amber's twin, whom I had never met before. So, yes, people can be fooled by identical twins.

Jesus' twin brother. He looked and sounded so much like Jesus that she thought he was Jesus. Meanwhile, for whatever reason—maybe he liked all the adulation (on the other hand, considering that the leaders wanted Jesus dead, maybe being mistaken for Him would not be a good idea)—the brother decided to let people think that he was the resurrected Christ, even though, again, no one was expecting a resurrected Messiah.

And when Jesus miraculously appeared in the upper room, it was not the real Jesus but actually His twin. "Then, the same day at evening, being the first day of the week, when the doors were shut where the disciples were assembled, for fear of the Jews, Jesus came and stood in the midst, and said to them, 'Peace be with you.' When He had said this, He showed them His hands and His side. Then the disciples were glad when they saw the Lord" (verses 19, 20).

Jesus' twin fooled them, as well as Mary, though—besides the question of how he slipped into the shut room—how did the twin brother get the scars on his hands and on his side? Did he, as part of the deception, purposely injure himself so that people would think he really was Jesus, who had just been crucified? Then one could ask about how the wounds could have turned to scars in just a few days if he really hadn't been resurrected. Also, he must have not only looked like Jesus but also talked like Him and said things that sounded like Jesus because he had them all convinced that, yes, he was Jesus.

Then, too, how does one explain what John wrote, when after Thomas had finally seen Jesus (or his twin) and believed? "And truly Jesus did many other signs in the presence of His disciples, which are not written in this book; but these are written that you may believe that Jesus is the Christ, the Son of God, and that believing you may have life in His name" (verses 30, 31). Other signs in the presence of the disciples? Thus, Jesus' twin not only looked like Him but also was able to do miracles or signs, as did Jesus?

Most anyone could be fooled, at least at first, by a twin, but after a while, the disciples would have caught on, wouldn't they? After all, according to the book of Acts, the resurrected Jesus remained with them for almost six weeks. Talking about Jesus, Luke wrote that "He also presented Himself alive after His suffering by many infallible proofs, being seen by them during forty days and speaking of the things pertaining to the kingdom of God" (Acts 1:3). Forty days with them and no one caught on that this really wasn't Jesus but a twin? Or maybe that was because Jesus' twin was giving them "infallible proofs"?

Please, the twin theory makes *Dave* look plausible.

And what about the empty tomb? In order to pull off this charade, the twin would have had to slip past the guards by himself (unless he had some cohorts, though even then it would be difficult), move the rock, steal the body of Jesus, and then bury it where it would never be found.

Not impossible but seriously unlikely.

Also, how does one explain the following if one accepts the twin theory? "Now when He had spoken these things, while they watched, He was taken up, and a cloud received Him out of their sight. And while they looked steadfastly toward heaven as He went up, behold, two men stood by them in white apparel, who also said, 'Men of Galilee, why do you stand gazing up into heaven? This same Jesus, who was taken up from you into heaven, will so come in like manner as you saw Him go into heaven' " (verses 9–11).

One can't explain it with the twin theory, which means that either the theory is wrong or the author was lying. And if lying, we are back to the hoax theory and all the attendant problems with it.

Who was this twin anyway? Jesus did have brothers, at least four:

- "Is this not the carpenter's son? Is not His mother called Mary? And His brothers James, Joses, Simon, and Judas?" (Matthew 13:55).
- " 'Is this not the carpenter, the Son of Mary, and brother of James, Joses, Judas, and Simon? And are not His sisters here with us?' So they were offended at Him" (Mark 6:3).

However, considering the miraculous birth of Jesus (Luke 1:34, 35) and not a hint of twins in the manger either, none of these boys shared the lineage of both parents, which makes the idea of one looking so much like Him that he fooled all the close associates of Jesus seem ridiculous.

The twin theory, in short, is no more plausible than the other implausible theories conjured up to explain what cannot be denied: many people believed that they had encountered Jesus Christ risen from the grave.

J ust when you think arguments against the resurrection of Jesus can't get more far-fetched (The twin theory? Come on!) they do. In the era of such cinematic marvels as *The Giant Spider Invasion*, *Zombies of the Stratosphere*, and *Voyage to the Planet of Prehistoric Women*, it shouldn't be surprising that some have argued for an extraterrestrial element to the resurrection of Jesus. However, that notion is closer to the truth than any of the attempted naturalistic explanations for the belief in Christ's resurrection. "Now after the Sabbath, as the first day of the week began to dawn, Mary Magdalene and the other Mary came to see the tomb. And behold, there was a great earthquake; for an angel of the Lord descended from heaven, and came and rolled back the stone from the door, and sat on it. His countenance was like lightning, and his clothing as white as snow. And the guards shook for fear of him, and became like dead men" (Matthew 28:1–4).

Angel of the Lord? From heaven? It doesn't get more extraterrestrial than that.

Like all the others, the alien theory comes in variant shades and hues; it asserts that Jesus Himself was an alien, which explains the miracles from His birth to His resurrection. After all, who but an alien from a race advanced enough to get to the earth could have pulled off such things as turning water into wine, stilling the wind, and raising the dead?

According to an article in the United Kingdom's *Daily Express*, a Presbyterian minister named Dr. Barry Downing

argues the divine events depicted in the Bible are in fact evidence of extraterrestrial technologies that were interpreted by early humans.

In fact, Dr Downing even goes so far as to say Jesus Christ was actually an alien.[2]

As such, He had all sorts of powers, including the ability to resurrect Himself. "This alien power, Dr Downing believes, is also what Jesus used to resurrect himself after being crucified on the cross and his ascension from the Earth is argued to be a return to this home planet."[3]

In a book called *The Bible and Flying Saucers*, Downing pretty much attributes everything in the Bible to UFOs and aliens.[4] Others have floated a similar idea that Jesus was, perhaps, an extraterrestrial. "Whoever Jesus was, there can be no doubt that he was a most extraordinary, and possibly extraterrestrial being. How else can we explain the miracles he performed, the transfiguration, and eventually regeneration after being executed on the cross?"[5]

How else?

Unless a God exists who is not locked into and restricted by the natural laws He had created and now sustains.

However bizarre, even a tad wacky, the alien theory is in one way true. Like the angel descending to Christ's tomb, Jesus came from the Father in heaven—that is, from somewhere else in the cosmos or, perhaps, from a realm outside of the four-dimensional space-time that makes up the known (at least by us) universe. As Jesus said about Himself: "No one has ascended to heaven but He who came down from heaven, that is, the Son of Man who is in heaven" (John 3:13).

While the quixotic folks at SETI* aim their sensitive listening devices into the cosmos in search of a text or a tweet from intelligent life out there, Scripture is replete with the idea of not only intelligences existing in another part of the cosmos but also of their interest in, and even influence on, life here.

Paul, talking about powers in another part of the cosmos, writes that he was given grace to preach "to the intent that now the manifold wisdom of God might be made known by the church to the principalities and powers in the heavenly places" (Ephesians 3:10).

The book of Job states:

> Now there was a day when the sons of God came to present themselves before the LORD, and Satan also came among them. And the LORD said to Satan, "From where do you come?"
>
> So Satan answered the LORD and said, "From going to and fro on the earth, and from walking back and forth on it" (Job 1:6, 7).

Or as depicted in the Gospel of Luke: "And the angel answered and said to him, 'I am Gabriel, who stands in the presence of God, and was sent to speak to you and bring you these glad tidings' " (Luke 1:19).

And in the book of Revelation: "And war broke out in heaven: Michael and his angels fought with the dragon; and the dragon and his angels fought, but they did not prevail, nor was a place found for them in heaven any longer. So the great dragon was cast out, that serpent of old, called the Devil and Satan, who deceives the whole world; he was cast to the earth, and his angels were cast out with him" (Revelation 12:7–9).

Scripture is unequivocal not only about the existence of extraterrestrials but also about their interaction with us here. Some believe that the best way to understand the state of our world, including the origin and pervasiveness of evil, is in the context of these foreign (that is, foreign to Earth) powers.

One evangelical theologian, Gregory Boyd, wrote in *God at War*, "The warfare worldview thus presupposes the reality of relatively autonomous free creatures, human and angelic, who can and do act genuinely on their own, and who can and do sometimes go against God's will."[6]

---

* SETI is the acronym for the Search for Extraterrestrial Intelligence.

"In the New Testament," writes Greek Orthodox theologian David Bentley Hart, "our condition as fallen creatures is explicitly portrayed as a subjugation to the subsidiary and often mutinous authority of angelic and demonic 'powers,' which are not able to defeat God's transcendent and providential governance of all things, but which certainly are able to act against him within the limits of cosmic time."[7]

Theologian Michael Brown talks about a "cosmic conflict"[8] that involved not just angels but humans as well.

The only thing that the alien theory has in common with the biblical narrative is the inclusion of an intelligent and purposeful reality existing beyond the earth's crust. Given the vastness of the cosmos, to think that intelligent life exists only here, or that all reality can be explained by and is limited to what science and the "scientific method"* can potentially reveal, represents an unwarranted dogmatism for beings whose experiences are played out almost exclusively on something as small, limited, isolated, and contingent as the earth's crust.

---

* A great deal of debate exists among philosophers of science regarding the very idea of the scientific method. That is, little consensus exists about what exactly the scientific method is or, in fact, if there even is one.

With the exception of the cosmic element, the biblical narrative is radically different from the little green men and UFOs that permeate the alien theory, which, along with the twin theory, reveal how far some will go to try and explain what can't seem to be justifiably denied: many people believed that they had seen Jesus arisen from the tomb. That these views are wacky and far-fetched is precisely why their inclusion is so revealing. *Something* has to explain the belief in the risen Jesus, and if one rejects even the possibility that Jesus had been raised from death, and if one finds the hoax theory, the swoon theory, or the hallucination theory lacking, then what else is there?

So Jesus had a twin brother or was a space alien. Talk about divergent explanations! However divergent (one earthly, one cosmic), both views show a dogged determination to deny the biblical explanation for the sightings. Think about how powerful and convincing evidence for them must be for people to come up with ideas like Jesus had a twin brother or was a space alien, all in order to try to explain, without God and the supernatural, those sightings of the resurrected Jesus, or at least the belief by so many that they did see Him.

None of this should be surprising. Jesus warned us before His death that people would not believe and that His followers would face persecution for promoting it. "Then they will deliver you up to tribulation and kill you, and you will be hated by all nations for My name's sake" (Matthew 24:9). And central to their witness for His "name's sake" was Christ's resurrection.

Another time, working from what must have been a common myth, Jesus told a fictional story about two men—one an unnamed rich man "who was clothed in purple and fine linen and fared sumptuously every day" (Luke 16:19), and the other a beggar named Lazarus, "full of sores" (verse 20). Both died; first, the beggar, then the rich man. In torment in Hades, the rich man looked up and saw the beggar safely and happily ensconced in "Abraham's bosom" (verse 22), an image reflecting a rabbinic tradition that the faithful dead would rest by Abraham's side. The rest of the parable has the rich man begging Abraham to let Lazarus go back and warn his family: "Then he said, 'I beg you therefore, father, that you would send him to my father's house, for I have five brothers, that he may testify to them, lest they also come to this place of torment.' Abraham said to him, 'They have Moses and the prophets; let them hear them.' And he said, 'No, father Abraham; but if one goes to them from the dead, they will repent.' But he said to him, 'If they do not hear Moses and the prophets, neither will they be persuaded though one rise from the dead' " (verses 27–31).

Whatever spiritual truths can be mined from this tale, for our immediate purposes, the last verse is crucial. If they don't believe the Bible ("Moses and the prophets"); that is, if they don't believe what the Bible says about repentance, salvation, and their eternal destiny (the context of the parable), then even if someone were to return from the grave, which Jesus did, they still wouldn't believe. This rejection happened with many of the priests and leaders. Though

Jesus did "rise from the dead," they closed their hearts and minds to that truth, despite being some of the few people in history to hear eyewitness testimony to His actual resurrection.

It's the same today. How else to explain ideas like Jesus had a twin brother or that He was a space alien, if not as attempts to justify disbelief? The issue isn't so much rationality, logic, science—no matter the convenient excuses they seemingly provide—because nothing is irrational, illogical, or anti-scientific* about the idea that God, the Creator of nature and natural laws, occasionally works outside of nature and of those laws, as in the case of Christ's resurrection.

The issue, instead, is moral, personal, and subjective. It's based on that nagging itch that implies, if Jesus was resurrected, then God is real, which means that, yes, a transcendent moral code exists, and people are going to answer to this God for having violated it. To answer for that and for a host of other things that most would rather forget and hope have been obliterated into whatever metaphysical nonstate the past becomes.

However, all of these theories, from hoaxes to aliens, even if they had any plausibility, can't account for what many would argue is Scripture's most powerful and convincing testimony to the risen Christ.

Saul of Tarsus.

1. *Dave*, directed by Ivan Reitman (1993, Burbank, CA: Warner Bros. Pictures, 2010), DVD.
2. Tom Fish, "Easter 2019: Was Jesus Christ an Alien Prophet? SHOCK Theory Is 'Increasingly Likely,' " *Express*, April 21, 2019, https://www.express.co.uk/news/weird/1117007/easter-2019-was-jesus-christ-alien-prophet-conspiracy-theory-ufo-proof.
3. Fish, "Easter 2019."
4. Barry Downing, *The Bible and Flying Saucers* (New York: Avon, 1968).
5. Tom Slemen, "Was Jesus an . . . Extraterrestrial?" Biblioteca Pleyades, May 1999, https://www.bibliotecapleyades.net/biblianazar/esp_biblianazar_68.htm.
6. Gregory Boyd, *God at War: The Bible and Spiritual Conflict* (Downers Grove, IL: IVP Academic, 1997), 58. See also Ellen G. White, *The Great Controversy Between Christ and Satan* (Nampa, ID: Pacific Press®, 2005).
7. David Bentley Hart, *The Doors of the Sea: Where Was God in the Tsunami?* (Grand Rapids, MI: Eerdmans, 2005), 65.
8. Michael T. Brown, *Job: The Faith to Challenge God* (Peabody, MA: Hendrickson, 2019), 30.

* Science, we are told, doesn't deal with these things, so how could they be "anti-science" any more than the claim that George Washington lived in Mount Vernon could be anti-physics?

Saul of Tarsus

In 1994, well-respected cosmologist Frank Tipler published *The Physics of Immortality*,[1] which, he writes, is "a description of the Omega Point Theory, which is a testable physical theory for an omnipresent, omniscient, omnipotent God who will one day in the far future resurrect every single one of us to live forever in an abode which is in all essentials the Judeo-Christian Heaven."[2] How well Tipler proved his "Omega Point Theory" is debatable. Well, maybe not debatable; physicists excoriated the book, and one reviewer called it "a masterpiece of pseudoscience."[3]

In 2007, Dr. Tipler published a sequel (of sorts)—*The Physics of Christianity*[4]—which, as the title says, promotes his claims that physics can explain much of Christianity, from Jesus' miracles to the fulfillment of end-time prophecies. And even God Himself. "The Cosmological Singularity is the Judeo-Christian God,"[5] he writes in the introduction; the "Cosmological Singularity" is the infinitely hot and infinitely dense whatever-it-was that supposedly exploded at the big bang and out of which space, time, matter, and energy—at least the space, time, matter, and energy of *our* universe—emerged.

Voilà! Yahweh Himself, as Creator, reduced to modern physics.

In the book, Tipler also uses science to show, for instance, how Jesus walked on water:

> If Jesus had a mass of 178 pounds, or about 80.8 kilograms (I shall justify this mass shortly), then the force that must be exerted to support his weight against the force of gravity is $F = Mg = (80.8 \text{ kg})(9.80 \text{ m/sec}^2) = 792$ newtons. But the force is the momentum p carried away by the neutrinos per unit time, and for nearly massless particles, such as neutrinos, the momentum equals the energy divided by the speed of light. But if the energy of the neutrinos comes from the annihilation of matter, then this energy equals the mass of the matter annihilated times the speed of light squared ($E = mc^2$). Thus $p/t = (E/c)/t = (mc^2/c)/t = mc/t = Mg$. Thus, the amount of mass that must be annihilated per second, or m/t, must equal $Mg/c = (792$ Newtons)$/(3.00 \times 10^8 \text{ m/sec}) = 2.64$ milligrams per second. Thus, if the field responsible for converting matter into neutrinos extends a short distance into the water below Jesus' feet, and if this field is capable of directing all the neutrinos downward, Jesus would walk on water. Or ascend into the clouds after His Resurrection.[6]

This isn't a caricature, farce, nor satire. He's serious!

Jesus' resurrection, he says, can be explained by physics as well. Tipler writes about such things as baryon annihilation and electroweak tunneling, which "would convert all the matter in Jesus' body into neutrinos, which interact so weakly with matter that a person in a room with Jesus would see Jesus vanish."[7]

However, he then says that "reversing the process could carry out materialization apparently out of nothing. The Resurrection is then merely an example of the first dematerialization of Jesus' dead body, followed by the materialization of a living body."[8]

However well-meaning Tipler's intent, his book represents how powerful scientism is. *Scientism* is the idea—a philosophical (not a scientific) idea, wrong in every aspect—that "natural science does or soon will constitute the entire domain of truth."[9]

Yet it's a myth. (You think that ours is the only era that doesn't believe in myths? *But it's not myth*, you say, *it's true because it is science.* But that sentiment itself—that because it's science, it must be true—is the great myth of the modern age.) Thus, the "entire domain of truth" includes the resurrection of Jesus, which, as Tipler argues, comes down to physics. Once we understand the physics, even the resurrection of Jesus Christ becomes more believable.

Yet one doesn't need to understand baryon annihilation and electroweak tunneling to believe in the resurrection of Jesus. We have been given powerful reasons to believe, without the fanciful physics of a quixotic cosmologist. We have eyewitness testimony and multiple historical sources, and even these far-fetched and ad hoc attempts to deny it (Space aliens? Hallucinations? Jesus' twin brother?), which have had the opposite effect, help to make the resurrection of Christ the most plausible explanation for the events. After all, these are what these people have to come up with to try to explain it!

And we have even more evidence as well: the testimony and witness of Saul of Tarsus (a.k.a. the apostle Paul).

One of the ironies of truth (yes, truth can be ironic) is that the most explicitly detailed theological explanation in Scripture of the meaning of Christ's death and resurrection came from someone who wasn't there for any of it and didn't appear in Scripture until years after it all happened.

Saul of Tarsus wasn't among the original Twelve. He wasn't at the baptism of Jesus; he didn't hear the voice from heaven: "This is My beloved Son, in whom I am well pleased" (Matthew 3:17).

Saul was nowhere near when Jesus spoke the Beatitudes, when He healed the lepers, or when He raised Lazarus from the dead. Where was Saul when, in the upper room, "as they were eating, Jesus took bread, blessed and broke it, and gave it to them and said, 'Take, eat; this is My body' " (Mark 14:22)?

Saul was not in the Garden when Judas betrayed Jesus with a kiss. Saul was not there when Jesus was interrogated by Herod, Pilate, or the high priest. He didn't see the scourging, nor was he present when Jesus was mocked by the soldiers: "And having blindfolded Him, they struck Him on the face and asked Him, saying, 'Prophesy! Who is the one who struck You?' " (Luke 22:64).

Who knows where Saul of Tarsus was when Jesus was led to the cross and was crucified, crying out:

"Father, forgive them, for they do not know what they do."
And they divided His garments and cast lots (Luke 23:34).

Where was Saul when, after Jesus died, His body was taken down and put in Joseph's tomb? Where was Saul when Mary, having seen the empty tomb, ran and told the disciples about it? Where was Saul when, on Sunday morning, the women came to the empty tomb?

And when Jesus first emerged after His resurrection, to whom did He appear? Not to Saul of Tarsus, but to Mary, to a group of women, to the two travelers on the road to Emmaus, and to those in the shut room. "Then, the same day at evening, being the first day of the week, when the doors were shut where the disciples were assembled, for fear of the Jews, Jesus came and stood in the midst, and said to them, 'Peace be with you.' When He had said this, He showed them His hands and His side. Then the disciples were glad when they saw the Lord" (John 20:19, 20).

Saul of Tarsus, wherever he was, was not among them, and so he neither saw nor experienced any of these events.

Nor was Saul there when Jesus later appeared at the Sea of Galilee.

Jesus then came and took the bread and gave it to them, and likewise the fish.
This is now the third time Jesus showed Himself to His disciples after He was raised from the dead (John 21:13, 14).

And where was Saul of Tarsus during the final days of Christ's earthly ministry, when the resurrected Christ "presented Himself alive after His suffering by many infallible proofs, being seen by them during forty days and speaking of the things pertaining to the kingdom of God" (Acts 1:3)?

There's no record of Saul's presence during the outpouring of the Holy Spirit at Pentecost or when Peter stood up before the crowd and preached Jesus. And, certainly, Saul of Tarsus was not among those early Jews who, hearing the preaching of Peter, accepted Jesus and were baptized. "Then those who gladly received his word were baptized; and that day about three thousand souls were added to them" (Acts 2:41).

During all of these world-changing events, Saul of Tarsus, at least according to the biblical texts, was a nonperson—a no-show. He had nothing to do with any of the incidents regarding the birth, life, ministry, death, resurrection, and early post-resurrection appearances of Jesus of Nazareth. Nothing at all.

Instead, Saul of Tarsus's chronological debut in Scripture doesn't occur until a few years later, with the stoning of Stephen—the first recorded martyr in the church.

An early Jewish follower of Jesus, Stephen was besting his Jewish contemporaries over discussions of whether or not Jesus was the Messiah. "Then there arose some from what is called the Synagogue of the Freedmen (Cyrenians, Alexandrians, and those from Cilicia and Asia), disputing with Stephen. And they were not able to resist the wisdom and the Spirit by which he spoke" (Acts 6:9, 10). Unable to "resist the wisdom," his opponents—having convinced people to lie about him (as they had with Jesus)—did the next best thing: they had him arrested and brought before a tribunal where the charges against him were similar to what Jesus had been charged with. "This man does not cease to speak blasphemous words against this holy place and the law; for we have heard him say that this Jesus of Nazareth will destroy this place and change the customs which Moses delivered to us" (verses 13, 14).

Unlike Jesus before His accusers, Stephen then began a monologue recounting the history of the Hebrew people as revealed in Scripture. Starting with Abraham, he worked his way through: from Joseph going alone into Egypt to Moses with the whole Hebrew nation leaving it, their entrance into the Promised Land, and to King David and then King Solomon, who built the first temple.

Then, after quoting Isaiah about the transcendence and sovereignty of God, Stephen shifted gears abruptly. Something must have happened, not recorded, between him and the council because, instead of continuing the history (he never got to other major events, such as the Babylonian destruction of Jerusalem, the return from captivity, and the rebuilding of the temple), Stephen suddenly aimed his discourse directly at the tribunal: "You stiff-necked and uncircumcised in heart and ears! You always resist the Holy Spirit; as your fathers did, so do you. Which of the prophets did your fathers not persecute? And they killed those who foretold the coming of the Just One, of whom you now have become the betrayers and murderers, who have received the law by the direction of angels and have not kept it" (Acts 7:51–53).

In short, your fathers killed those who prophesized about the Messiah, but you—you killed the Messiah Himself!

It's hard to imagine a more direct attack, telling these people that instead of being the guardians of the truth that they had been entrusted with—"who have received the law by the direction of angels" (verse 53)—they, like their forefathers, had worked against it, even though nothing their ancestors had done compared to betraying and murdering Jesus.

"Cut to the heart" (verse 54)—that is, furious (perhaps with some unconscious guilt?)—they revealed that fury when "they gnashed at him with their teeth" (verse 54). Probably not helping matters was Stephen, who was then gazing upward toward heaven and proclaiming, "Look! I see the heavens opened and the Son of Man standing at the right hand of God!" (verse 56). *Claiming to see the Messiah in heaven next to the Father?* In a rage, the crowd "ran at him with one accord; and they cast him out of the city and stoned him" (verses 57, 58).

It was amid this outrageous fury and this expression of the antagonism and hatred against these early Jewish believers in Jesus—it is now, at this moment, when these leaders made "official" their rejection of Jesus—that Saul of Tarsus first appears.

In the movie *Tinker Tailor Soldier Spy*, two British secret agents during the Cold War were discussing their number one Soviet nemesis, code-named "Karla."[10] One agent told how, years earlier, British intelligence had confronted the man in India, long before he became the infamous "Karla," and though they had offered him a new life in the West, he refused, choosing to return to Russia, even though he probably would be executed. As both expressed amazement at his dedication, one of the Brits, George Smiley, said he knew then that Karla could be beaten. Why? Because "he was a fanatic," said Smiley. "And the fanatic is always concealing a secret doubt."

Could something similar have been happening with Saul of Tarsus, when he first appears, which is at the stoning of Stephen?

Having enraged the leaders, Stephen was taken out to be killed. "Then they cried out with a loud voice, stopped their ears, and ran at him with one accord; and they cast him out of the city and stoned him" (verses 57, 58). At this ugly juncture, Saul of Tarsus enters sacred history: "And the witnesses laid down their clothes at the feet of a young man named Saul" (verse 58).

Stoning someone to death is a bloody, dirty, and sweaty way to kill, the likely reason why they shed some of their garments, which they then placed at the feet of Saul, obviously complicit in the affair. Never named in the Gospels, Saul is named now, in the book of Acts, for the first time.

And as soon as he is named, the story resumes, with Stephen crying out, "Lord Jesus, receive my spirit" (verse 59). *Calling the crucified Galilean peasant "Lord"?* This was an in-your-face act of defiance; it was also an act of faith, revealing his certainty of who Jesus was. Then came the famous words: "Lord, do not charge them with this sin" (verse 60). Having a powerful connection with God, Stephen revealed that connection by how he related to humanity, even to those killing him.

How Saul was impacted by this powerful testimony, which he surely witnessed, Scripture doesn't say. But one can extrapolate.

The first text after Stephen died, though beginning in the next chapter, fits better with the previous chapter about the stoning of Stephen. It reads, "Now Saul was consenting to his death" (Acts 8:1). The Greek word *suneudokōn*, translated as "consenting," means "to be in approval of, to agree with." He was, no doubt, a willing participant. As Paul himself later described it to King Agrippa: "Many of the saints I shut up in prison, having received authority from the chief priests; and when they were put to death, I cast my vote against them. And I punished them often in every synagogue and compelled them to blaspheme; and being exceedingly enraged against them, I persecuted them even to foreign cities" (Acts 26:10, 11).

Yet what went through Saul's mind when he saw Stephen's face as "the face of an angel" (Acts 6:15)? What did Saul think as he listened to Stephen's faithful recounting of Jewish history? Or when he heard Stephen, facing death, declare with passion that he saw "the heavens opened and the Son of Man standing at the right hand of God!" (Acts 7:56)? Or when Stephen cried out, "Lord, do not charge them with this sin" (verse 60), what effect did this amazing witness have on Saul, who was a very spiritual man?

After all, Saul, "a Pharisee, the son of a Pharisee" (Acts 23:6), had been a passionate and faithful Jew, "zealous toward God" (Acts 22:3). This passion was manifestly revealed later through his tireless and selfless ministry after he came to understand who this God really was. Was not some of that sincerity and openness to truth there before his change of heart and conversion experience? Had not his conscience been pricked by what he saw these people, such as Stephen, endure for this Jesus?

Also, Saul had studied under the renowned and respected Pharisee Gamaliel (Acts 22:3), presented in Acts as a wise and prudent man, who had cautioned his fellow council members about reacting too harshly to the nascent movement of Jews proclaiming Jesus of Nazareth as the Messiah. After talking about some other men who had amassed followings that came to nothing, Gamaliel warned them: "And now I say to you, keep away from these men and let them alone; for if this plan or this work is of men, it will come to nothing; but if it is of God, you cannot overthrow it—lest you even be found to fight against God" (Acts 5:38). (Which, unfortunately, is what they would end up doing anyway.) Did Saul hear these words directly or hear about them later, if at all? We don't know, but we can assume that the wisdom of this teacher had impacted his brilliant student and must have, to some degree, influenced Saul's thinking about these followers of Jesus.

Whatever doubts Saul might have harbored, or perhaps, because of these doubts—and despite Gamaliel's caution (assuming he heard it, which he probably did)—Saul became a violent opponent of Jesus and His followers. "As for Saul, he made havoc of the church, entering every house, and dragging off men and women, committing them to prison" (Acts 8:3). He was depicted later as initiating action against them, having approached the high priest for authority to go to Damascus, and "if he found any who were of the Way, whether men or women, he might bring them bound to Jerusalem" (Acts 9:2). This hardly sounds like a man who was pushed to do what he didn't want to do. Later, Paul described himself as having "persecuted the church of God beyond measure and tried to destroy it" (Galatians 1:13; see also 1 Corinthians 15:9; Philippians 3:6).

It is in this context that Saul of Tarsus, a.k.a. the apostle Paul, enters biblical history.

Ａnd yet, what? This same Saul of Tarsus became a passionate believer not only in Jesus as the Messiah but also in Christ's resurrection from the dead. Saul, who at one point was "breathing threats and murder against the disciples of the Lord" (Acts 9:1), became the author, the prophet (for, surely, Paul was the major prophetic voice of the New Covenant), who wrote more of the New Testament than did any other of the founders of the faith. And, too, he became the chief exponent of the reality and significance of Christ's resurrection:

> For I delivered to you first of all that which I also received: that Christ died for our sins according to the Scriptures, and that He was buried, and that He rose again the third day according to the Scriptures. . . .
> . . . But if there is no resurrection of the dead, then Christ is not risen. And if Christ is not risen, then our preaching is empty and your faith is also empty. Yes, and we are found false witnesses of God, because we have testified of God that He raised up Christ, whom He did not raise up—if in fact the dead do not rise. For if the dead do not rise, then Christ is not risen. And if Christ is not risen, your faith is futile; you are still in your sins! (1 Corinthians 15:3, 4, 13–17).

> Therefore we were buried with Him through baptism into death, that just as Christ was raised from the dead by the glory of the Father, even so we also should walk in newness of life.
> For if we have been united together in the likeness of His death, certainly we also shall be in the likeness of His resurrection (Romans 6:4, 5).

And he preached Jesus—the risen Jesus—to the Jews:

> "And though they found no cause for death in Him, they asked Pilate that He should be put to death. Now when they had fulfilled all that was written concerning Him, they took Him down from the tree and laid Him in a tomb. But God raised Him from the dead. He was seen for many days by those who came up with Him from Galilee to Jerusalem, who are His witnesses to the people" (Acts 13:28–31).

Saul of Tarsus preached the resurrected Christ to the Gentiles as well.

> "Therefore, since we are the offspring of God, we ought not to think that the Divine Nature is like gold or silver or stone, something shaped by art and man's devising. Truly, these times of ignorance God overlooked, but now commands all men everywhere to repent, because He has appointed a day on which He will judge the world in righteousness by the Man whom

He has ordained. He has given assurance of this to all by raising Him from the dead" (Acts 17:29–31).

And to King Agrippa:

"Therefore, having obtained help from God, to this day I stand, witnessing both to small and great, saying no other things than those which the prophets and Moses said would come—that the Christ would suffer, that He would be the first to rise from the dead, and would proclaim light to the Jewish people and to the Gentiles" (Acts 26:22, 23).

How does one explain this radical change? Skeptics have a hard time defending, from natural means only, the transformation of Saul of Tarsus into the apostle Paul.

Also, as already stated, though all four Gospels emphasize the resurrection of Jesus, none give any explicit theological explanation of what it meant and the great hope that it offers. The disciples told only about His rising and appearing to them but little about just how important it was to the promise of eternal life—a strange omission had they been making it all up in order to start a new religion or save face.

It's not Peter, who had seen the resurrected Jesus numerous times right after it happened; nor John, who also had seen the resurrected Jesus numerous times in those early days; nor any of the other eyewitnesses to the resurrected Christ, who ended up giving the world the deepest and most explicit theological explanation about Christ's resurrection. Instead, it was a man who not only had not been present during the Resurrection saga but who, by his own admission, thought it a heretical lie. And yet, Paul's absence at these events and his initial rejection of them all serve to make his witness and testimony that much more difficult to refute.

What happened to Saul, and how does his experience provide powerful evidence for the resurrection of Jesus?

Central to Paul's life and ministry was his claim to have seen the resurrected Christ, who had appeared to him on the road to Damascus. As he himself explained it years later, he was on his way, "with authority and commission from the chief priests" (verse 12), to arrest believers in Jesus who were, at that time, already in Damascus, indicative of how fast the early church was growing and the fear that it must have created in religious leaders such as Saul, who was walking from Jerusalem to Damascus in order to fight against these believers. According to his own account, about noon, "suddenly a great light from heaven shone around me. And I fell to the ground and heard a voice saying to me, 'Saul, Saul, why are you persecuting Me?' So I answered, 'Who are You, Lord?' And He said to me, 'I am Jesus of Nazareth, whom you are persecuting' " (Acts 22:6–8).

For years, this man had been persecuting those who believed in Jesus, even unto death in some cases. His antagonism to the church was so well known that, after his conversion, when he went to Jerusalem to meet with the disciples, they didn't trust him at first. "But they were all afraid of him, and did not believe that he was a disciple" (Acts 9:26).

Yet what happened to Saul the persecutor after he met Christ on the road to Damascus? He instantly replied, "What shall I do, Lord?" (Acts 22:10).

There was no *Wait a minute, you cannot be the Messiah because the Messiah is not crucified and risen.*

Nor, *Whoa, I must be delirious because Jesus of Nazareth was a false prophet leading people astray, so how can He be the one before me?*

Nor, *How do I know you are who you say you are?*

Instead, once Jesus identified Himself to Saul (again, as far as we know, Saul had never seen Jesus before), Saul didn't question His identity. It's as if—just below the anger, zeal, and violence—there were secret doubts that came to the surface at that moment, and Saul came to believe, instantly, spontaneously, that this Jesus was the Messiah, which was why someone like Stephen, "his face as the face of an angel" (Acts 6:15), could die so full of faith.

Instead of questioning Jesus, arguing with Him, or denying Him, Saul instantly submitted to Him as to God Himself. "What shall I do, Lord?" Those are the words of a man who now believed that the Person before him in the blinding light, Jesus of Nazareth, was the Messiah.

And though Saul had been "trembling and astonished" (Acts 9:6) at the appearance of Christ, and though Jesus first confronted Saul as a persecutor— "Saul, Saul, why are you persecuting Me?" (Acts 22:7) and "I am Jesus of Nazareth, whom you are persecuting" (verse 8)—Christ's presence must not have been threatening but loving and accepting, which Saul sensed. Even amid the drama, the intensity of the moment, and the accusation against Saul, Christ's love—the same love that had manifested itself to His flawed and, at times, faithless disciples—must have been made manifest to Saul, His persecutor, who instantly submitted to and surrendered before it.

Then Saul, blinded by the light, was led by the hand to the house of someone named Judas, where Saul did not eat or drink for three days. Three days with no food and no drink (and blind to boot), Saul had plenty of time to ponder all that had come before, including his role in the stoning of Stephen.

Next, a disciple named Ananias was told by the Lord to go to Saul of Tarsus, who "in a vision . . . has seen a man named Ananias coming in and putting his hand on him, so that he might receive his sight" (Acts 9:12). Ananias's reaction gives more evidence about Saul's well-known antipathy. "Lord, I have heard from many about this man, how much harm he has done to Your saints in Jerusalem. And here he has authority from the chief priests to bind all who call on Your name" (verses 13, 14). Nevertheless, Ananias, at the Lord's beckoning, does what he is told: he sets hands on Saul, who receives back his sight, then gets up, and even before eating, he is baptized.

Then what?

Immediately he preached the Christ in the synagogues, that He is the Son of God.

Then all who heard were amazed, and said, "Is this not he who destroyed those who called on this name in Jerusalem, and has come here for that purpose, so that he might bring them bound to the chief priests?" (verses 20, 21).

Yes, it was "he who destroyed those who called on" the name of Jesus. Only now, instead of attacking those who called on the name of Jesus, Saul of Tarsus, also known as Paul, proclaimed "the name of Jesus" as the crucified and risen Christ, and he did so for the rest of his life until that proclamation cost him his life.

However dramatic, these events are not hard to explain if you believe in a God who can perform miracles. The risen Christ, who had appeared years earlier to all of those others, now—in a different manner (amid a blinding light)—appeared to Saul, just as the New Testament teaches.

The New Testament has provided the only "official" depiction of Saul of Tarsus, first as a persecutor of Christians and then as one of the greatest promoters of Christianity. There are two main sources in it: the book of Acts, by Luke, and then the letters of Saul (Paul) himself.

Saul appears in Acts 8 like this: "As for Saul, he made havoc of the church, entering every house, and dragging off men and women, committing them to prison" (verse 3). By Acts 9, Saul "preached the Christ in the synagogues, that He is the Son of God" (verse 20). And before Acts 9 is over, instead of Saul seeking to kill or imprison Jews who believed in Jesus, some Jews were seeking to kill Saul for believing in Jesus: "And he spoke boldly in the name of the Lord Jesus and disputed against the Hellenists, but they attempted to kill him" (verse 29).

Paul's letters also make mention of his persecution of the church: "For I am the least of the apostles, who am not worthy to be called an apostle, because I persecuted the church of God" (1 Corinthians 15:9).* In Acts 22, he is depicted as describing his actions: "I persecuted this Way to the death, binding and delivering into prisons both men and women, as also the high priest bears me witness, and all the council of the elders, from whom I also received letters to the brethren, and went to Damascus to bring in chains even those who were there to Jerusalem to be punished" (verses 4, 5).

Few serious historians doubt the existence of a Saul of Tarsus, a fervent opponent of the early church, who became the apostle Paul. Opponents of the Resurrection will admit, they have to, that there was a Saul of Tarsus who claimed that the resurrected Christ had appeared to him, just as they have to admit that the early disciples thought the same thing. If, however, the risen Christ could not have appeared to him on the road to Damascus because there was no risen Christ to appear to anyone (dead people don't come back to life), then how does one explain the extraordinary phenomenon of Saul of Tarsus, someone who had persecuted those who believed in Jesus, suddenly becoming persecuted for believing in Jesus? The one who hated the church becoming the greatest church planter? The one who had taught that belief in Jesus was a heresy becoming the greatest promoter of faith in Jesus?

If one doesn't believe that Christ appeared to Saul, then what happened to him instead?

---

* He also wrote that he was "circumcised the eighth day, of the stock of Israel, of the tribe of Benjamin, a Hebrew of the Hebrews; concerning the law, a Pharisee; concerning zeal, persecuting the church; concerning the righteousness which is in the law, blameless" (Philippians 3:5, 6).

To begin, there's the conspiracy theory, only now, instead of applying it to the Gospels—a move that came with numerous problems—it has to be applied to the conversion and ministry of Saul as well. In other words, the whole thing was a lie, well meaning perhaps, but a lie, deliberate and calculated, nonetheless.

Because we have limited sources for Saul's conversion experience and because these are explicit about what happened, they would have to be outright deceptions then. If Luke, for instance, had made up the narrative about Paul, why trust him on anything in the book of Acts, which means that his biblical account of the early Christian church could be nothing but fables. From the outpouring of the Holy Spirit at Pentecost to the conversion of Saul to his missionary journeys, none of it could be trusted as accurate, or perhaps even having occurred.

Much in the book of Acts deals with the ministry of Paul, which began with his conversion. But if that account—that is, the appearance of the resurrected Jesus to Saul (Paul) on the road to Damascus, the event upon which all else about Paul rested—were false, a lie, then probably everything else he wrote about Paul could be as well.

The first question, however, would be the same one regarding the Gospels: What personal advantage did anyone have following Jesus in an environment that opposed Christians, openly and violently? Whoever Luke was, as a follower of Jesus, he would have faced the same threat of persecution that so many others did, maybe even more because he was a person of influence in the church (after all, he wrote what came to be two books of the New Testament). He was also, it appears, someone who worked with Paul, even during Paul's jail time, and thus could have easily faced similar persecution.* So why endure whatever persecution he faced, or even the potential of persecution, for what he knew was a lie—a lie that he himself helped fabricate about the conversion of Saul?

Regardless of how one explains the rise of the early Christian church—whether the supernatural actions of God, which included the resurrection of Jesus, or the result of machinations conceived by liars and charlatans—no one denies the fervent opposition that the church faced.

Roman historian Tacitus gives one example of what Christians suffered for their faith. His account tells about Nero, who had, perhaps (historians still debate it), started a fire in Rome in order to facilitate his own building ambitions. Needing someone to blame for the conflagration, he found them in the followers of a small religious sect, arising from the hated Judea, called Christians.

---

* Paul mentions Luke three times (Colossians 4:14; 2 Timothy 4:11; Philemon 24), giving the idea that he was with Paul in his labors and travels. "Only Luke is with me. Get Mark and bring him with you, for he is useful to me for ministry" (2 Timothy 4:11). And what Paul wrote in Philemon: "As do Mark, Aristarchus, Demas, Luke, my fellow laborers" (Philemon 24). Two of these three letters are known as Paul's "prison letters," which implies Luke's association with him during his imprisonment.

Consequently, to get rid of the report [that he had caused it], Nero fastened the guilt and inflicted the most exquisite tortures on a class hated for their abominations, called Christians by the populace. Christus, from whom the name had its origin, suffered the extreme penalty during the reign of Tiberius at the hands of one of our procurators, Pontius Pilatus, and a most mischievous superstition, thus checked for the moment, again broke out not only in Judea, the first source of the evil, but even in Rome, where all things hideous and shameful from every part of the world find their centre and become popular. Accordingly, an arrest was first made of all who pleaded guilty; then, upon their information, an immense multitude was convicted, not so much of the crime of firing the city, as of hatred against mankind. Mockery of every sort was added to their deaths. Covered with the skins of beasts, they were torn by dogs and perished, or were nailed to crosses, or were doomed to the flames and burnt, to serve as a nightly illumination, when daylight had expired.

Nero offered his gardens for the spectacle, and was exhibiting a show in the circus, while he mingled with the people in the dress of a charioteer or stood aloft on a car. Hence, even for criminals who deserved extreme and exemplary punishment, there arose a feeling of compassion; for it was not, as it seemed, for the public good, but to glut one man's cruelty, that they were being destroyed.[11]

Nero's reign ended with his death in AD 68, which means that some eyewitnesses to Jesus Himself or to the events in Acts could have easily been among those tortured and killed, if not in this specific massacre but in others.

We don't know what happened, ultimately, to Luke. But why spread something about Saul of Tarsus—that he became a believer in Jesus—that he knew was a lie and that, even if it didn't directly lead to his own persecution or death, certainly helped lead to the persecution and death of other adherents to what Tacitus, probably reflecting common Roman thought, deemed a "mischievous superstition" composed of people known for their "hatred against mankind"? And look at what they suffered, too, for their belief in Luke's lies: "Covered with the skins of beasts, they were torn by dogs and perished, or were nailed to crosses, or were doomed to the flames and burnt, to serve as a nightly illumination."[12]

All of this suffering for lies that Luke promoted about Saul, knowing that they were lies?

Again, imagine Mary Shelley not only facing persecution for promoting the historicity of Frankenstein's monster but letting others—those who believed her story—suffer and die as well for what she knew was a lie? The conspiracy theory claims just that for Luke: he fabricated the story (among others) of Christ's appearance to Saul, and then he let many people suffer and die for their beliefs in this fabrication.

The argument that Luke was part of some conspiracy to get people to believe in Jesus' resurrection by lying about Saul's conversion crosses into the absurd, and gets even more so the further one looks.

After all, the apostle Paul himself would also have to be in on Luke's conspiracy. Otherwise, how could Luke concoct the persecutor-turned-apostle tale without the persecutor-turned-apostle's consent, even complicity? Sooner or later, people would catch on that the stories Luke was spreading about Saul as a believer were not true if Saul were not a believer. That is, unless Saul were in on the lies as well.

Was Paul, then, faking his belief in Jesus as the crucified and risen Messiah? Hence, all that he had faced and experienced were part of a hoax—a conspiracy between him and Luke and also with Peter and James and all the other apostles whom he met in Jerusalem, who, themselves, had been perpetrating the Jesus hoax for years already?

Then, too, what about all the letters Paul wrote in the New Testament—Romans, Corinthians, Galatians, Ephesians, Philippians, Colossians, Thessalonians, Timothy, Titus, and Philemon—which form, in many ways, the theological basis of the entire Christian faith? Were all of these outright lies by Paul as part of some grand conspiracy to get people to believe in Jesus and thus suffer wrath from the Romans?

Was Paul openly perpetrating a deception when he wrote such things as, "Christ died and rose and lived again, that He might be Lord of both the dead and the living" (Romans 14:9)? Or, "Let this mind be in you which was also in Christ Jesus, who, being in the form of God, did not consider it robbery to be equal with God, but made Himself of no reputation, taking the form of a bondservant, and coming in the likeness of men. And being found in appearance as a man, He humbled Himself and became obedient to the point of death, even the death of the cross" (Philippians 2:5–8)?

If it were a deception, then the one who wrote, "Whatever things are true, whatever things are noble, whatever things are just, whatever things are pure, whatever things are lovely, whatever things are of good report, if there is any virtue and if there is anything praiseworthy—meditate on these things" (Philippians 4:8) was simultaneously concocting stories that were false, ignoble, unjust, impure, of bad report, unvirtuous, and unpraiseworthy. If Paul's life and teachings were a deliberate scheme, then he would have to be one of the most deceitful con men in all history, even though he also (as seen above) penned some of history's most beautiful moral teachings.

Unless, of course, that was all part of the conspiracy? Perhaps, Paul, thinking of ways to keep the hoax going, thought something like this: *I will write all these uplifting and beautiful moral truths that will dupe people into believing that I am sincere. That is, who's going to believe that the person who writes, for instance, "Let no corrupt word proceed out of your mouth" (Ephesians 4:29), or "Let nothing be done through selfish ambition or conceit, but in lowliness of mind let each esteem others better than himself" (Philippians 2:3) is spreading the lie about the resurrected Christ? What a great way to dupe these fools!*

Not impossible but surely unlikely.

Also, as with the authors of the Gospels, what worldly advantage did Paul get from his belief in Jesus? This young Pharisee, apparently an up-and-coming star in the Jewish religion, became such an outcast that, at one point, a cabal of more than forty Jewish men had bound themselves under oath that they would "eat nothing until [they had] killed Paul" (Acts 23:14). This is the kind of animus and danger that Paul was willing to let himself face—all in order to get people to believe that Jesus was really the Messiah when Paul knew all along that Jesus wasn't the Messiah and that the belief in Jesus as the Messiah would lead to great suffering for himself and for those who believed what he said and wrote about Jesus as the Messiah?

What had Paul faced for his continued promotion of a story that he knew was a lie?

> From the Jews five times I received forty stripes minus one. Three times I was beaten with rods; once I was stoned; three times I was shipwrecked; a night and a day I have been in the deep; in journeys often, in perils of waters, in perils of robbers, in perils of my own countrymen, in perils of the Gentiles, in perils in the city, in perils in the wilderness, in perils in the sea, in perils among false brethren; in weariness and toil, in sleeplessness often, in hunger and thirst, in fastings often, in cold and nakedness—besides the other things, what comes upon me daily: my deep concern for all the churches (2 Corinthians 11:24–28).

That is, unless all of these events—the stripes, the beatings, the shipwrecks, the perils, all for Christ's sake—never happened to begin with. Rather, those accounts were lies promulgated by Luke, which again leads to the same question: Why? What did Luke gain by making up this account or any of the other things he wrote about Paul?

Or maybe Paul was lying, and Luke wrote down the lies? But why? If one could argue that, after the ignominious death of Jesus, the early believers and the disciples concocted the story to save face or even to save the Jesus movement itself—that's one thing (which doesn't particularly work). But that motivation to save the movement, even as improbable as it was for the disciples, can't be applied to Paul, who was nowhere to be seen during the ministry of Jesus and, even years after Christ's death, had been a fervent opponent of the movement. He didn't make this stuff up to try to save a movement that he had persecuted for years.

Whatever Paul's supposed motives for concocting the story of Christ's resurrection, fabricated first by Christ's early disciples, his motives were certainly not the same as theirs. They lied, for their own reasons; Paul lied, for his own reasons; then (if one accepts this theory), they eventually got together and must have said something like this: *Hey, since we are all promoting the same lie about the resurrected*

Christ and since it seems to be working so well, let's collude to keep it going.

Was that possible? Perhaps? But like the chances of an egg returning to a fully restored shell after it has been splattered on the floor, Paul lying about the whole thing, though possible, is—like the egg returning to its shell—ridiculous.

If, however, Paul hadn't lied about the resurrection of Jesus for the same reasons the first disciples lied about it—that is, to save the movement—then what other reasons might he have had to make up the story and then spend the rest of his life promoting it?

Maybe he wanted to be part of a despised and vilified cult, openly and violently opposed by the Roman authorities?

Maybe Paul decided that he didn't like being a rising star in the Jewish religion? As he himself had written, he had been "circumcised the eighth day, of the stock of Israel, of the tribe of Benjamin, a Hebrew of the Hebrews; concerning the law, a Pharisee; concerning zeal, persecuting the church; concerning the righteousness which is in the law, blameless" (Philippians 3:5, 6). But by joining himself with the followers of Jesus, he no longer had to worry about being a respected Pharisee. Thus, he made up the story of the risen Christ appearing to him as a way of getting out of his career path as an up-and-coming religious leader.

Or, maybe, Paul made up the Resurrection story because he liked being hated and vilified by his own people, who began to persecute him for his faith in Jesus. "Then Jews from Antioch and Iconium came there; and having persuaded the multitudes, they stoned Paul and dragged him out of the city, supposing him to be dead" (Acts 14:19). Or later, as we have already seen, when "some of the Jews banded together and bound themselves under an oath, saying that they would neither eat nor drink till they had killed Paul" (Acts 23:12).

Or, perhaps, sensing that this Jesus movement was the wave of the future, Paul made up the story of Christ's appearance to him so that he, too, could become part of the Jesus movement? After all, at one point, even many priests believed: "Then the word of God spread, and the number of the disciples multiplied greatly in Jerusalem, and a great many of the priests were obedient to the faith" (Acts 6:7). (Two problems, though. First, you didn't need to have witnessed the resurrected Christ in order to become a Christian. Second, during his life and for years afterward, the movement faced great opposition and, from a human standpoint at least, seemed destined to fail.)

Or he, too—along with such liars and deceivers as Peter, James, John, and others who claimed to have seen the resurrected Christ—was a sadist? They all kept on promoting what they knew was not true—that is, the resurrection of Jesus—because they enjoyed seeing people who believed their lies face jail, torture, and death?

Or Paul simply reveled in the struggle, maybe? The imprisonments, the beatings, the shipwrecks, the attacks, and the attempts on his life. He simply got a kick out of the trials and tribulations that he had faced after concocting the story of Christ appearing to him.

If none of these options seem valid explanations for the persecutor-turned-apostle phenomenon, then something has to explain it. But what?

The hallucination theory, what else? Saul was not lying about his belief in the resurrected Jesus. He truly thought that the risen Christ had appeared to him on the road to Damascus. However, because Christ could not have risen from the dead (unless God exists, which means that miracles can too), Saul of Tarsus must have suffered a psychological breakdown—some kind of psychosis (perhaps guilt induced over his persecution?)—that caused him to believe he had seen Jesus.

When applied to Saul, the hallucination theory doesn't require mass hallucinations either. No need to posit something as far-fetched, if not ludicrous, as hundreds of people having the same psychotic experience at once. Instead, it was just one man, usually how these things work anyway. However, this one man just happened to have a similar hallucination, the resurrected Jesus, as all these other people had experienced years earlier?

Really?

Unless the disciples had been lying all along? Which would mean that Saul, not knowing that they were lying, nevertheless had a hallucination that, as luck would have it, just happened to jibe with their lie. Then, later, he joined up with them, actually believing in the resurrected Jesus when the others knew it was a lie but said nothing to him. After all, what a stroke of good fortune to have such a firebrand like Paul, once an enemy who believed that they were liars, now suddenly on their side and sincerely promoting their lie! Thus, based on the lies of a handful of men and the psychotic event of one other man, Christianity was founded.

Either way, the idea of Saul having hallucinated the Damascus road experience is promulgated today as one non-supernatural explanation for his sudden conversion. Experts and nonexperts alike, across more than nineteen hundred years, have diagnosed Paul's experience on the road to Damascus as some sort of psychotic episode, brought about by any number of possible things: stress, guilt, anxiety, heat, too much Syrian wine, or whatever.

According to Jews for Judaism, a group designed to keep Jews from believing in Jesus, what happened to Saul was some kind of seizure, out of which he thought that he had seen the risen Christ. "In the midst of a seizure Paul hallucinated, believing that out of a blinding light he heard a voice which identified itself as that of Jesus (Acts 9:3–7, 22:6–9, 26:13–15)."[13]

Jack Kent wrote a book called *The Psychological Origins of the Resurrection Myth*,[14] which claims Paul's experience was all some kind of mental disorder. Writing about Kent's approach, historian Gary Habermas said that, according to Kent, Paul "experienced inward conflict and turbulence because he participated in the death of Stephen and because of his persecution of Christians. As a result, he underwent a 'conversion disorder,' a recognized psychiatric malady that accounts for his conversion on the road to Damascus, which included his stumbling and blindness in particular."[15]

Decades ago, Albert Schweitzer, rejecting many of the historical aspects of Jesus as depicted in the Gospels,[16] argued that Paul was a sick man who, on the road to Damascus, faced some kind of brain malady. "The most natural hypothesis," Schweitzer wrote, "is that Paul suffered from some kind of epileptiform attacks."[17]

The *Journal of Neurology, Neurosurgery, and Psychiatry* published a piece, "St Paul and Temporal Lobe Epilepsy,"[18] arguing that the explanations not only of Paul's experience on the road to Damascus but of his claims of other supernatural spiritual experiences could have been "manifestations of temporal lobe epilepsy" or of "complex partial seizures, some of which progressed to generalised convulsions."[19]

From this assumption, as opposed to anything supernatural, the article first analyzes what Paul wrote to the Corinthians: "I know a man in Christ who fourteen years ago—whether in the body I do not know, or whether out of the body I do not know, God knows—such a one was caught up to the third heaven. And I know such a man—whether in the body or out of the body I do not know" (2 Corinthians 12:2, 3).

Though Paul, of course, depicted it as a supernatural event, as one of "these surpassingly great revelations" (verse 7, NIV) that he claims to have been given, D. Landborough in the *Journal of Neurology, Neurosurgery, and Psychiatry*—working from the erroneous philosophical presupposition that only natural causes can explain natural events—said the account "bears a close resemblance to the psychic and perceptual experience of a temporal lobe seizure, albeit of spiritual significance for Paul."[20] In other words, Paul's vision wasn't from God above but from an epileptic seizure within.

The article then looks at his conversion and claim that the resurrected Christ had appeared to him. It compared them to supposedly similar epileptic phenomena as seen in other patients, including his temporary blindness, and concluded that with temporal lobe epilepsy (TLE) "as a hypothesis for the cause of his ecstatic visions it is suggested that his 'thorn in the flesh' was the occasional supervention of grand mal attacks, and that he may have had an attack of TLE on the road to Damascus, followed by post-ictal blindness."[21]

In short, though claiming to have seen the resurrected Christ, proclaiming this event as central to his faith, and promoting the Damascus road encounter for the rest of his life, Paul was, really, a victim of a mental disorder: temporal lobe epilepsy or some kind of post-traumatic stress disorder (PTSD). These, or any of dozens of other potential neurological problems, could have caused his hallucination. That's all his experience was, a hallucination, and all the theology and morality and teaching that forms so much of the New Testament canon was based on Paul's misunderstanding of what had happened to him. Having some kind of epileptic fit, Paul thought he had met God.

As one skeptic of the Resurrection wrote: "So, what happened to Paul on the

Damascus Road? The fact is that the data in the NT [New Testament] on this experience is so limited, that it's impossible to make any definitive conclusion. It could have been an illusion which led to auditory hallucinations, it could have been a seizure caused by TLE, or it could have been some other phenomena. In any case, a supernatural encounter with a risen Jesus is not required to understand Paul's radical conversion."[22]

Maybe not required, as in an absolute formal logical sense, but "a supernatural encounter" remains the most logical and the most, if not the *only*, plausible explanation for Paul's "radical conversion."

Why?

S cripture gives three specific depictions of Saul's conversion to Jesus. All occur in Acts. The simple question is, Do these depictions sound like hallucinations? First, here is Luke's depiction of the Damascus road experience.

> Then Saul, still breathing threats and murder against the disciples of the Lord, went to the high priest and asked letters from him to the synagogues of Damascus, so that if he found any who were of the Way, whether men or women, he might bring them bound to Jerusalem.
>
> As he journeyed he came near Damascus, and suddenly a light shone around him from heaven. Then he fell to the ground, and heard a voice saying to him, "Saul, Saul, why are you persecuting Me?"
>
> And he said, "Who are You, Lord?"
>
> Then the Lord said, "I am Jesus, whom you are persecuting. It is hard for you to kick against the goads."
>
> So he, trembling and astonished, said, "Lord, what do You want me to do?"
>
> Then the Lord said to him, "Arise and go into the city, and you will be told what you must do."
>
> And the men who journeyed with him stood speechless, hearing a voice but seeing no one. Then Saul arose from the ground, and when his eyes were opened he saw no one. But they led him by the hand and brought him into Damascus. And he was three days without sight, and neither ate nor drank (Acts 9:1–9).

What follows is Luke's recounting of Paul telling about the same event, this time before a mob intent on killing him. Paul began by talking about his training under Gamaliel and his own zealousness toward God, and then he included his journey to Damascus in order to persecute followers of Jesus.

> "Now it happened, as I journeyed and came near Damascus at about noon, suddenly a great light from heaven shone around me. And I fell to the ground and heard a voice saying to me, 'Saul, Saul, why are you persecuting Me?' So I answered, 'Who are You, Lord?' And He said to me, 'I am Jesus of Nazareth, whom you are persecuting.'
>
> "And those who were with me indeed saw the light and were afraid, but they did not hear the voice of Him who spoke to me. So I said, 'What shall I do, Lord?' And the Lord said to me, 'Arise and go into Damascus, and there you will be told all things which are appointed for you to do.' And since I could not see for the glory of that light, being led by the hand of those who were with me, I came into Damascus" (Acts 22:6–11).

And finally, here is Luke's depiction of Paul, again, telling what had happened
to him but now to King Agrippa. After giving Agrippa a bit of background
concerning his life, in which he claims to have been known for his piety and
strictness in the Jewish faith, he also told about his persecution of those who
followed Jesus. Then he goes into what happened on the road to Damascus.

"At midday, O king, along the road I saw a light from heaven, brighter than
the sun, shining around me and those who journeyed with me. And when
we all had fallen to the ground, I heard a voice speaking to me and saying
in the Hebrew language, 'Saul, Saul, why are you persecuting Me? It is hard
for you to kick against the goads.' So I said, 'Who are You, Lord?' And He
said, 'I am Jesus, whom you are persecuting. But rise and stand on your feet;
for I have appeared to you for this purpose, to make you a minister and a
witness both of the things which you have seen and of the things which I
will yet reveal to you. I will deliver you from the Jewish people, as well as
from the Gentiles, to whom I now send you, to open their eyes, in order
to turn them from darkness to light, and from the power of Satan to God,
that they may receive forgiveness of sins and an inheritance among those
who are sanctified by faith in Me' " (Acts 26:13–18).

How well, then, does the hallucination theory cut it regarding Saul's radical
change?

For starters, it would mean that, unlike Christ's early disciples who supposedly all hallucinated the resurrected Christ out of their own disappointment about His death, Paul would have hallucinated the resurrected Christ out of—what?

Disappointment over Christ's death as well?

Obviously not. Whatever caused Saul to hallucinate the risen Jesus, it was not what caused the disciples to have the same hallucinatory phenomenon. For reasons opposite from the disciples, Saul nevertheless had the same hallucination?

This argument reflects what philosopher of science Karl Popper warned about decades ago. Rejecting Marxism as science (which many claimed that it was), Popper said that it didn't matter what the theory was dealing with, A or -A, Marxism could be used to explain it. That is, the same theory could be used to explain opposite occurrences, which Popper saw as making it all suspect, at least as something that could be deemed science. "A Marxist could not open a newspaper without finding on every page confirming evidence for his interpretation of history; not only in the news, but also in its presentation—which revealed the class bias of the paper—and especially of course in what the paper did *not* say."[23]

Though not dealing with the exact situation here, we are supposed to believe that, for opposing reasons, both the passionate followers of Jesus and this man, the most rabid opponent of Jesus, had hallucinated the same thing: Jesus resurrected? That is, opposite causes brought the same effect? Though not impossible, that argument seems overtly ad hoc.

Though evidence exists that, yes, Saul had misgivings about what he had been doing,* to argue that these misgivings, suddenly and unexpectedly, manifested themselves with a life-changing hallucination—one that reverses the direction of his life—remains highly suspect.

---

* For example, Christ's very words to Saul, "It is hard for you to kick against the goads" (Acts 9:5), do seem to reveal that Saul was, in his actions, fighting against his conscience.

Also, how does one explain the outward physical events that were manifested during Saul's supposed hallucination? It's one thing if Saul himself, for whatever reasons (guilt, epilepsy, trauma, PTSD?) suffered from a sudden psychotic episode. It happens. But how does that move explain the physical phenomena that all three accounts depicted? All the people with Saul saw a light, all heard (if not all understood) a voice,* and at one point, all fell to the ground, afraid.

A hallucinating Paul doesn't work. (Unless, of course, they all were simultaneously suffering the same hallucination, which is what supposedly happened years earlier to the first disciples after the death of Jesus. In this case, Paul and those with him hallucinated the light and voice together, which caused them all to fall to the ground, though only Paul understood the auditory part of their common hallucination.)

Some, however, have sought to explain the physical phenomena experienced on the Damascus road as an astronomical occurrence—a meteorite. A paper in 2015 by William K. Hartmann, based on observations of recent meteorites ("the Chelyabinsk event, the Tunguska event"), speculated that a "fireball" meteorite, such as what happened in Russia in 2013, could explain almost everything that occurred on the road to Damascus: the light, the sound, their falling down, their fear, and Saul's blindness. William K. Hartmann wrote,

> The first-century book, *Acts of the Apostles*, gives three separate descriptions of a bright light "from heaven," which occurred probably in the 30s (C.E.) near Damascus, Syria. The details offer a strikingly good match to a Chelyabinsk-class or Tunguska-class fireball. Among the most impressive, unexpected consistencies with modern knowledge is the first-century description of symptoms of temporary blindness caused by exposure to intense radiation, matching a condition now known as photokeratitis. An analysis of the re-entry of debris from the Russian Zond IV over the eastern United States in 1968 shows how actual *perceived* phenomena in an unfamiliar natural celestial apparition are often *conceived* by the observer in terms of current cultural conceptions, and it is suggested that this happened also in the first-century case.[24]

The "first-century case" being, of course, Saul's conversion experience on the road to Damascus.

Commenting on Hartmann's theory, an article in *New Scientist* was headlined:

---

* At first glance, there seems to be a contradiction in the accounts, with one saying that the others around Saul heard the voice, and the other saying that they didn't hear the voice but saw the light. The Greek here can be helpful. In Acts 9:7, the word translated as "voice" (*tēs phōnēs*) is in the genitive case, meaning that they heard the sound but did not necessarily the content of what was said (cf. John 12:29). In Acts 22:9, "voice" is in the accusative case (*tēn . . . phōnēn*), making clear that they did not understand what was said to Paul. In short, all saw the light, heard a sound, and fell to the ground. But only Saul understood what the voice was saying.

"Falling Meteor May Have Changed the Course of Christianity." It went on: "The early evangelist Paul became a Christian because of a dazzling light on the road to Damascus, but one astronomer thinks it was an exploding meteor."[25]

For argument's sake, what would have had to have taken place if this theory were accepted? A meteorite drops from the sky ("a light shone around him from heaven") and crashes into the ground. The men see it, hear it, and perhaps, from shock waves or from fear of the fireball itself—all drop to the ground.

Then, suddenly, for some reason (perhaps caused by the trauma of a meteorite?), Saul of Tarsus starts hallucinating that someone began speaking to him, calling him by name and saying, "Saul, Saul, why are you persecuting Me?" And Saul, speaking back to the hallucination, asks who this was. And the hallucination responds, "I am Jesus, whom you are persecuting." Meanwhile, the others, though hearing the voice, don't understand it. How, though, could they have heard (even if not understand) a voice that Saul was only hallucinating?

According to Hartmann, these celestial events are conceived "in terms of current cultural conceptions"; that is, people see a meteorite or something like it, and they understand it in their own context. An ancient Greek might have conceived of the crashing fireball as a divine act of Helios, the sun god. An ancient Mesopotamian might have interpreted it as from Shamash, their sun god. A Muslim might have construed it as a sign from Allah.

If so, then why would Saul of Tarsus receive this event as a supernatural revelation of Jesus of Nazareth—someone whom he believed was an impostor and a fraud? Why not interpret it in line with what he already believed, that perhaps the angel Gabriel was speaking to him? In this case, however, we are supposed to believe that Saul had some kind of hallucination—brought on, perhaps, by the trauma of the fireball—about, of all things, Jesus of Nazareth? And then, suddenly, based on this illusion, Saul refers to Him as "Lord" and even submits to Him as well ("Lord, what do You want me to do?")? And this experience, a meteorite-induced psychotic event, with both auditory and visual manifestations, became the foundation, the basis, for his spending the rest of his life promoting Jesus as the crucified and risen Messiah?

In this context, the hallucination theory (even coupled with the meteorite theory) doesn't provide a viable explanation for what most everyone, even skeptics of the Resurrection, believe: that Saul of Tarsus, once an enemy of Jesus, became His greatest proponent based on the belief that Jesus had been raised from the dead and had appeared to him.

M eanwhile, how does one, adhering to the hallucination theory (along with the meteorite one as well), deal with the events immediately *following* Saul's Damascus road "temporal lobe seizure" or "grand mal" epileptic fit—or whatever neurological event is theorized, hypothesized, postulated, and diagnosed (from afar) in order to explain the change of Saul? According to Luke, about the time of Paul's "seizure," something happened to a disciple, a believer in Jesus, named Ananias who lived in Damascus, the place where Paul was going to arrest people like Ananias or, perhaps, even Ananias himself.

> Now there was a certain disciple at Damascus named Ananias; and to him the Lord said in a vision, "Ananias."
> And he said, "Here I am, Lord."
> So the Lord said to him, "Arise and go to the street called Straight, and inquire at the house of Judas for one called Saul of Tarsus, for behold, he is praying. And in a vision he has seen a man named Ananias coming in and putting his hand on him, so that he might receive his sight."
> Then Ananias answered, "Lord, I have heard from many about this man, how much harm he has done to Your saints in Jerusalem. And here he has authority from the chief priests to bind all who call on Your name."
> But the Lord said to him, "Go, for he is a chosen vessel of Mine to bear My name before Gentiles, kings, and the children of Israel. For I will show him how many things he must suffer for My name's sake" (Acts 9:10–16).

How does one, from the hallucination-theory standpoint, explain this? Hallucination theorists would have to argue that, about the same time that Paul had his seizure or hallucination, this man Ananias, miles away in Damascus, had, coincidentally enough, a seizure or hallucination as well. Even more coincidentally and astonishingly, Ananias's seizure or seizure-induced hallucination just happened to tell him about a man named Saul of Tarsus, who himself was hallucinating about a man named Ananias who was coming to restore his sight. In short, Paul hallucinates about Ananias, and Ananias hallucinates about Paul.

If the idea of different people, the early disciples, having the same hallucination was a bit too much to take seriously, then what about the idea that around the same time that Saul had hallucinated about "a man named Ananias" coming to him, a man named Ananias hallucinated that he should go to Saul?

However preposterous, how else do hallucination theorists explain what happened? Given the premise that miracles cannot occur, whatever did occur could not have been God actually giving Ananias a vision of the blind Saul, as both Luke and later Paul (as recorded by Luke) claimed. Instead, they must argue that both men had hallucinations that coincided with each other so well that their psychotic events brought the two men together on the street called Straight in Damascus. "And Ananias went his way and entered the house; and laying his hands on him he said, 'Brother Saul, the Lord Jesus, who appeared to you on the road as you came, has sent me that you may receive your sight and be filled with the Holy Spirit.' Immediately there fell from his eyes something like scales, and he received his sight at once; and he arose and was baptized" (verses 17, 18).

Ananias went to where his hallucination told him to go, and coincidentally and astonishingly enough, he finds at that specific place Saul of Tarsus—blind and waiting for him to restore his sight—just as Ananias and Saul both had hallucinated. Meanwhile, how did Ananias, in his hallucination, know what Saul had seen on the road—that is, Jesus appearing to him—especially if Saul only hallucinated Jesus to begin with? In short, Ananias hallucinated about Saul hallucinating about Jesus. And their hallucinations brought them together, and then, exactly as both hallucinated, Ananias healed Saul.

If this doesn't work, what other option then? That Luke was lying and that none of this happened—not Paul's experience on the road to Damascus, not Ananias coming to him, none of it? That move, though, brings us back to the conspiracy theory, which itself contains so many problems that few scholars, even atheists, take it seriously today. After all (and again), it would take, among other things, Paul and Luke conspiring together to promote a lie, perhaps first started by Peter, that not only endangered their lives but the lives of those who believed their lies. Though not as ludicrous as the above scenario, with Saul and Ananias each hallucinating about each other, it's still not a viable explanation for the life and ministry of Paul.

Remember, again, what this is all about. Skeptics of Christ's resurrection claim that it did not happen because, based on their philosophical presuppositions, it could not have happened. Or they don't want to believe that it happened because of the moral implications involved (judgment, obedience, the Ten Commandments, etc.). Unconsciously, perhaps, they camouflage their fear under the emotionless rules of deduction: miracles don't happen; the resurrection of Jesus was a miracle; ergo, Jesus was not resurrected. The logic works great, but if the premise ("miracles don't happen") is false, the conclusion, however logically deduced, can be wrong too. (This is what logicians depict as a *valid* but not a *sound* argument.) Whatever the motives, skeptics still have to explain why Saul of Tarsus, once a fervent, even violent enemy of the early church, became its greatest champion.

If, as already shown, the idea of a conspiracy—that is, the early disciples, and then, later, Paul, together promoted what they all knew was a lie: that Jesus had been resurrected from the dead and that this resurrection proved He was the Messiah—if that doesn't work, then how to explain what happened to Saul?

The other attempted explanation was that Saul hallucinated it. Yet this move, even when coupled with the meteorite theory, flounders embarrassingly right out of the gate, both as an explanation for what happened to Saul on the road to Damascus and then, especially, for his interaction with Ananias.

How, too, does this hallucination idea explain what Paul wrote, perhaps twenty years later, to the Corinthians about the resurrection of Jesus?

> For I delivered to you first of all that which I also received: that Christ died for our sins according to the Scriptures, and that He was buried, and that He rose again the third day according to the Scriptures, and that He was seen by Cephas, then by the twelve. After that He was seen by over five hundred brethren at once, of whom the greater part remain to the present, but some have fallen asleep. After that He was seen by James, then by all the apostles. Then last of all He was seen by me also, as by one born out of due time (1 Corinthians 15:3–8).

Here Paul twice referred to the Scriptures, the Hebrew Bible (as he often did), which would mean, then, that though he hallucinated everything, he just happened (luckily enough for him) to find scriptural support for his hallucination? For centuries since then, millions of Christians and many Jews have found Messianic prophecies in the Old Testament for the death and resurrection of Jesus, which is all rather strange if the most explicit and influential explanation in the New Testament for the death and resurrection of Jesus came from someone who had only hallucinated the idea to begin with.[26]

Then, after stressing the scriptural basis for the death and resurrection of

Jesus, Paul starts naming those to whom the resurrected Jesus had (he believed) appeared: Cephas (Peter); then the Twelve (that is, Peter and the eleven others but not necessarily at the same time); then "over five hundred brethren *at once*" (verse 6; emphasis added); James; then all the apostles; and finally, himself.

If Paul were lying, again, there's the question of motive. Also, if he were, it would mean that he must have assumed that these others were in on the lie as well, and so they all would have collaborated on it. (Truly a vast conspiracy if there ever were one!) Why? Because he stresses, at least with the more than five hundred brethren, that, though some have "fallen asleep"—that is, died—"the greater part remain to the present" (verse 6). What he seems to be saying is, *Look, don't take my word for it. Jesus appeared to all of these people; many are still alive. Go ask them for yourselves.*

If that's unlikely for someone who had concocted the whole thing, how much more unlikely for someone who had *hallucinated* it instead? Years after his first hallucination, he's so sure it's real that he all but dares people to track down and find others who will corroborate what he hallucinated?

Unless, of course, they all had the same hallucination as Paul? Or they all were part of a conspiracy, including those remaining among the five hundred, and they all simply took advantage of their great fortune in having someone as sharp, dynamic, and knowledgeable as Paul having hallucinated their lie and becoming a powerful proponent of it?

None of these theories, even when amalgamated (the others made up the story, while Paul hallucinated it), credibly explain what happened to Saul of Tarsus.

hat's left? The swoon theory, which teaches that Jesus didn't really die on the cross but only swooned and then later revived, and those who saw the revived Jesus thought He had been raised from the dead. If that notion, as we saw, failed with those who claimed to have seen Him in the days and weeks right after the cross, how much more would it fail with Saul?

That is, unless one wants to believe, perhaps, a combined swoon-meteorite theory? Saul is on his way to Damascus, a meteorite falls from the sky, and at the moment it crashed into terra firma, the revived Jesus (by now long healed) just happened to be there and confronted Saul for his perfidy, who then believed that the resurrected Jesus had appeared to him.

There's the twin theory. Maybe Jesus' purported twin just happened to show up on the road to Damascus at the same time the meteorite fell, and he duped Saul into believing that he was the resurrected Christ?

Finally, who can forget the alien theory of the already mentioned and inimitable Barry Downing, the Presbyterian minister and author of *The Bible and Flying Saucers*? For him, what happened to Saul was that a UFO came down with Jesus in it—that is, after it took Jesus away from Earth (the "Ascension"*)—and from this UFO, Jesus chided Saul for being such a scalawag. "It seems consistent to argue," wrote Downing, "that if Jesus 'ascended' in some sort of UFO, the same vehicle brought him to Paul's company on the Damascus Road."[27]

Again, the preposterousness here reveals just how convincing the evidence must be. Forced to accept the events—that after the death of Jesus, many people believed that they saw the resurrected Jesus, and Saul of Tarsus, once a fervent opponent of Jesus, became one of His most devoted disciples—skeptics have to come up with something nondivine to explain these events. Fraud, hallucination, a swooning Jesus, a twin brother, a meteorite, UFOs, aliens—anything and everything except for what the Bible, and the numerous eyewitness testimonies in the Bible, teaches.

---

* "Now when He had spoken these things, while they watched, He was taken up, and a cloud received Him out of their sight. And while they looked steadfastly toward heaven as He went up, behold, two men stood by them in white apparel, who also said, 'Men of Galilee, why do you stand gazing up into heaven? This *same* Jesus, who was taken up from you into heaven, will so come in like manner as you saw Him go into heaven' " (Acts 1:9–11; emphasis added). According to Reverend Downing, this, too, was the result of aliens and UFOs.

What does the Bible teach?

First, the Bible teaches that Jesus of Nazareth, God in human flesh, died on the cross as a human being. "Let this mind be in you which was also in Christ Jesus, who, being in the form of God, did not consider it robbery to be equal with God, but made Himself of no reputation, taking the form of a bondservant, and coming in the likeness of men. And being found in appearance as a man, He humbled Himself and became obedient to the point of death, even the death of the cross" (Philippians 2:5–8). The God who created the cosmos certainly could, if He chose, "shrink down" and become a human baby who grew into adulthood and who then died on the cross.

However astonishing the notion, however much it recasts and reinterprets the creation in a whole new light,* nothing is illogical, irrational, or impossible about the idea of Christ on the cross. It becomes that way only for those whose worldview is confined by atheistic materialism.

Next, the Bible teaches that, by His death, Jesus, equal to God, atoned for the sins of all the world. He died for each of us, individually, whether we asked for it or not and whether we acknowledge it or not. "For He made Him who knew no sin to be sin for us, that we might become the righteousness of God in Him" (2 Corinthians 5:21). "For when we were still without strength, in due time Christ died for the ungodly" (Romans 5:6). "All we like sheep have gone astray; we have turned, every one, to his own way; and the Lord has laid on Him the iniquity of us all" (Isaiah 53:6).

People are afraid of the moral implications of God existing (judgment, obedience, the Ten Commandments, etc.)—yes, a God who might make us answer for our deeds. That fear is, indeed, grounded in reality. "For God will bring every work into judgment, including every secret thing, whether good or evil" (Ecclesiastes 12:14). We feel guilty because we are guilty. That irksome pricking of our conscience isn't our imagination.

Yet the Bible teaches that the death of Jesus on the cross means that God Himself, in the Person of Jesus, suffered the judgment and the punishment for all the evils that we, however subtly, even subconsciously, fear that we'll have to answer for. This God whom we fear, and rightly so, put all of our evils upon Jesus, which means that He was punished for all of those things that we have done, even when knowing that they were wrong and that follow us around like slivers under our skulls.

Let us hear the conclusion of the whole matter:

Fear God and keep His commandments,

---

* That is, the universe is something more than the mere chance creation of a mindless explosion in which all matter and life arose, purely by chance, with no ends or purposes in mind.

For this is man's all (Ecclesiastes 12:13).

Yet the Bible teaches that the good news, the gospel, is that, by faith in Him, by claiming what He did for us, we are instantly forgiven those evil things—all of them. To use a theological term, we are "justified," accounted as righteous in the sight of God—despite the harsh fact that we don't deserve it and that there's nothing we could do to make us deserve it. That it took the sacrifice of God Himself on the cross in order to atone for our sins reveals just how bad those sins are and how useless human works are for solving the problems caused by them. The penalty for what caused our death—sin—has been paid by Jesus because we could never pay it ourselves.

"Knowing that a man is not justified by the works of the law but by faith in Jesus Christ, even we have believed in Christ Jesus, that we might be justified by faith in Christ and not by the works of the law; for by the works of the law no flesh shall be justified" (Galatians 2:16). "For by grace you have been saved through faith, and that not of yourselves; it is the gift of God, not of works, lest anyone should boast" (Ephesians 2:8, 9). And "therefore by the deeds of the law no flesh will be justified in His sight, for by the law is the knowledge of sin" (Romans 3:20).

And the Bible teaches that because Jesus has been resurrected from the dead, we, who must die because of sin, have the promise of our own resurrection from the dead as well. "When Christ who is our life appears, then you also will appear with Him in glory" (Colossians 3:4).

Your dead shall live;
Together with my dead body they shall arise.
Awake and sing, you who dwell in dust;
For your dew is like the dew of herbs,
And the earth shall cast out the dead (Isaiah 26:19).

"For as in Adam all die, even so in Christ all shall be made alive. But each one in his own order: Christ the firstfruits, afterward those who are Christ's at His coming" (1 Corinthians 15:22, 23). "Jesus said to her, 'I am the resurrection and the life. He who believes in Me, though he may die, he shall live' " (John 11:25).

Otherwise, if we all die, which we all do, and if all the people who ever knew us will die, which they all will, too, it's all for nothing, isn't it? Frenchman Jean-Paul Sartre wrote that "when you have lost the illusion of being eternal,"[28] life itself then loses all meaning. But why have that illusion of eternity to begin with?

Although humans long to be remembered—to have at least an illusion of being eternal—reality shows us otherwise. "Thingless we came into the world," wrote poet Charles Wright, "and thingless we leave."[29] The apostle Paul observed, "For we brought nothing into this world, and it is certain we can carry nothing out" (1 Timothy 6:7). As the patriarch Job said: "Naked I came from my mother's womb, and naked shall I return there" (Job 1:21). And King Solomon:

> As he came from his mother's womb, naked shall he return,
> To go as he came;
> And he shall take nothing
> From his labor which he may carry away in his hand (Ecclesiastes 5:15).

And poet Wallace Stevens: "For the listener, who listens in the snow, and, nothing himself, beholds nothing that is not there and the nothing that is."[30]

Thingless on the way in, thingless out, nothing in, nothing out, naked in, naked out. We are, to quote Goethe's *Faust*, "the earthworm's dust-engendered brood,"[31] and there's nothing we can do about it, or as Samuel Beckett's character Estragon said, "Nothing to be done,"[32] because nothing can be done, at least by us, no matter how hard we try to latch on to eternity as opposed to being devoured by it.

The Bible teaches, however, that we don't need to try. Jesus earned eternity for us. That's what the cross and the resurrection of Jesus were about: Christ doing for us what we could never do for ourselves. From the four-thousand-year-old *Epic of Gilgamesh*,[33] in which Gilgamesh goes on a fruitless quest for eternal life, to the Soviets' attempt to bring Vladimir Lenin back to life,[34] to freezing heads in vats of liquid nitrogen—it doesn't work.

It doesn't need to, not with Jesus having died for us and then having been resurrected for us. What has been needed to offer us eternal life has been accomplished by Jesus.

The only question is, Do we accept it for ourselves?

Why not, especially when the evidence for Christ's resurrection is so convincing that skeptics have to resort to such things as mass hallucinations, vast conspiracies, meteorites, twin Jesuses, UFOs, hallucinations-cum-meteorites, and so forth to try and explain it away?

1. Frank Tipler, *The Physics of Immortality: Modern Cosmology, God and the Resurrection of the Dead* (New York: Anchor Books, 1995).

2. Tipler, 1.

3. George Ellis, "Piety in the Sky," review of *The Physics of Immortality: Modern Cosmology, God and the Resurrection of the Dead*, by Frank Tipler, *Nature* 371, no. 115 (September 1994), https://www.nature.com/articles/371115a0.

4. Frank Tipler, *The Physics of Christianity* (New York: Doubleday, 2007).

5. Tipler, introduction to *The Physics of Christianity*, 1.

6. Tipler, 200.

7. Tipler, 199.

8. Tipler, 199.

9. Austin L. Hughes, "The Folly of Scientism," *New Atlantis*, Fall 2012, https://www

.thenewatlantis.com/publications/the-folly-of-scientism. For a recent powerful critique of scientism, see Richard N. Williams and Daniel N. Robinson, eds., *Scientism: The New Orthodoxy* (New York: Bloomsbury Academic, 2015).

10. *Tinker Tailor Soldier Spy*, directed by Tomas Alfredson (2011, London: Focus Features, 2011), DVD.

11. Tacitus, *Annals and Histories*, trans. Alfred John Church and William Jackson Brodribb (New York: Alfred A. Knopf, 2009), 353, 354.

12. Tacitus, 354.

13. Gerald Sigal, "Does Paul's Claim That Jesus Appeared to Him Establish That Jesus Was Resurrected?" Jews for Judaism, accessed August 17, 2020, https://jewsforjudaism.org/knowledge/articles/does-pauls-claim-that-jesus-appeard-to-him-establish-that-jesus-was-resurrected/.

14. Jack A. Kent, *The Psychological Origins of the Resurrection Myth* (London: Open Gate, 1999).

15. Gary R. Habermas, "Explaining Away Jesus' Resurrection: Hallucination," Christian Research Institute, June 9, 2009, https://www.equip.org/article/explaining-away-jesus-resurrection-hallucination/.

16. "The Jesus of Nazareth who came forward publicly as the Messiah, who preached the ethic of the kingdom of God, who founded the kingdom of heaven upon earth and died to give his work its final consecration, never existed." Albert Schweitzer, *The Quest of the Historical Jesus*, ed. John Bowden, trans. W. Montgomery, J. R. Coates, Susan Cupitt, and John Bowden (Minneapolis, MN: Fortress Press, 2001), 478.

17. Schweitzer, 152.

18. D. Landsborough, "St Paul and Temporal Lobe Epilepsy," *Journal of Neurology, Neurosurgery, and Psychiatry* 50, no. 6 (June 1987): 659–664, https://jnnp.bmj.com/content/jnnp/50/6/659.full.pdf.

19. Landsborough, "Temporal Lobe Epilepsy," 659.

20. Landsborough, "Temporal Lobe Epilepsy," 659.

21. Landsborough, "Temporal Lobe Epilepsy," 663.

22. Ken Pulliam, "Did Paul Hallucinate on the Road to Damascus?—Part Two," *Why I De-converted From Evangelical Christianity* (blog), April 25, 2010, http://formerfundy.blogspot.com/2010/04/did-paul-hallucinate-on-road-to_25.html.

23. Karl Popper, *Conjectures and Refutations: The Growth of Scientific Knowledge* (New York: Routledge, 2002), 46; emphasis in the original.

24. William K. Hartmann, "Chelyabinsk, Zond IV, and a Possible First-Century Fireball of Historical Importance," abstract, *Meteoritics & Planetary Science* 50, no. 3 (March 12, 2015), https://onlinelibrary.wiley.com/doi/full/10.1111/maps.12428; emphasis in the original.

25. Jacob Aron, "Falling Meteor May Have Changed the Course of Christianity," Space, *New Scientist*, April 22, 2015, https://www.newscientist.com/article/mg22630183-700-falling-meteor-may-have-changed-the-course-of-christianity/.

26. See Jacques Doukhan, *On the Way to Emmaus: Five Major Messianic Prophecies Explained* (Clarksville, MD: Lederer Books, 2012).

27. Barry Downing, *The Bible and Flying Saucers* (New York: Avon, 1968), 134.

28. Jean-Paul Sartre, *The Wall (Intimacy) and Other Stories*, trans. Lloyd Alexander (New York: New Directions, 1975), 12.

29. Charles Wright, *Apologia Pro Vita Sua*, in *Black Zodiac* (New York: Farrar, Straus and Giroux, 1997), 6.

30. Wallace Stevens, "The Snow Man," in *The Collected Poems* (New York: Vintage Books, 1982), 10.

31. Johann Wolfgang von Goethe, *Faust: A Tragedy*, 2nd ed., ed. Cyrus Hamlin, trans. Walter Arndt (New York: W. W. Norton, 2001), 19.

32. Samuel Beckett, *Waiting for Godot* (New York: Grove Press, 1982), 17.

33. *The Epic of Gilgamesh* (New York: Penguin Books, 1999).

34. "Whoever may have been responsible, the decision to embalm Lenin involved more than political calculation. The God-builders had a magical faith in the power of science, which they believed could conquer death. One of these—Leonid Krasin (1870–1926)—attempted to freeze Lenin, with the ultimate aim of returning him to life. Like Gorky, Krasin was a devotee of the philosophy of God-building. He was also a believer in scientific resurrection." John Gray, *The Immortalization Commission: Science and the Strange Quest to Cheat Death* (New York: Farrar, Straus and Giroux, 2011), 158.

This Piddling Few

When Christianity talks about the end-time resurrection of the dead, it's not dealing just with still-warm corpses. It's dealing with all the dead, even those who, after dissolving for weeks in salt water, were eaten by various and sundry sea creatures, from bacteria to barracudas, twenty-five hundred years ago. (In this context, "seafood" takes on a whole new meaning.) Belief in the resurrection is belief in something neither obvious nor attested to by nature. This is why one doesn't have to be a twenty-first-century materialist-atheist skeptic to still question the resurrection of the dead.

"The Romans," wrote Stephen Cave, "were well aware of the Christians' belief that they would one day rise bodily from the grave and did everything they could to mock and hinder those hopes. A report of a persecution in Gaul in 177 CE records that the martyrs were first executed, then their corpses left to rot unburied for six days before being burned and the ashes thrown into the river Rhône—'Now let us see whether they will rise again,' the Romans are reported to have said."[1]

That little object lesson in theological skepticism, however compelling, is beside the point; it proved nothing about the biblical promise of the resurrection.

About twenty-six hundred years ago, in ancient Greece and the surrounding areas, philosophers wondered about the nature of reality. What are things, at their most basic level, made of, apart from how they appear to us and before being parsed, analyzed, systematized, and filtered by our debatable senses? What is the most prime building block of nature—the smallest possible entity that can't be broken down into anything other than smaller proportions of itself because nothing else exists other than smaller portions of itself?

Among the theories in which things such as water, fire, air, and even numbers were picked as the ultimate entity, Democritus and Leucippus, two Greeks who lived hundreds of years before Christ, theorized that all matter was composed of tiny invisible particles called *atoms*, from a Greek word meaning "that which cannot be split." Atomic physics has, surely, progressed since Democritus and Leucippus, though their term *atom* has endured, even though, of course, atoms can be split.

In fact, atoms are composed of two classes of smaller particles: quarks and leptons. For now, quarks and leptons are deemed the long-sought-for ultimate entities, the building blocks of all physical reality—even if, according to quantum physics, they really are quantum waves but assume particle-like attributes only when we measure them. (As physicist Philip Ball explains, it's one thing to say that a tennis ball is moving 100 miles per hour [mph] when I measure it; it's quite another to say that it's "travelling at 100 mph *because* I measured it"[2]).

Now, if our present existence as carbon-based protoplasm is, indeed, it, and our "threescore years and ten" (Psalm 90:10, KJV)—possibly a bit more if we don't smoke or get hit by lightning—is all that we get, ever, we're in pretty tough shape. We die, everyone who ever knew us dies, every memory of us vanishes, everything we ever accomplished vanishes, and eventually, it will be as if we had never existed to begin with. In, perhaps, Scripture's only existentialist dread riff, Solomon, musing about the meaninglessness of this life in and of itself, wrote: "I have seen all the works that are done under the sun; and indeed, all is vanity and grasping for the wind" (Ecclesiastes 1:14). Which is, again, why even the apostle Paul, who wrote so much about God's love for us—"For I am persuaded that neither death nor life, nor angels nor principalities nor powers, nor things present nor things to come, nor height nor depth, nor any other created thing, shall be able to separate us from the love of God which is in Christ Jesus our Lord" (Romans 8:38, 39)—warned that, without the promised resurrection, "your faith is futile; you are still in your sins! Then also those who have fallen asleep in Christ have perished" (1 Corinthians 15:17, 18).

In other words, without the resurrection, after you die, you rot forever, or at least for as long as it takes to get as decomposed as people can decompose.

Still, though, the dead resurrected? Like those dissolved in the sea and then eaten by barracuda, which themselves have been dead for twenty-five hundred years? That's asking people to believe in an awful lot, isn't it?

It is an awful lot, but not logically impossible.

Reality, at some level, is information or filled with information, especially in the living world. In a fascinating (though flawed) book, Paul Davies wrote, "The thing that separates life from non-life is *information*."[3] Google, for instance, how much information exists in a single cell, and you'll get the idea. One website expressed it like this: "The DNA of a single cell contains so much information that if it were represented in printed words, simply listing the first letter of each base would require over 1.5 million pages of text!"[4] Wrote Davies too: "What does the surprise factor tell us about how much information an organism contains? . . . Every cell in your body contains about a billion DNA bases arranged in a particular sequence of the four-letter biological alphabet. The number of possible combinations is 4 raised to the power of 1 billion, which is one followed by about six hundred million zeros. Compare that to the paltry number of atoms in the universe—one followed by about eighty zeros."[5]

So if the physical world that we arose from and exist in is, at the core, quarks and leptons, couldn't the God who not only created and sustains that world just reconfigure the quarks and leptons when the time comes to resurrect us? Without taking the computer analogy too far, if mere zeros and ones themselves, when combined with the information in a software package, can do all the amazing stuff that computers do, imagine what the Living God could do with all the information He has about us.

Mocking the resurrection, atheist Bertrand Russell asked what happens to those whom cannibals ate, because their bodies were now part of the cannibals', and so who gets what in the resurrection?[6] But suppose the Creator simply grabs quarks and leptons, the ultimate building blocks of existence, from wherever and, based on the information that He possesses about each one of us, reconstructs us from those quarks and leptons on up? He doesn't need the ones originally in bodies eaten by crabs a thousand years ago or burned by the Romans. Any will do. Or He could just speak new quarks and leptons into existence and then go from there.

However God does it, what's the result?

"For this corruptible must put on incorruption, and this mortal must put on immortality. So when this corruptible has put on incorruption, and this mortal has put on immortality, then shall be brought to pass the saying that is written: 'Death is swallowed up in victory' " (1 Corinthians 15:53, 54).

If not, the option always remains of freezing our brains in vats of liquid nitrogen in the hope of having someone upload our neural connections so that we can "exist" as computer programs in massive hard drives. On the other hand, perhaps our hopes should be placed not on futurist science fiction but on the historical facts of Jesus' death and resurrection, especially considering how flabby the attempts to debunk that death and resurrection are and get only more so the more one looks at them.

Numerous times Jesus of Nazareth had predicted His own death and resurrection:

- "From that time Jesus began to show to His disciples that He must go to Jerusalem, and suffer many things from the elders and chief priests and scribes, and be killed, and be raised the third day" (Matthew 16:21).
- "And He began to teach them that the Son of Man must suffer many things, and be rejected by the elders and chief priests and scribes, and be killed, and after three days rise again" (Mark 8:31).
- "But He answered and said to them, 'An evil and adulterous generation seeks after a sign, and no sign will be given to it except the sign of the prophet Jonah. For as Jonah was three days and three nights in the belly of the great fish, so will the Son of Man be three days and three nights in the heart of the earth' " (Matthew 12:39, 40).
- "Jesus answered and said to them, 'Destroy this temple, and in three days I will raise it up.'

  "Then the Jews said, 'It has taken forty-six years to build this temple, and will You raise it up in three days?'

  "But He was speaking of the temple of His body. Therefore, when He had risen from the dead, His disciples remembered that He had said this to them; and they believed the Scripture and the word which Jesus had said" (John 2:19–22).

Now, if one believes the Bible is the Word of God, and that Jesus is the Son of God, and that He came here purposely to die and to be resurrected as a sacrifice for human evil—all in fulfillment of Old Testament scriptures—then the idea of His having predicted beforehand His death and resurrection is no big deal.

In contrast, if one doesn't believe that Jesus was resurrected after His death, one isn't going to believe that He had predicted both His death and resurrection beforehand, which then happened just as He had predicted. These texts, after all, were written years after the purported events, and were written by those who either concocted the story of His death and resurrection or, for some reason (hallucinations?), really believed that they had happened. The inclusion of these predictions in the Gospels, then, proves nothing. How easy, all of those years later, to have just made them up and stick them in.

However, if Jesus hadn't been resurrected, why did the writers of the Gospels lie that He had been, and then add to that lie by saying that He had predicted it too? No one expected a resurrected Messiah, so why concoct one, especially one who had died in the most ignoble way possible—on a cross as did the worst of criminals? What worldly advantage did they get from promoting not only the lie that He had been resurrected but the lie that He had predicted that He would be?

Also, Jesus warned of His impending death, and the disciples all refused to believe Him. Certainly, if making up the story of His prediction that He would die and be resurrected, they could have made themselves look better than the disbelieving and unfaithful buffoons portrayed in their own lies.

Or, if they had hallucinated it all, then we have to believe that, decades later, still deceived by this mass hallucination, they wrote down His predictions even though they never actually happened? It's far-fetched enough to believe that they all, amid the trauma of His unexpected death, hallucinated that He had risen from the grave. Not only that, but they must have also hallucinated that He had predicted His own death and resurrection as well. Or, perhaps, decades later, still hallucinating about Jesus, they hallucinated that He had predicted His own death and resurrection before they happened, and then they wrote down their hallucination of His prediction in the Gospels.

Possible but, insanely, improbable.

Or, perhaps, duped by Jesus' twin, decades later, they concocted the accounts of Him making these predictions about His death and resurrection, kind of a twin-conspiracy theory combined. Or Jesus, who did not die on the cross, appeared to them the next day, and now, decades later, they just make up this stuff about His having years earlier predicted His resurrection in a combination swoon-conspiracy theory. In either scenario, if they made up the account of Christ's predictions, the same question—that of their motives—remains unanswered.

These options get only more ludicrous as an explanation for what cannot be denied: the biblical accounts of those who believed in Christ's death and resurrection. If they are not true, then how does one explain those accounts?

In the Gospels, as we saw, Jesus is recorded as predicting His own death and resurrection. Suppose in the same place, the Gospels, Jesus is also recorded as having predicted things that happened long after He had died—things that people today can read about and see that what Jesus had predicted about the future has, amazingly enough, come to pass. Though not proving the truth about His own predictions regarding His death and resurrection, these accounts prove only that what the authors put in Christ's mouth certainly and amazingly, at least in these cases, came to pass and did so long after they had been first written.

The Gospels were written in the decades following the death of Jesus. All are dated to the first century AD, when Christianity, though growing, was still a sect hated by many of the leaders in Israel and, even more importantly, by the Roman masters of the universe. Starting with Nero in the 60s, sporadic persecution, some worse than others, continued through the next two centuries, with the worst coming under Emperor Diocletian (284–305),[7] who tried to eradicate the faith. Thus, whenever in the first century the Gospels were written, they were written long before Christianity dominated the ancient Western world.

In this context, one of Jesus' most famous speeches occurred on the Mount of Olives in Jerusalem. At this time, what was the situation with Jesus and His followers? They were a small, rag-tag group of outsiders. Before long, Jesus Himself would be killed, His followers fleeing in fear. From all human perspective, Christ and His motley crew should have evaporated into oblivion long ago.

However, the Gospels—written in the first century AD—record Jesus, the Leader of a small group of nobodies, saying to these nobodies: "Heaven and earth will pass away, but My words will by no means pass away" (Matthew 24:35). His words, *such as these very words themselves*—"Heaven and earth will pass away, but My words will by no means pass away"—will always remain? The mere fact of them being read right now, almost two thousand years later, is a fulfillment of His prediction.

All of Christ's recorded words had been spoken at a time when He and His followers were soon to be pariahs in a nation itself that was one small and unimportant province amid the vast Roman Empire. How could Jesus at that time have known that His words would live on for so long? When His words were being written down by the Gospel writers, the church was facing persecution from Rome that would get only worse before getting better *centuries later*. Considering the circumstances, both during the time that Jesus had said those words, and the time that they had been written, it was an astonishing prediction that, to this day, is being fulfilled.

Or was it a lucky guess? Or His followers had conjured it up, and voilà, it came true anyway? Or maybe they hallucinated it, and voilà, their hallucination came true? Or instead, Jesus as the Messiah, knowing the future, made this prediction, which we today help fulfill by simply reading His words?

In the same talk on the Mount of Olives, Jesus was recorded as predicting something else that, at the time, seemed ludicrous. "For many will come in My name, saying, 'I am the Christ,' and will deceive many" (verse 5). Many will come in "*My name*"? At that time, the name of Jesus was known primarily in the small area where He had lived and ministered. Because of the circumstances in which it was said, and then later recorded, it was an astonishingly bold, even outrageous, prediction, especially considering that later, as Christianity was being vilified and persecuted, His name was hated both by Jews and Romans.

And yet, what? The world has been littered with the wreckage caused by those who, as Jesus said two thousand years ago, came in His name, claiming to be the Christ and who, indeed, have deceived many. Christian history, from the first century AD up through the twenty-first century, reveals that many have come and gone, claiming to be Christ (from *christos*, the Greek word for "Messiah"), just as Jesus predicted. Anyone can search the internet for the history of false christs and false messiahs and see that what Jesus was recorded as saying has come amazingly true. *National Geographic* has an online article, dated July 2017, titled "Meet Five Men Who All Think They're the Messiah." The article continues, "These men say they're the Second Coming of Jesus Christ. Their disciples agree."[8] Claiming to be Jesus? Deceiving people? Exactly as Jesus was reported as saying almost two thousand years ago.

Another lucky guess by Jesus or by the Gospel authors who put those words in His mouth as part of a conspiracy? More hallucinations? Or Jesus as the Messiah, knowing the future, told what He knew?

Finally, at that same meeting on the Mount of Olives, Jesus made another prediction that seemed, at that time, as impossible as the other two. He said, "And this gospel of the kingdom shall be preached in all the world for a witness unto all nations; and then shall the end come" (verse 14, KJV).

When Jesus made that prediction, what was the status of "this gospel," not even in terms of being spread into "all the world" but of simply being understood? His own followers didn't understand who He was or that He was to face death and then resurrection—all in fulfillment of Old Testament prophecies. At first, they didn't even believe that He had even been resurrected, much less that this event was central to the "everlasting gospel" (Revelation 14:6).

Also, how many were believers in Jesus when He spoke those words? Whatever handfuls of Jews and few scattered Gentiles who believed in Him, they were a piddling few in contrast to the world's millions. And even this piddling few weren't yet sure just whom it was they believed in or what it meant to believe in Him. Also, when Jesus made that prediction, Judas hadn't yet turned Him in, nor did He yet face the reaction of His followers at His arrest: "Then they all forsook Him and fled" (Mark 14:50). Hardly an auspicious beginning for a movement whose message was to be heralded worldwide.

Yet today Christianity—"this gospel" (in one form or another), as Jesus said—has gone into almost "all the world." Christianity is the world's largest religion. Reading the text now, with Christianity having more adherents than any other faith and a presence in almost every country, one can easily forget what a bold, even daring, prediction that this was when spoken and when recorded decades later.

Here's Jesus, surrounded by a handful of followers, in a world that mostly had never heard of Him and was often hostile when it did. Which is why the prediction that He had made then seemed so outrageously implausible. *The soon-to-be-killed leader of a small and undistinguished group of Jewish monotheists immersed in a vast world of paganism and polytheism made this prediction about how far and wide His teaching would be made known, and He did so when that prediction seemed so far-fetched as to be laughable?*

However skeptical one can be about the resurrection of Jesus, what one cannot be skeptical about is that some of the Gospel writers, in the first century AD, wrote down that Jesus said (whether one believes that He said it or not) that "this gospel" would go into all the world.

Another lucky guess? Another lie of the apostles putting words in His mouth? More hallucinations? Or Jesus, as divine, correctly predicted the future many centuries in advance, just as He did about being crucified and resurrected?

As if Resurrection skeptics didn't have enough problems, how do they deal with the conversion of Jesus' brother James? And His other brothers too? As far as the biblical record goes, James had previously—that is, before the resurrection of Jesus—not been a believer in his own Brother as anything other than, perhaps, being a bit strange. Later, though, he is depicted as a church leader and, in even a nonbiblical source, it seems, was willing to die for his faith.

For starters, despite the extraordinary circumstances surrounding His own birth, Jesus had brothers and sisters. Because He was the firstborn son of Mary (Matthew 1:25; see also Luke 2:7), these siblings obviously came later as the children of Mary and (most likely) of Joseph. How many in total can be only speculated about but at least six (Matthew 13:55, 56).

In one incident, Jesus was preaching in His native land in the synagogue. Knowing His family background (at least partially), the locals were astonished at both His wisdom and works, saying, "Where did this Man get this wisdom and these mighty works? Is this not the carpenter's son? Is not His mother called Mary? And His brothers James, Joses, Simon, and Judas? And His sisters, are they not all with us? Where then did this Man get all these things?" (verses 54–56; see also Mark 6:3). According to the texts, Jesus had four brothers, among them James, and at least two sisters. Other texts refer to Christ's siblings as well (Matthew 12:46, 47; Mark 6:3; Luke 8:19).

His brothers, however, are not depicted as sympathetic. "For even His brothers did not believe in Him" (John 7:5). Worse, after Jesus had performed some miracles, He met resistance from His own. "When his family heard about this, they went to take charge of him, for they said, 'He is out of his mind' " (Mark 3:21, NIV).* Exactly what they intended to do after they took "charge of him" isn't specified, but this text, along with what John wrote, shows that His family members were not among Jesus' first disciples.

If making up all of these stories as part of a plot to dupe people into believing in Jesus, why would the Gospel writers have mentioned this negativity from Jesus' immediate family? Especially the author John, whose whole purpose in his Gospel was to get people to believe in Jesus? Why, then, would they have depicted Christ's own family not only as not believing in Him but even as thinking Him to be "out of his mind"? This makes little sense because they, the ones making up the story, had every incentive to depict Jesus' closest relatives as believing in Him—whether they did or not.

It's not until after the death and resurrection of Jesus that His brothers appear again, only now as believers in Jesus.

What, then, happened?

---

* Though the word *family* isn't there in the original Greek (it reads more literally in the Greek "his own"), evidence points to it being His own relatives, as reflected in the NIV translation.

To begin, in an early account of Christ's resurrection, Paul wrote that, after Christ's death and resurrection, "He was seen by Cephas, then by the twelve. After that He was seen by over five hundred brethren at once, of whom the greater part remain to the present, but some have fallen asleep. After that He was seen by James, then by all the apostles. Then last of all He was seen by me also, as by one born out of due time" (1 Corinthians 15:5–8).

Paul specifically mentioned Christ's appearance to James. Why to James and no other family members, Paul didn't say. Nor did Paul say how James responded after seeing his resurrected Brother. Everyone else named, it seemed, believed in Him after the Resurrection, so most likely, James did as well. Otherwise, why would Paul have mentioned it?

The book of Acts, after the final departure of the resurrected Christ, immediately depicts a number of Jesus' earliest followers together in "the upper room where they were staying" (Acts 1:13). Then, wrote Luke: "These all continued with one accord in prayer and supplication, with the women and Mary the mother of Jesus, and with His brothers" (verse 14).

His brothers? The ones who hadn't believed in Him and even thought Him "out of his mind"? They are now depicted with Peter, James, John, their mother, and others together in prayer and in "one accord"? Obviously, these brothers, at least the ones in the room, had a change of heart. Before the Resurrection, they are depicted as not believing in Jesus; and after it, as believing in Him.

In his letter to the Corinthians, Paul wrote, "Do we have no right to take along a believing wife, as do also the other apostles, the brothers of the Lord, and Cephas?" (1 Corinthians 9:5). Though these brothers are not named, their inclusion shows that at least some were now believers, listed with the apostles and Peter himself.

In Acts 12, after having been miraculously freed from jail, Peter came to the house of fellow Messianic Jews. "But motioning to them with his hand to keep silent, he declared to them how the Lord had brought him out of the prison. And he said, 'Go, tell these things to James and to the brethren.' And he departed and went to another place" (verse 17). By this time, still early in the formation of the church, James is counted among the faithful, singled out by Peter as if of special import.

In Acts 15, Luke writes about an early dispute in the church regarding non-Jews who believed in Jesus (at this point, the church was predominately Jews). One side, Pharisees who had accepted Jesus demanded that the Gentile believers be circumcised; others, such as Paul and Peter, said no. "But some of the sect of the Pharisees who believed rose up, saying, 'It is necessary to circumcise them, and to command them to keep the law of Moses' " (verse 5). The dispute came to a head in Jerusalem when, after the opposing arguments, James interceded. The next nine verses (verses 13–21) consist of James speaking, with authority, on what should be done, which included the following directive: "We write to them to abstain from things polluted by idols, from sexual immorality, from things strangled, and from blood" (verse 20). Interestingly enough, a letter about the matter was soon sent to the churches, saying that, in regard to the Gentiles who join, they should "abstain from things offered to idols, from blood, from things strangled, and from sexual immorality" (verse 29). James, then, is not only part of the church but, apparently, an influential leader.

In recounting his own story, Paul told how he eventually went to Jerusalem "to see Peter, and remained with him fifteen days. But I saw none of the other apostles except James, the Lord's brother" (Galatians 1:18, 19). James the Lord's brother, one of the apostles? James is depicted here not only as a believer in Jesus but as an "apostle" as well, which could help explain his leadership role in the dispute over the Gentiles in the church.

In the same letter, Paul wrote that he went up to Jerusalem, and those who "seemed to be pillars" (Galatians 2:9) in the church saw what God had done in Paul (remember, at first other Messianic Jews were skeptical, even afraid, of Paul), and so "they gave me and Barnabas the right hand of fellowship" (verse 9). And whom did Paul name as those pillars? "James, Cephas, and John" (verse 9).

Acts later records the following: "And when we had come to Jerusalem, the brethren received us gladly. On the following day Paul went in with us to James, and all the elders were present" (Acts 21:17, 18). This was a meeting with the leaders of the church in Jerusalem, and James was, again, specifically mentioned, apparently in a leading role, as he was distinguished from "all the elders."

The point?

S omething changed Jesus' brothers from unbelievers to believers, with James even assuming a leadership role. But what? Though some, perhaps all, possibly came to believe in Jesus before the cross, no mention of that happening was made, which is strange considering that, if their unbelief had been recorded, why not their belief?

Also, if they weren't believers before the cross, what about the cross would have convinced them to become believers? No one expected a crucified Messiah, and if Christ's own followers so completely misunderstood what it meant that they abandoned Him, it makes no sense that His unbelieving brothers would have been converted to the cause by the brutal and shameful execution of Jesus.

What, then, accounted for this radical change?

Only after the Resurrection, after He had appeared to James, are they depicted, numerous times, too, as believers. It must have been the resurrected Jesus who convinced them, especially because they were now part of a small group of Jews whose whole faith rested on the resurrection of Jesus. It's hard to imagine the brothers, in Jerusalem itself, preaching a resurrected Christ as the Messiah if they hadn't seen Him resurrected, or at least believed that they had seen Him. Either that, or they had trusted in the testimony of those who had seen Him resurrected or, again, believed that they had. More than likely, though, had Christ appeared to all of these other people, as Paul claimed, He would have eventually appeared to His own brothers as well.

Paul's mention of Jesus having appeared specifically to James, who is later depicted as a church leader, is powerful. It's hard to imagine Paul overtly lying about someone so prominent in the church and who could have easily refuted what Paul had said about Jesus appearing to him were it a lie.

James's brother Jesus is shamefully killed by the authorities. James, then, came to believe in his Brother as the resurrected Messiah, *even though Jesus had not really been resurrected?* Meanwhile, as a leader of a small group openly promoting what they know is a lie—that is, Jesus as the resurrected *Mashiach*—James is willing to face hatred, persecution, and rejection from his own people? Here, too, the conspiracy theory makes no sense.

What's particularly interesting about James is that he is depicted in a nonbib-lical source, Flavius Josephus's writings, not only as a follower of Jesus and His brother but also as, apparently, a martyr for Him.

Josephus wrote concerning events dating about AD 60: "Festus was now dead, and Albinus was but upon the road; so he assembled the sanhedrin of judges, and brought before them the brother of Jesus, who was called Christ, whose name was James, and some others, [or, some of his companions]; and when he had formed an accusation against them as breakers of the law, he delivered them to be stoned."[9]

Though the charge against them was not specifically explained, other than being "breakers of the law," two things should be noted. First, James was singled out as "the brother of Jesus, who was called Christ," and "Christ" is another name for the Messiah—an idea that many of the Jewish leaders found worthy of death. That is, by merely referring to Jesus as "Christ," Josephus showed that what His followers believed about Jesus got many of them in trouble. Second, because the church was being persecuted and because James was a leader of the church, he was most likely delivered "to be stoned" (as was Stephen) because of his faith in Jesus. And this was a faith that, it seems, he acquired only after seeing his own Brother resurrected from the dead.

Unless, perhaps, James, along with his brothers, hallucinated the resurrected Christ, as did Peter, John, and the rest? Or Jesus, having only swooned on the cross, escaped the tomb, slipped past the Romans, and reappeared to His followers? And so, James and his brothers, along with the disciples, believed Him to be the risen Messiah? Or one of their other brothers, Jesus' twin, faked being the resurrected Jesus while the real Jesus rotted away somewhere else?

Or, maybe, aliens in UFOs duped them?

Another problem for deniers: the empty tomb. To dismiss the account of Christ's burial in Joseph's tomb as just more conspiracy or myth making runs headlong into the perennial and unanswered question of motive. Why conjure up a story that only added to the disciples' woes as outcasts and promoted a hated and vilified narrative? And why make up a story that had Joseph of Arimathea and Nicodemus, members of their greatest enemy at that time—the Sanhedrin—as the two heroes who put Jesus in Joseph's tomb while depicting the other disciples and themselves as having ignominiously flown the coop?

And if the first apostles were lying about the empty tomb as part of their conspiracy to promote a resurrected Messiah, whom no one had expected to begin with, why didn't the religious leaders just go to the tomb, get the body of Jesus, and present it publicly? *Here's your resurrected Messiah!* That move alone would have shut down the whole Jesus-as-the-resurrected-Christ account in its infancy.

Instead, after the soldiers guarding the tomb reported what had happened, how did the chief priests respond to the guards? "You are to say, 'His disciples came during the night and stole him away while we were asleep' " (Matthew 28:13, NIV). Strange words for people who were not convinced themselves that the tomb was empty. Even more fascinating is that Matthew, many years later, when recounting this event, added this line: "And this story has been widely circulated among the Jews to this very day" (verse 15, NIV). What story? That the disciples stole the body.

In other words, even the enemies of the gospel conceded the truth of the empty tomb, and were still doing so decades later. With Christ in the tomb, the claim that He had been resurrected becomes absurd beyond measure. The undeniable fact of the apostles preaching Christ—and successfully too—*in Jerusalem*, where the tomb existed, remains powerful evidence for it being empty.

Otherwise, how could Peter, on the Day of Pentecost, get away with proclaiming, "This Jesus God has raised up, of which we are all witnesses" (Acts 2:32) if "this Jesus" were still rotting in a nearby tomb? How could it be written that same day that "about three thousand souls were added to them" (verse 41), that "believers were increasingly added to the Lord, multitudes of both men and women" (Acts 5:14), and that "a great many of the priests were obedient to the faith" (Acts 6:7) if central to the faith was a resurrected Jesus who was, however, still in the tomb? The early success of the church in Jerusalem, with thousands of Jews—contrary to the commonly held assumptions about the Messiah—believing that Jesus died and was resurrected, presents overwhelming evidence that Christ's tomb was empty. If it weren't, the movement most likely would have died out before starting.

It would be as if the Lubavitch today who believe that Rabbi Schneerson is the Messiah were claiming that, though the Rebbe's corpse is still in his tomb, he had been resurrected anyway. Not likely to convince many people, especially those who, like the early Jews at the time of Christ, never expected a dead and resurrected Messiah to begin with.

ohn Dominic Crossan, however, takes a unique approach to the empty tomb. He argues that the biblical story of the empty tomb was false because a poor wretch crucified by the Romans in Judea "was usually left on the cross to be consumed eventually by the wild beasts"[10] or was unceremoniously dumped "in a shallow grave barely covered with dirt and stones, [where] the dogs were waiting."[11] Perhaps that is what usually happened to the poor wretches crucified by the Romans. But that practice hardly demands that exceptions never occurred. It's like saying that because the homeless who die in the United States are, usually, cremated, then someone, a relative perhaps, couldn't come and bury the body.

Mark depicted Joseph's approach to Pilate to get the body of Jesus like this: "Joseph of Arimathea, a prominent council member, who was himself waiting for the kingdom of God, coming and taking courage, went in to Pilate and asked for the body of Jesus" (Mark 15:43). The verse said that he took "courage." The Greek word translated as "courage" there, *tolmao*, implies boldness and daring.* What Joseph was asking was, perhaps, out of order, not the common run of things, which is why it took *tolmao*. Hence, Crossan's argument that the story was a mere fabrication because that wasn't how the crucified dead were commonly disposed of means nothing.

Meanwhile, the hallucination theory gets pretty far-fetched here as well. Though the empty tomb doesn't demand a resurrected Christ, a resurrected Christ demands an empty tomb. So they hallucinate not only the resurrected Jesus but His empty tomb as well? And then, what? Based on their corporate hallucinations, they go around preaching that Jesus had been resurrected, even though He's still in the tomb? How well would that have worked?

"And with great power the apostles gave witness to the resurrection of the Lord Jesus" (Acts 4:33). Though they all only hallucinated the resurrected Jesus, who was, in fact, lying in a tomb right there in Jerusalem, the hallucinating apostles were, nevertheless, able "with great power" to witness in Jerusalem to the resurrection of Jesus? This isn't a serious explanation.

Jesus' supposed twin brother, meanwhile, even if he had been inclined (for whatever reason) to convince people that he was really the resurrected Jesus, would have had a few problems as an impostor had the real Jesus still been in the tomb—though some might have chosen to believe the twin's lie.

The swoon theory could explain the empty tomb. Jesus, not dead but only injured enough to lose consciousness, somehow—despite His wounds, despite being wrapped in linen and covered in spices, and despite being in a sealed tomb closed by a large rock guarded by Roman soldiers—managed by Himself to shed what they wrapped Him in, get up, move the rock, break the seal, and sneak past the Romans. And then, outside the tomb, He presents Himself as the risen Christ, who, again, no one was expecting, and this convinced His followers that,

---

* The King James Version translates it as Joseph going in "boldly."

yes, Jesus was the Messiah who had conquered death. However little this story has going for it, at least, unlike the others, it "explains" the empty tomb.

Of course, one could always resort to the alien option. Aliens from outer space, maybe in a UFO, took away the body of Jesus, or even miraculously resurrected it, which explains the empty tomb and Christ's appearances as well.

S ome might remember the old TV police show *Dragnet*,[12] with Sergeant Joe Friday's iconic line, which supposedly went like this: "Just the facts, ma'am."* What, then, are "just the facts" regarding Jesus and His supposed resurrection?

The question isn't moot or irrelevant. If Jesus was not resurrected from the grave, then unless someone can come up with another solution to our eternal death, we're all, ultimately, fertilizer, if even that much. In contrast, if Jesus has been resurrected, then God exists, the supernatural exists, and so does the promise of eternal life.

As Jesus Himself said, the same Jesus who was recorded as predicting that false christs would come in His name (they have); the same Jesus recorded as predicting that His words won't pass away (they haven't); the same Jesus recorded as predicting that the gospel would go into all the world (it has)—this same Jesus is also recorded as predicting, even promising, "I am the resurrection and the life. He who believes in Me, though he may die, he shall live" (John 11:25). With this same Jesus so right on all of those other predictions, "we who must die"[13] ought to think long and hard about His prediction, His promise even, that though we die, in Him we can live again, even eternally, because this same Jesus also promised that whoever believed in Him would "have eternal life" (John 3:15).

Eternal—as in forever and as opposed to "eternal destruction" (2 Thessalonians 1:9, ESV). In short, balanced over each of us is eternal life or eternal death. We, each one of us alone, tip it one way or the other.

With something so crucial balanced above us (in contrast, who will win the Super Bowl or World Cup seems trivial), what are "just the facts"?

1. Jesus Christ was crucified by the Romans.
2. After His crucifixion, many of Christ's earliest followers, and then others, believed (or at least claimed they believed) that they had seen the resurrected Christ.
3. These early Jewish disciples, proclaiming Jesus as the risen Messiah, founded the Christian church, despite sometimes violent opposition.
4. Saul of Tarsus, a violent opponent of the church, became one of its most passionate promoters.

How can these facts, mostly uncontested by historians, even those opposed to the Resurrection, be explained?

A conspiracy by Christ's early followers?

At first glance, it sounds reasonable enough, especially for those whose philosophical predilections incline them to believe in only what can, at least in principle, be explained by the laws, known and unknown, of physics and chemistry. The biblical accounts of miracles—from the supernatural birth of Jesus to His

---

* Actually, the line was "All we want [or "know"] are the facts, ma'am."

resurrection (none of which these people believe could be true)—were simply stories made up by Christ's earliest followers, most likely as a way to salvage what was left of their movement after the death of Jesus. What else could explain the written accounts of things that, according to the laws of physics and chemistry, cannot happen?

However, the conspiracy theory, on closer examination, is so fatuous, so crammed full of incredible coincidences, superharmonized lies, and detailed syncopations of deceptions that it couldn't pass as lousy, far-fetched pulp fiction, let alone as a serious explanation for the historical facts. It would be one thing if, after the unexpected death of Jesus, His disgruntled followers, trying to rescue something of the movement, concocted the cockamamie notion of a Messiah who, rather than throwing the Romans out of Judah, was crucified by them instead. (After all, that is what really happened.) If they stopped there, turning their Messiah into a mere martyr, upon whose untimely death they superimposed all sorts of spiritual and theological meaning, that would be one thing, even a fairly reasonable thing, actually, especially considering how common crucified Jews were to begin with.

But a resurrected Jew? If only the disciples had left the new Messiah in the tomb. Instead, they have Him rising from the dead—an idea deemed as incredible then as it is now. And they first made up this story and first promoted it *in Jerusalem*—the easiest place on Earth to have rebutted the claim? And then they kept the lie going decade after decade, even though it caused them and those who believed their lie suffering, persecution, and in some cases, death?

Which means, then, that these early disciples concocted a lie of such gigantic proportions, a lie of one finely honed level of theological bunkum upon another, culminating, climaxing, in the claim that not only was Jesus resurrected but also His resurrection created the only hope of humanity that their death, their inevitable, tragic death—the one thing that, surely, promises to dunk into the cosmic trash bin whatever meaning and purpose that they might have clawed and fought out of their existence here—that this death, thanks to the resurrection of Jesus, is only a chemical* rest from all the clawing and fighting until, as Paul (in on the conspiracy with those he once violently opposed) wrote, "The dead in Christ will rise first" (1 Thessalonians 4:16)? And rise to eternal life? It took a lot of chutzpah on the part of a few Jewish bumpkins (and one disfellowshiped Pharisee) to make it all up—and then to pull it all off too.

Or it was hallucinations. Dozens, if not hundreds of people, all hallucinating

---

* "After death, the human body undergoes the decomposition process and its constituents: 64% water, 20% proteins, 10% lipids, 1% carbohydrates and 5% minerals are broken down into simpler compounds, until they reach their building block ingredients, i.e. C, H, O, N, P and S." Beatrice Ioan et al., "The Chemistry Decomposition in Human Corpses," *Revista de Chimie* 68, no. 6 (June 2017), https://www.researchgate.net/publication/318772231_The_Chemistry_Decomposition_in_Human_Corpses.

the same unexpected and unheard-of thing (a crucified and resurrected Messiah), and then, based on their own hallucinations, they convinced thousands to believe that these psychotic events were the truth of the universe. And decades later, despite opposition from every corner, they still preached about the hallucinations and, by so doing, changed the world? (The mere fact that you are reading these words, and not doing something else, is a result of a few traumatized Jewish peasants who almost two thousand years ago had a psychotic breakdown that caused them to hear and see things that never happened?)

Or Jesus didn't really die but, surviving the cross, escaped the tomb and duped all of His followers and hundreds of others into believing that He was the resurrected Messiah. (Perhaps, while in the tomb, the idea came to Him: *If I could only get out of this place. Then I can convince everyone that I rose from the dead, and maybe that will make them think I am the Messiah.*)

None of these explanations work, which leaves—what? A twin brother? Aliens? Or, for Paul, a meteorite duping him into thinking that Jesus, whom he hated, was the Messiah after all? These options either skirt the edges of absurdity or, from the start, plunge headlong beyond them.

What, then, explains what no one denies?

After all, two trillion galaxies burnish the cosmos. That's 2,000,000,000,000. Approximately one hundred million stars comprise each galaxy. That's 100,000,000 Two trillion galaxies, of one hundred million stars each, come to 200,000,000,000,000,000,000 (two hundred quintillion) stars.[14]

These numbers appeared in chapter 2 to make a point, and they're repeated now to make a different one.

Assuming that the universe and the trillions of galaxies in it didn't arise from nothing (contrary to the scientific speculation that it might have[15]) or that the universe and all of those galaxies in it didn't create themselves (contrary to the scientific speculation that they might have[16]), then something else, or Someone else, must have created them all. "If the theory of the Big Bang is correct," wrote author Michael Frayn, "and the universe had a beginning, then there does seem to be a rather extensive state of affairs that has come into being without any precedents to account for it at all."[17]

Something had to create, and even now sustain, the creation. And if one assumes that the precedent for the universe and all that it contains—that is, the One who created and sustains it—is the God depicted in the Bible, then one has the answer to the resurrection of Jesus, without having to resort to such things as meteorites converting Saul of Tarsus into a Christian. God, the Creator of the natural world and of the natural laws that run it, simply acted outside those natural laws and resurrected Jesus from death. For the God who created and sustains two hundred quintillion (200,000,000,000,000,000,000) stars, it probably would have been a cinch.

Also, an estimated one hundred billion people have lived on the earth. A pittance, really, in contrast to these other numbers. We're only one galaxy worth of stars in a cosmos with what—two *trillion* galaxies?

Of course, the existence of two trillion galaxies of one hundred million stars each doesn't prove that the same God who created and sustains those galaxies will raise the dead. But it simply shows that the God who created and sustains two trillion galaxies of one hundred million stars each would (it would seem) have the power to raise only about one galaxy or so worth of the dead if He chose to. And according to the Bible, He has chosen to and raised Jesus from the dead to prove that He will.

Otherwise, what? We don't remember our birth, and the one corpse that we never have to see is our own,* and so all that's ours are the troubles between being a fetus and cadaver. And then—what? We're gone. We and the oysters. The raccoon roadkill too.

And if that all sounds meaningless, it's because it is—unless there is the hope of something beyond, such as the hope offered to us in the New Testament, where the promise of eternal life, everlasting life, is given over and over:

---

* "It was on one of those days that I realized that the only corpse I couldn't bear to look at would be the one I would never have to see." Michael Herr, *Dispatches* (New York: Vintage Books, 1991), 77.

- "To those who are going to believe on Him for everlasting life" (1 Timothy 1:16).
- "Eternal life through Jesus Christ our Lord" (Romans 5:21).
- "Lay hold on eternal life" (1 Timothy 6:12).
- "In hope of eternal life which God, who cannot lie, promised before time began" (Titus 1:2).
- "He who believes in the Son has everlasting life" (John 3:36).
- "And this is the promise that He has promised us—eternal life" (1 John 2:25).
- "Looking for the mercy of our Lord Jesus Christ unto eternal life" (Jude 21).
- "That whoever believes in Him should not perish but have everlasting life" (John 3:16).

And though that promise is wonderful, many fear being judged by the God who offers it. They should—that is, unless they have claimed Christ's death on their behalf. If so, they're covered. Therefore, because of Christ's resurrection (unless they opt for the conspiracy, hallucination, twin, swoon, alien, meteorite, or any combination theory thereof), they can rest, even now, in the promise, in the guarantee, of their own.

"The last enemy that will be destroyed is death" (1 Corinthians 15:26).

This current tragedy will end then, not with death, but with the end of death—the only end that spares us the fetus-to-corpse farce that's, otherwise, ours.

---

1. Stephen Cave, *Immortality: The Quest to Live Forever and How It Drives Civilization* (New York: Skyhorse, 2017), 104, 105.

2. Philip Ball, *Beyond Weird: Why Everything You Thought You Knew About Quantum Physics Is Different* (Chicago: University of Chicago Press, 2018), 33; emphasis in the original.

3. Paul Davies, *The Demon in the Machine: How Hidden Webs of Information Are Solving the Mystery of Life* (Chicago: University of Chicago Press, 2019), 24; emphasis in the original.

4. *3 Billion Base Pairs per Cell*, video, 0:07 of 0:30, Endowment for Human Development, accessed August 13, 2020, https://www.ehd.org/movies/3/3-Billion-Base-Pairs-per-Cell.

5. Davies, *Demon in the Machine*, 38.

6. See Bertrand Russell, *A History of Western Philosophy* (New York: Simon and Schuster, 1972), 461.

7. *Encyclopædia Britannica*, s.v. "Diocletian: Roman Emperor," by Jean Cousin, accessed August 13, 2020, https://www.britannica.com/biography/Diocletian.

8. Jonas Bendiksen and Jeremy Berlin, "Meet Five Men Who All Think They're the Messiah," *National Geographic*, July 11, 2017, https://www.nationalgeographic.com/magazine/2017/08/new-messiahs-jesus-christ-second-coming-photos/.

9. Flavius Josephus, *Josephus: The Complete Works*, trans. William Whiston (Nashville, TN: Thomas Nelson, 1998), 645.

10. John Dominic Crossan, *Jesus: A Revolutionary Biography* (New York: HarperCollins, 1994), 143.

11. Crossan, 174.

12. *Dragnet*, directed by Jack Webb (Universal City, CA: NBC, 1951–1959, 1967–1970).

13. W. H. Auden, *For the Time Being*, in *Collected Poems* (New York: Vintage Books, 1991), 353.

14. See Elizabeth Howell, "How Many Stars Are in the Universe?" Space.com, May 18, 2017,

https://www.space.com/26078-how-many-stars-are-there.html.

15. See Lawrence Krauss, *A Universe From Nothing: Why There Is Something Rather Than Nothing* (New York: Atria Paperback, 2012).

16. See Paul Davies, *The Mind of God* (New York: Simon and Schuster, 1992), 39–72.

17. Michael Frayn, *The Human Touch: Our Part in the Creation of the Universe* (London: Faber and Faber, 2006), 73.